IFIP Advances in Information and Communication Technology 441

IFIP – The International Federation for Information Processing

IFIP was founded in 1960 under the auspices of UNESCO, following the First World Computer Congress held in Paris the previous year. An umbrella organization for societies working in information processing, IFIP's aim is two-fold: to support information processing within its member countries and to encourage technology transfer to developing nations. As its mission statement clearly states,

> IFIP's mission is to be the leading, truly international, apolitical organization which encourages and assists in the development, exploitation and application of information technology for the benefit of all people.

IFIP is a non-profitmaking organization, run almost solely by 2500 volunteers. It operates through a number of technical committees, which organize events and publications. IFIP's events range from an international congress to local seminars, but the most important are:

- The IFIP World Computer Congress, held every second year;
- Open conferences;
- Working conferences.

The flagship event is the IFIP World Computer Congress, at which both invited and contributed papers are presented. Contributed papers are rigorously refereed and the rejection rate is high.

As with the Congress, participation in the open conferences is open to all and papers may be invited or submitted. Again, submitted papers are stringently refereed.

The working conferences are structured differently. They are usually run by a working group and attendance is small and by invitation only. Their purpose is to create an atmosphere conducive to innovation and development. Refereeing is also rigorous and papers are subjected to extensive group discussion.

Publications arising from IFIP events vary. The papers presented at the IFIP World Computer Congress and at open conferences are published as conference proceedings, while the results of the working conferences are often published as collections of selected and edited papers.

Any national society whose primary activity is about information processing may apply to become a full member of IFIP, although full membership is restricted to one society per country. Full members are entitled to vote at the annual General Assembly, National societies preferring a less committed involvement may apply for associate or corresponding membership. Associate members enjoy the same benefits as full members, but without voting rights. Corresponding members are not represented in IFIP bodies. Affiliated membership is open to non-national societies, and individual and honorary membership schemes are also offered.

Jonathan Butts   Sujeet Shenoi (Eds.)

Critical Infrastructure Protection VIII

8th IFIP WG 11.10 International Conference, ICCIP 2014
Arlington, VA, USA, March 17-19, 2014
Revised Selected Papers

 Springer

Volume Editors

Jonathan Butts
Air Force Institute of Technology
Wright-Patterson Air Force Base
Dayton, OH 45433-7765, USA
E-mail: jonathan.butts@afit.edu

Sujeet Shenoi
University of Tulsa
Tulsa, OK 74104-3189, USA
E-mail: sujeet@utulsa.edu

ISSN 1868-4238   e-ISSN 1868-422X
ISBN 978-3-662-52616-3   e-ISBN 978-3-662-45355-1 (eBook)
DOI 10.1007/978-3-662-45355-1
Springer Heidelberg New York Dordrecht London

Typesetting: Camera-ready by author, data conversion by Scientific Publishing Services, Chennai, India

Printed on acid-free paper

Springer is part of Springer Science+Business Media (www.springer.com)

Contents

Contributing Authors

Mohammad Ababneh recently received his Ph.D. degree in Information Technology from George Mason University, Fairfax, Virginia. His research interests include information security and assurance, command and control, semantic web and information systems.

Richard Agbeyibor is an M.S. student in Electrical Engineering at the Air Force Institute of Technology, Wright-Patterson Air Force Base, Ohio. His research interests include computer and network security, digital systems and avionics.

Carlos Aguayo Gonzalez is the Founder and Chief Technology Officer of PFP CyberSecurity, Vienna, Virginia. His research interests include cyber security, critical infrastructure protection, side channel information, machine learning and signal processing.

Cristina Alcaraz is a Marie Curie Postdoctoral Researcher at the School of Mathematics and Information Security at Royal Holloway, University of London, London, United Kingdom. Her research interests include critical information infrastructure protection, SCADA systems, smart grids and wireless sensor networks.

Abdullah Alsubaie is a Ph.D. student in Electrical Engineering at the University of British Columbia, Vancouver, Canada; and a Researcher at King Abdulaziz City for Science and Technology, Riyadh, Saudi Arabia. His research interests include power systems operation, smart grids and critical infrastructure simulation.

Kishore Angrishi is an IT Consultant with T-Systems International in Hamburg, Germany. His research interests include security and traffic engineering in data networks.

Stefano Armenia is a Research Fellow in the Department of Computer, Control and Management Engineering at Sapienza University of Rome, Rome, Italy. His research interests include cyber security, critical infrastructure protection, policy modeling, risk management, system dynamics and complex systems analysis.

Chad Arnold is a Ph.D. student in Computer Science at Wright State University, Dayton, Ohio. His research interests include computer and network security, critical infrastructure protection and malware analysis.

James Arnold received his M.S. degree in Geography from the University of Utah, Salt Lake City, Utah. His research interests include spatial analysis, geographic information systems and remote sensing.

Pierluigi Assogna is a Senior Consultant with Theorematica SpA, Rome, Italy. His research interests include knowledge management, control systems and decision support systems.

Malek Athamnah is a Ph.D. student in Computer Science at Temple University, Philadelphia, Pennsylvania. His research interests include information security and voice-based services.

Marco Bardoscia is a Postdoctoral Fellow at the Abdus Salam International Centre for Theoretical Physics, Trieste, Italy. His research focuses on applications of statistical physics to socio-economic systems.

Roberto Bellotti is an Associate Professor of Experimental Physics at the University of Bari Aldo Moro, Bari, Italy. His research interests include econophysics, medical physics and astroparticle physics.

Russell Bent is a Research Scientist in the Energy and Infrastructure Analysis Group at Los Alamos National Laboratory, Los Alamos, New Mexico. His research focuses on algorithms for planning, operating and designing the next generation of critical infrastructure systems.

Fabio Bisogni is a Member of the Board of the FORMIT Foundation, Rome, Italy. His research interests include information security economics, critical infrastructure protection and information disclosure policy.

Elisabeth Brein is a Researcher at the Rotterdam School of Management, Erasmus University Rotterdam, Rotterdam, The Netherlands. Her research focuses on the identification of social system variables, such as human behavior and leadership, during crisis situations.

Aaron Burkhart is an M.S. student in Computer Science at the University of Colorado at Colorado Springs, Colorado Springs, Colorado; and a Software Engineer Associate at Lockheed Martin in Colorado Springs, Colorado. His research interests include web programming, cloud computing, computer graphics and software architectures.

Jonathan Butts, Chair, IFIP Working Group 11.10 on Critical Infrastructure Protection, is an Assistant Professor of Computer Science and the Research Director of the Center for Cyberspace Research at the Air Force Institute of Technology, Wright-Patterson Air Force Base, Ohio. His research interests include critical infrastructure protection and cyber-physical systems security.

Alvaro Cardenas is an Assistant Professor of Computer Science at the University of Texas at Dallas, Richardson, Texas. His research interests include the security and privacy of cyber-physical systems and network security monitoring.

Camillo Carlini is a Research Fellow in the Department of Computer, Control and Management Engineering at Sapienza University of Rome, Rome, Italy. His research interests include system dynamics, critical infrastructure protection, policy modeling, simulation, cyber security and complex systems analysis.

Simona Cavallini is the Head of the Research and Innovation Area at the FORMIT Foundation, Rome, Italy. Her research interests include critical infrastructure protection, interdependency analysis, economics of security and macroeconomics modeling.

Edward Chow is a Professor of Computer Science at the University of Colorado at Colorado Springs, Colorado Springs, Colorado. His research focuses on improving the performance, reliability and security of networked systems.

Paulo Costa is an Associate Professor of Systems Engineering and Operations Research at George Mason University, Fairfax, Virginia. His research interests are in the area of Bayesian probabilistic reasoning, with a focus on decision support and multi-source data fusion.

Zhonghua Dai is a Researcher at the China Information Technology Security Evaluation Center, Beijing, China. His research focuses on industrial control system security.

Cristina d'Alessandro is a Senior Researcher at the FORMIT Foundation, Naples, Italy. Her research interests include critical infrastructure protection, urban and transportation infrastructures, innovation and technology transfer.

Salvatore D'Antonio is an Assistant Professor of Web Systems at the University of Naples Parthenope, Naples, Italy. His research interests include network and information security, critical infrastructure protection and cloud security.

Antonio Di Pietro is a Researcher with ENEA, Rome, Italy. His research interests include critical infrastructure modeling, decision support systems and data fusion.

Paul Fergus is a Senior Lecturer of Computer Science at Liverpool John Moores University, Liverpool, United Kingdom. His research interests include artificial intelligence, semantic web, bioinformatics and data science.

Chiara Foglietta is a Researcher at the University of Roma Tre, Rome, Italy. Her research interests include industrial control systems (especially energy management systems), critical infrastructure interdependencies and data fusion techniques.

Valerio Formicola is a Postdoctoral Researcher in the Department of Engineering at the University of Naples Parthenope, Naples, Italy. His research interests include network and information security, critical infrastructure protection and cyber-physical systems.

Haihui Gao is a Researcher at the China Information Technology Security Evaluation Center, Beijing, China. His research interests include critical infrastructure protection, network testbeds, cyber-physical systems and information processing.

Wei Gao is an Industrial Control Systems Security Research Engineer at Siemens Corporation, Atlanta, Georgia. His research interests include SCADA system security, malware analysis and software vulnerability discovery.

Michael Grimaila is an Associate Professor of Systems Engineering at the Air Force Institute of Technology, Wright-Patterson Air Force Base, Ohio. His research interests include computer and network security, data analytics, quantum information, quantum key distribution and systems engineering.

Xuefeng Han is a Researcher at the China Information Technology Security Evaluation Center, Beijing, China. His research interests include industrial control system security and security testing.

Alan Hinton is a Principal Systems Engineer at PFP CyberSecurity, Vienna, Virginia. His research interests include side channel information processing for cyber security applications and signal processing architectures.

William Hurst is a Senior Lecturer of Computer Science at Liverpool John Moores University, Liverpool, United Kingdom. His research interests include cyber security, data classification and critical infrastructure simulation.

Mohammed Talat Khouj is a Postdoctoral Fellow in the Department of Electrical and Computer Engineering at the University of British Columbia, Vancouver, Canada. His research interests include the real-time simulation of complex systems with a focus on resource allocation optimization in interdependent systems.

Marina Krotofil is a Research Assistant at the Institute for Security in Distributed Applications, Hamburg University of Technology, Hamburg, Germany. Her research interests include cyber-physical system security and process-aware risk assessment of industrial control systems.

Hanjing Li is an M.E. student in Electronic Information Engineering at the Beijing University of Technology, Beijing, China. Her research interests include signal processing and digital image processing.

Steve Linger is an R&D Engineer at Los Alamos National Laboratory, Los Alamos, New Mexico. His research interests include electric power systems, water systems and atmospheric modeling.

Cesar Lopez is a Ph.D. student in Electrical and Computer Engineering at the University of British Columbia, Vancouver, Canada. His research interests include the real-time simulation of complex systems with a focus on infrastructure interdependencies in problems involving energy systems and disaster response scenarios.

Jose Marti is a Professor of Electrical and Computer Engineering at the University of British Columbia, Vancouver, Canada. His research interests include complex systems, power systems and critical infrastructures.

Logan Maynard is an Instructor and Researcher with Navy Cyber Forces in Colorado Springs, Colorado. His research interests include space systems security, self-healing networks and anti-jamming techniques.

Madjid Merabti is the Director and Head of Research at the School of Computing and Mathematical Sciences, Liverpool John Moores University, Liverpool, United Kingdom. His research interests include distributed multimedia systems, computer networks, operating systems and computer security.

Robert Mills is an Associate Professor of Electrical Engineering and the Director of the Center for Cyberspace Research at the Air Force Institute of Technology, Wright-Patterson Air Force Base, Ohio. His research interests include network security and management, cyber situational awareness and electronic warfare.

Thomas Morris is an Associate Professor of Electrical and Computer Engineering and the Director of the Critical Infrastructure Protection Center at Mississippi State University, Mississippi State, Mississippi. His research interests include industrial control systems and power system security.

Okan Pala is a Ph.D. student in Software and Information Systems at the University of North Carolina at Charlotte, Charlotte, North Carolina. His research interests include intelligent software systems, spatial decision support systems, geographic information systems, critical infrastructure protection, computational geometry and accuracy assessment.

Stefano Panzieri is an Associate Professor of Engineering and the Head of the Automation Laboratory at the University of Roma Tre, Rome, Italy. His research interests include industrial control systems, robotics and sensor fusion.

Yong Peng is a Research Fellow at the China Information Technology Security Evaluation Center, Beijing, China. His research interests include critical infrastructure protection, SCADA systems and complex systems analysis.

Riccardo Santini is a Ph.D. student in Computer Science and Automation at the University of Roma Tre, Rome, Italy. His research interests are in the area of control theory with an emphasis on renewable resources, smart grids, robotics and data fusion techniques.

Sarbjit Sarkaria is a Sessional Lecturer of Electrical and Computer Engineering at the University of British Columbia, Vancouver, Canada. His research interests include machine learning and critical infrastructure protection.

Krishnaprasad Thirunarayan is a Professor of Computer Science and Engineering at Wright State University, Dayton, Ohio. His research interests include big data analytics, Web 3.0, information retrieval, trust networks and programming languages.

Margherita Volpe is a Researcher at the FORMIT Foundation, Rome, Italy. Her research interests include critical infrastructure protection, crisis management, public-private entity interactions, international law and macroeconomics policies.

Ting Wang is a Researcher at the China Information Technology Security Evaluation Center, Beijing, China. Her research focuses on industrial control system security.

Goitom Weldehawaryat is a Ph.D. student in Information Security at the Norwegian Information Security Laboratory, Gjovik University College, Gjovik, Norway. His research interests include the modeling and analysis of critical infrastructure networks, Byzantine fault tolerance and digital forensics.

Richard White is the Director of Academic Programs at Everest University Online in Colorado Springs, Colorado. His research interests include risk management and critical infrastructure protection.

Duminda Wijesekera is a Professor of Computer Science at George Mason University, Fairfax, Virginia. His research interests include information security, safety and security of wireless-controlled trains, security and privacy of healthcare applications, and financial crime.

David Wilson is an Associate Professor of Software and Information Systems at the University of North Carolina at Charlotte, Charlotte, North Carolina. His research interests include intelligent software systems and the application of intelligent systems techniques to geographic, multimedia, database, Internet and communications systems.

Stephen Wolthusen is a Professor of Information Security at the Norwegian Information Security Laboratory, Gjovik University College, Gjovik, Norway; and a Reader in Mathematics at Royal Holloway, University of London, London, United Kingdom. His research interests include the modeling and analysis of critical infrastructure networks, and distributed systems security.

Preface

The information infrastructure – comprising computers, embedded devices, networks and software systems – is vital to operations in every sector: information technology, telecommunications, energy, banking and finance, transportation systems, chemicals, agriculture and food, defense industrial base, public health and health care, national monuments and icons, drinking water and water treatment systems, commercial facilities, dams, emergency services, commercial nuclear reactors, materials and waste, postal and shipping, and government facilities. Global business and industry, governments, indeed society itself, cannot function if major components of the critical information infrastructure are degraded, disabled or destroyed.

This book, *Critical Infrastructure Protection VIII*, is the eighth volume in the annual series produced by IFIP Working Group 11.10 on Critical Infrastructure Protection, an active international community of scientists, engineers, practitioners and policy makers dedicated to advancing research, development and implementation efforts related to critical infrastructure protection. The book presents original research results and innovative applications in the area of infrastructure protection. Also, it highlights the importance of weaving science, technology and policy in crafting sophisticated, yet practical, solutions that will help secure information, computer and network assets in the various critical infrastructure sectors.

This volume contains seventeen edited papers from the Eighth Annual IFIP Working Group 11.10 International Conference on Critical Infrastructure Protection, held at SRI International in Arlington, Virginia, USA on March 17–19, 2014. The papers were refereed by members of IFIP Working Group 11.10 and other internationally-recognized experts in critical infrastructure protection.

The chapters are organized into five sections: control systems security, infrastructure security, infrastructure modeling and simulation, risk and impact assessment, and advanced techniques. The coverage of topics showcases the richness and vitality of the discipline, and offers promising avenues for future research in critical infrastructure protection.

This book is the result of the combined efforts of several individuals and organizations. In particular, we thank Zach Tudor, Richard George, Heather Drinan and Nicole Hall Hewett for their tireless work on behalf of IFIP Working Group 11.10. We gratefully acknowledge the Institute for Information Infrastructure Protection (I3P), managed by Dartmouth College, for its sponsorship of IFIP Working Group 11.10. We also thank the Department of Homeland Security, the National Security Agency and SRI International for their support of IFIP Working Group 11.10 and its activities. Finally, we wish to note that all opinions, findings, conclusions and recommendations in the chapters of this book are those of the authors and do not necessarily reflect the views of their employers or funding agencies.

JONATHAN BUTTS AND SUJEET SHENOI

I

CONTROL SYSTEMS SECURITY

Chapter 1

DETECTING INTEGRITY ATTACKS ON INDUSTRIAL CONTROL SYSTEMS*

Chad Arnold, Jonathan Butts, and Krishnaprasad Thirunarayan

Abstract   Industrial control systems monitor and control critical infrastructure assets such as the electric power grid, oil and gas pipelines, transportation systems and water treatment and supply facilities. Attacks that impact the operations of these critical assets could have devastating consequences to society. The complexity and interconnectivity of industrial control systems have introduced vulnerabilities and attack surfaces that previously did not exist. The numerous communications paths and ingress and egress points, technological diversity and strict operating requirements provide myriad opportunities for a motivated adversary. This paper investigates the detection of integrity errors in industrial control systems by correlating state values from field devices. Specifically, it considers a formulation of the classic Byzantine Generals Problem in the context of industrial control systems. The results demonstrate that leveraging physical system properties allows the inference of system states to identify integrity compromises.

Keywords: Control systems, integrity attacks, Byzantine Generals Problem

1.   Introduction

On June 26, 1996, an oil pipeline operator in Fork Shoals, South Carolina acted on erroneous data that conflicted with the true state of the pipeline system [5]. To relieve pressure in the pipeline, the operator sent a remote signal to start a pump. Although the operator's console revealed that the pump had started, it was a faulty indication and the pump had not been activated. As the pressure readings continued to increase, the operator was confused by the anomaly and took actions that exacerbated the problem. The pipeline ultimately ruptured, spilling 957,600 gallons of oil into a nearby river and surrounding areas, and causing more than 20 million dollars in damage.

---

*The rights of this work are transferred to the extent transferable according to title 17 U.S.C. § 105.

J. Butts and S. Shenoi (Eds.): Critical Infrastructure Protection VIII, IFIP AICT 441, pp. 3–13, 2014.

Industrial control systems monitor and control infrastructure assets that are vital to society – the electric power grid, oil and gas pipelines, transportation systems and water treatment and supply facilities. Attacks that impact the operations of these critical assets can have devastating consequences. The complexity and interconnectivity of control systems have introduced vulnerabilities and attack surfaces that previously did not exist, resulting in a significant increase in security incidents during the past few years [6, 7]. Indeed, researchers have demonstrated that a number of critical infrastructure systems have been exposed to malicious process manipulation [1, 8].

Industrial control devices inherently trust system inputs for proper operation [4]. Few, if any, advanced decision support systems are available to assist operators in identifying anomalous data and determining the best course of action in the presence of conflicting information about process systems. As a result, accidental or malicious manipulations of system parameters can cascade to produce incorrect functionality and possibly induce system failures.

The Byzantine Generals Problem (BGP) [2] is a classic problem in distributed computing that seeks to determine the appropriate course of action when there is no consensus among the actors. Indeed, this problem is relevant to industrial control systems where operators often have to make important process control and management decisions in the presence of bad data. This paper considers a formulation of the Byzantine Generals Problem in the context of industrial control systems. The goal is to draw inferences from the physical state of a system to help determine integrity compromises.

2.   Byzantine Generals Problem

The Byzantine Generals Problem was originally introduced as an abstract problem for understanding the reliability of computer systems and failures stemming from conflicting information [2]. The problem is described in the context of malicious actors who can modify messages to create discontinuity and conflict. In the classical formulation of the problem, Byzantine generals communicate with each another by messenger and must decide on a common course of action: attack or retreat. Messages can be manipulated by senders or while they are in transit from senders to receivers. Each receiver must gather and compare messages from all the neighboring generals before making a final decision to attack or retreat.

The original work by Lamport, *et al.* [2] evaluated solutions for resolving conflicting data. Each solution assumes different requirements, features and constraints when evaluating the overall reliability of a system. In the Byzantine Generals Problem, traditional oral messages sent between the generals correspond to the messages sent between computer systems. A common plan of action guarantees that a small number of "traitors" cannot negatively impact the system by enforcing a bad plan.

Valid solutions require more than two-thirds of the generals to be loyal. A valid solution enables generals to reach consensus or an agreed upon decision that cannot be negatively influenced by a limited number of traitors. Thus,

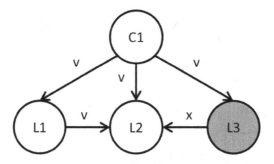

Figure 1. Byzantine Generals Problem.

when there are only three generals, no solution exists in the presence of even a single traitor. Lamport, *et al.* [2] proved that consensus can be reached when there are at least $3m + 1$ generals in the presence of at most m traitors. More generally, with $3m + 1$ total nodes, at most m nodes can suffer from Byzantine faults. That is, for $m = 1$, only one of the four nodes can be malicious for the solution to be valid.

Figure 1 shows a traditional Byzantine Generals Problem scenario where the commander $C1$ sends a consistent value (message v) to three lieutenants, $L1$, $L2$ and $L3$, where $L3$ is a traitor. $L2$ receives conflicting data from the commander and the other two lieutenants, $C1$, $L1$ and $L3$, and evaluates the values provided by $C1$, $L1$ and $L3$. Specifically, $L2$ identifies the inconsistency using a majority function that considers the three inputs (v, v, x). The inconsistent data source is identified and, in this case, $L3$ is identified as the traitor based on the set of three messages. Note that the majority function is the basis for conflict resolution in the Byzantine Generals Problem [2].

3. Control Systems and Byzantine Failures

An industrial control system is a hierarchical, distributed system with operators, controllers and sensors, often many miles apart. The control system enables an operator at a distant location to assess the current status of a process and to perform the appropriate control actions to manage the process. This activity can be automated or semi-automated and, depending on the situation, can require frequent, regular or immediate intervention. Effective communications with field devices are critical for the proper operation of an industrial control system.

This section demonstrates how the Byzantine Generals Problem applies to an industrial control environment. Instead of the generals passing messages, field devices in an industrial control system pass messages to a control layer. Each field device collects state values from sensors and transmits the values to the control layer. The decision authority in the control layer executes an algorithm that compares the inputs received from the field (device) layer. The algorithm identifies malicious nodes and presents the current state of the system

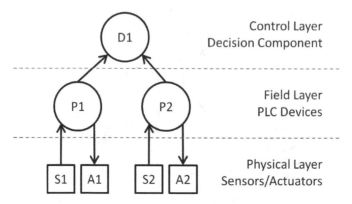

Figure 2.   Industrial control system components.

to enable an operator to make an informed decision when conflicting data is received. This may require the operator to modify system parameters for better performance or to restore the system to a stable state if it has become unstable as a result of a data integrity compromise.

3.1   Basic Notions

In the Byzantine Generals Problem, a contributing node is defined as a node that produces a state value to pass directly to other available nodes. In the original formulation of the problem, all the nodes are contributing nodes, including the lead commander and the lieutenants. However, in an industrial control system, only field layer devices are contributing nodes.

A decision authority is defined as a node that evaluates inputs and decides on the state of the system. In the original Byzantine Generals Problem, all the nodes with the exception of the lead commander are decision authorities. However, an industrial control system has a single decision authority that resides in the control layer.

In an industrial control system, all the nodes are generally known and trusted. However, a node can be compromised and its data may be manipulated in an integrity attack.

Figure 2 shows the major components of an industrial control system corresponding to the Byzantine Generals Problem framework. The framework has the following types of nodes:

- **Decision Component Node:** This corresponds to a control layer node. A single decision component node, also known as a decision authority, is present. The decision component node receives state values from field device nodes and executes an algorithm to identify inconsistencies.

- **PLC Node:** This corresponds to a field layer node. Multiple PLC (programmable logic controller) nodes, also known as contributing nodes, are present. The PLC nodes send state values to the single decision com-

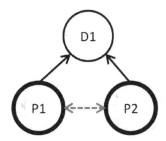

Figure 3. Industrial control system.

ponent node. Note that only PLC devices are considered in this paper. However, the approach is applicable to any type of industrial control device that reports status information to a central authority.

- **Sensor/Actuator Node:** This corresponds to a physical layer node. Multiple sensor (S_i) and actuator (A_i) nodes are present to monitor the process system and perform control actions on the process system, respectively. In an industrial control environment, the physical layer provides ground truth of the system state.

3.2   Industrial Control System Attributes

A Byzantine algorithm designed for an industrial control system must incorporate ground truth in order to correlate interdependencies between nodes. The ground truth is the actual state of a physical system. Given the state of one PLC, the decision component must infer the state of neighboring components. Inference is enabled by interdependent relationships between nodes. When neighboring components report state values, the decision component compares the reported state values with the anticipated state values.

Figure 3 shows a system with three nodes. Direct links exist from PLC nodes $P1$ and $P2$ to decision component node $D1$. Nodes $P1$ and $P2$ are contributing nodes.

To clarify the concepts, a simplified diagram of the original Byzantine Generals Problem is presented in Figure 4. The figure has three contributing nodes, $C1$, $L1$ and $L2$. The directional arrows in Figures 3 and 4 show the information flow between nodes. The solid lines in the two figures correspond to direct links along which messages are passed directly from one node to another; the messages may be manipulated by integrity attacks. The simplified industrial control system in Figure 3 uses a dotted line to represent an indirect link. The indirect link is not a physical link – it indirectly ties the two nodes together, enabling inferences to be made about the device state. Note that an indirect link cannot be compromised because it not a physical (actual) link.

To elaborate, the Byzantine Generals Problem in Figure 4 has direct links $C1 \rightarrow L1$, $C1 \rightarrow L2$, $L1 \rightarrow L2$ and $L2 \rightarrow L1$. The contributing nodes (bold circles) are $C1$, $L1$ and $L2$; the decision authorities are $L1$ and $L2$.

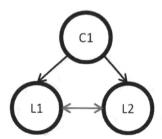

Figure 4. Byzantine Generals Problem.

The simplified industrial control system in Figure 3 has links $P1 \rightarrow D1$ and $P2 \rightarrow D1$. It has two contributing nodes, $P1$ and $P2$, which pass data to decision authority $D1$. Note that $D1$ is not a contributing node because it does not produce a state value that is sent to the other nodes.

The indirect link in Figure 3 is formed as a consequence of a direct physical relationship between the field devices. While direct links from contributing nodes can be compromised, an inferred link cannot be compromised; this reduces the attack surface. However, the interdependency captured by the inferred link enables the control layer to infer a change in state of a neighboring device. The interdependency arises from the ground truth of the system and the properties of dependent control system components.

As a practical example, consider a scenario where two sensors are attached to a bucket. One sensor detects the flow of water into the bucket while the other measures the weight of the bucket. If water does not leave the bucket as new water enters, the weight sensor should continually report an increase. The two sensors are, in fact, indirectly linked and their readings will always correlate if the system operates normally. However, if the system has an integrity error, the two sensors would not correlate; this inconsistency can lead to an unstable or undesired state. In the case of the bucket, the water will eventually overflow; in the Fork Shoals incident described above, the oil pipeline ruptured.

4.   Algorithm

In order to detect integrity errors, the decision authority in an industrial control system executes an algorithm after it receives local state values from the contributing nodes. A total of $(l + m)$ state values exist, one from each of the l loyal contributing nodes and the m malicious contributing nodes. By using inferred data, the algorithm identifies the m malicious nodes, where $m \geq 1$ and the total number of nodes $n \geq 4$, as long as there are a majority of $l > m$ loyal nodes. To assist in identifying loyal and malicious nodes, the function CONSISTENT is invoked. This function evaluates the state values to identify the inconsistent nodes. After the inconsistent nodes are identified, the integrity of the entire system is evaluated by comparing the number of malicious nodes with the number of loyal nodes.

Each contributing node receives an input from a physical device that represents ground truth; however, the contributing nodes can be loyal or malicious. It is assumed that physical devices work properly and have no faults, and all the inconsistencies are due to the malicious nodes. It is also assumed that the decision node has complete information about the design of the physical system. Specifically, it can determine if the contributing nodes are reporting consistent values or inconsistent values.

The algorithm uses two primary functions. After all the state values are collected, the function CONSISTENT is executed for each pair of contributing nodes to determine consistency. After all the nodes are analyzed for consistency, the function MAJORITY is executed to determine if the majority of nodes are consistent or inconsistent.

The input to the CONSISTENT function is (s_i, s_{i+1}) where s_i and s_{i+1} are state values for PLCs P_i and P_{i+1}, respectively. There are two possible return values for the CONSISTENT function, True or False, which reflect whether the state values are consistent or inconsistent, respectively. If both the state values are consistent, then the state determination t_i is assigned the consistent value C; if the values are inconsistent, the inconsistent value I is assigned. Note that, if the values are consistent, then the nodes are either both loyal or both malicious. If the values are inconsistent, then one of the nodes is malicious.

The MAJORITY function evaluates the results generated by the CONSISTENT function. The function returns an overall state for the system. The system is consistent if, over all the t_i, the number of C values is greater that the number of I values; otherwise, the system is inconsistent.

4.1   Evaluation

The algorithm, shown in Figure 5, begins by acquiring local state values from all the $l + m$ contributing nodes. If there are at least three contributing nodes, the first value is labeled as consistent; otherwise, the algorithm terminates because of the lack of a sufficient number of loyal nodes required to evaluate system state. Next, pairs of state values are evaluated for consistency in sequential order. Nodes are labeled for consistency based on their relationship to previous evaluations. After all the nodes are evaluated for consistency, the majority operation is performed. If the majority of the nodes are consistent, then the first node is loyal. As a result, all the consistent nodes are labeled as loyal and all the inconsistent nodes are labeled as malicious. Alternatively, if the majority of the nodes are inconsistent, the first node is malicious. These results hold as long as there are more loyal nodes than malicious nodes (i.e., $l > m$).

Figure 6 shows a three-node system with $P1$ as a malicious node and flagged with an integrity error $t_1 = I$. In the example, decision authority $D1$ receives inputs from PLC field devices $P1$ and $P2$. $P1$ reports a local state value $s_1 = b$, where b is the value of a system parameter. Meanwhile, $P2$ reports a local state value $s_2 = d$. $D1$ can infer, based on the state value reported by $P1$, that the state value reported by $P2$ should correlate with the state

Step	Description
1	Decision component collects local state values For each PLC P_i, $1 \leq i \leq (l+m)$, let s_i be the local state value from P_i sent to the decision component d.
2	If there are at least three contributing nodes ($l+m \geq 3$), assume first node is consistent ($t_1 = C$); Otherwise algorithm terminates due to lack of sufficient nodes.
3	Compare all node values for consistency (relative to initial state) for $i=1;\ i<(l+m);\ i++$ If *CONSISTENT*($s_i = s_{i+1}$) then ($t_{i+1} = t_i$); Else If $t_i = I$ then $t_{i+1} = C$; Else $t_{i+1} = I$
4	Execute majority function on set of flagged states; label loyal and malicious nodes If *MAJORITY* ($t_1, t_2, \ldots, t_{(l+m)}$) = C, then first node is loyal; If *MAJORITY* ($t_1, t_2, \ldots, t_{(l+m)}$) = I, then first node is malicious;

Figure 5. Algorithm for detecting integrity errors.

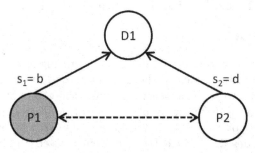

Figure 6. Impossibility of a solution for a system with less than four nodes.

c. Likewise, $D1$ can infer, based on the state value reported by $P2$, that the state value reported by $P1$ should be e. This discrepancy is caused by conflicting values from the two reporting field devices. An inconsistency is identified because CONSISTENT(s_1, s_2) = False. However, because of the small number of contributing nodes, $D1$ cannot determine the node that caused the integrity error.

The algorithm can accurately identify malicious nodes when there are a majority of loyal nodes ($l > m$). To demonstrate how the algorithm works, consider the basic case with $n = 4$. In this scenario, there are three contributing nodes and, as a result, $l > 1$ and $m < 2$ must be true for the algorithm to be successful.

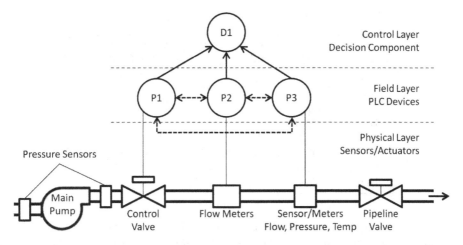

Figure 7. Oil pipeline representation.

Consider the case where $P3$ is flagged for an integrity problem. In the first step, $D1$ receives the state values: $s_1 = b$ from $P1$, $s_2 = c$ from $P2$ and $s_3 = f$ from $P3$. In the second step, since there are least three contributing nodes ($P1$, $P2$ and $P3$), the first node is labeled consistent ($t_1 = C$).

Next, the state values from $P1$ and $P2$ are compared for consistency. Specifically, CONSISTENT(s_1, s_2) = True. As a result, the integrity flag of $P2$ is set to the same value as $P1$ ($t_2 = C$). Next, CONSISTENT(s_2, s_3) = False. As a result, the integrity flag of $P3$ is set appropriately ($t_3 = I$).

Finally, the MAJORITY function is executed. Since MAJORITY(C, C, I) = C, the first node is loyal. As a result, all the nodes with $t_i = C$ are identified as loyal and all the nodes with $t_i = I$ are identified as malicious.

At this stage, using visual observations only, a control system operator may fail to identify the node with the integrity problem and could act on the invalid data, as in the case of the Fork Shoals pipeline rupture. Implementing this algorithm would have identified the faulty alert that led the pipeline operator to believe that the pump had started, when, in fact, it had not.

4.2   Application

The algorithm identifies integrity problems and a means for evaluating conflicting data. From a cyber security perspective, the integrity of field devices can be manipulated when components are networked to the Internet and targeted compromises or accidental manipulations occur. A field device can, thus, become compromised and report false data. If this occurs, the integrity of the data can be compromised. The following example highlights a scenario where devices provide inconsistent data, but the malicious device can be identified.

Figure 7 represents a notional oil pipeline with its associated connectivity and interdependencies. The physical layer components are several miles apart

Table 1.   Sample oil pipeline data.

Pressure P1	Valve P2	Flow P3	Consistent Yes/No	Malicious Node
Low	Open	Yes	Yes	None
High	Open	Yes	No	$P1$
Low	Open	No	No	$P3$
High	Open	No	No	$P2$
Low	Closed	No	No	$P1$
High	Closed	No	Yes	None
Low	Closed	Yes	No	$P2$
High	Closed	Yes	No	$P3$

and the components are managed by multiple PLCs that report to a single decision component. The distribution of PLCs makes it difficult for an operator to manually or visually verify the current state of every device. Nonetheless, the operator must rely on the system for situational awareness prior to making decisions or taking actions. Previous examples have demonstrated the negative effects of conflicting data.

In the example, a field device $P1$ monitors pressure, a field device $P2$ monitors a control valve and a field device $P3$ monitors flow. A change in state at $P1$ changes the physical layer and the corresponding states of the subsequent field devices $P2$ and $P3$. This is an important property, which enables the decision authority to infer the state of the subsequent field devices. For simplicity, pressure can be High or Low, the valve position can be Open or Closed, and the flow sensor shows a flow state of Yes or No. Each field device reports either the accurate local state or the false local state.

Data reported by each field device is evaluated for consistency to allow the decision component $D1$ to make decisions. Integrity problems are present if the field devices $P1$, $P2$ and $P3$ report conflicting state values. Table 1 lists various combinations of sensor readings that represent consistent and inconsistent states in the notional example. The table values are used for evaluating the CONSISTENT function and enabling inference.

When the pressure at $P1$ is Low, the valve position at $P2$ should be Open and the flow rate at $P3$ should be Yes. When the valve position at $P2$ is Closed, the pressure at $P1$ is High and the flow rate at $P3$ is No. Inconsistent sequences of the reported state values are detected by the algorithm.

For example, consider the second row in Table 1. In the first step, the decision component receives state values from field devices $P1$, $P2$ and $P3$. $P1$ reports the pressure as High, $P2$ reports the valve as Open and $P3$ reports the flow rate as Yes. In the second step, $P1$ is labeled as consistent ($t_1 = C$). In the third step, values from $P1$ and $P2$ are compared for consistency. CONSISTENT(s_1, s_2) = False, meaning that High pressure at $P1$ does not infer an Open valve position at $P2$. Since $P1$ and $P2$ are inconsistent, $P2$ is labeled as inconsistent ($t_2 = I$). Next, values from $P1$ and $P3$ are compared for consistency. CONSISTENT(s_1, s_3) = False, meaning a High pressure at $P1$ does not imply a flow rate of Yes at $P3$ and, therefore, $t_3 = I$. The comparison of state values from $P2$ and $P3$ reveals consistency. Since MAJORITY$(C, I, I) = I$, $P1$ is identified as malicious.

5. Conclusions

Human operators and automated decision components in industrial control environments often must make rapid decisions to react to system integrity errors. The application of the Byzantine Generals Problem to industrial control systems provides a formal mechanism for recognizing the presence of anomalous data and potentially identifying its sources. Using physical system properties, the resulting algorithm enables a decision authority to infer the system state and identify integrity compromises. A key constraint is that, when more than three field devices report the physical state of a system and when there are more trusted devices than compromised devices, it is possible to identify the specific devices that are compromised. The gas pipeline example demonstrates how the algorithm can identify and resolve conflicting data. As demonstrated, solutions to the Byzantine Generals Problem in the context of industrial control environments facilitate the resolution of inconsistent data that can result from cyber attacks against field devices and communications links.

References

[1] J. Finkle, "Irrational" hackers are growing U.S. security fear, *Reuters*, May 22, 2013.

[2] L. Lamport, R. Shostak and M. Pease, The Byzantine Generals Problem, *ACM Transactions on Programming Languages and Systems*, vol. 4(3), pp. 382–401, 1982.

[3] Y. Lindell, A. Lysyanskaya and T. Rabin, On the composition of authenticated Byzantine agreement, *Journal of the ACM*, vol. 56(6), pp. 881–917, 2006.

[4] T. Macaulay and B. Singer, *Cyber Security for Industrial Control Systems: SCADA, DCS, PLC, HMI and SIS*, CRC Press, Boca Raton, Florida, 2012.

[5] National Transportation Safety Board, Pipeline Accident Report, Pipeline Rupture and Release of Fuel Oil into the Reedy River at Fork Shoals, South Carolina, Report PB98-916502, NTSB/PAR-98-01, Washington, DC, 1996.

[6] F. Rashid, ICS-CERT: Response to cyber "incidents" against critical infrastructure jumped 52 percent in 2012, *Security Week*, January 10, 2013.

[7] U.S. Department of Homeland Security, ICS-CERT Incident Response Summary Report: 2009–2011, Washington, DC, 2012.

[8] Z. Zorz, Company's industrial heating system hacked via backdoor, *Help Net Security*, Kastav, Croatia, December 12, 2012.

Chapter 2

DETECTING MALICIOUS SOFTWARE EXECUTION IN PROGRAMMABLE LOGIC CONTROLLERS USING POWER FINGERPRINTING

Carlos Aguayo Gonzalez and Alan Hinton

Abstract   Traditional cyber security mechanisms, such as network-based intrusion detection systems and signature-based antivirus software, have limited effectiveness in industrial control settings, rendering critical infrastructure assets vulnerable to cyber attacks. Even four years after the discovery of Stuxnet, security solutions that can directly monitor the execution of constrained platforms, such as programmable logic controllers, are not yet available. Power fingerprinting, which uses physical measurements from a side channel such as power consumption or electromagnetic emissions, is a promising new technique for detecting malicious software execution in critical systems. The technique can be used to directly monitor the execution of systems with constrained resources without the need to load third-party software artifacts on the platforms.

This paper demonstrates the feasibility of using power fingerprinting to directly monitor programmable logic controllers and detect malicious software execution. Experiments with a Siemens S7 programmable logic controller show that power fingerprinting can successfully monitor programmable logic controller execution and detect malware similar to Stuxnet. Indeed, power fingerprinting has the potential to dramatically transform industrial control system security by providing a unified intrusion detection solution for critical systems.

Keywords: Industrial control systems, malware detection, power fingerprinting

1.   Introduction

Industrial control systems are computer-based systems that monitor and control process systems in critical infrastructure assets such as water treatment and distribution facilities, transportation systems, oil and gas pipelines,

J. Butts and S. Shenoi (Eds.): Critical Infrastructure Protection VIII, IFIP AICT 441, pp. 15–27, 2014.

electrical power transmission and distribution systems, and large telecommunications systems. Attacks against industrial control systems by a well-funded adversary can have devastating consequences to modern society.

Current industrial control system defenses involve updating and patching, strengthening the periphery and implementing other traditional information technology solutions. Unfortunately, these approaches have limited success in industrial control system environments [11], which render critical systems highly vulnerable to cyber attacks – as Stuxnet famously demonstrated [13]. Consider, for example, intrusion detection systems that rely on traffic analysis. Such systems are notoriously ineffective against advanced persistent threats, which leverage attacks that are immune to signature detection, minimize network utilization and mimic legitimate network traffic [6, 12, 19]. Furthermore, the systems are incapable of detecting malicious software whose execution does not generate traditional network traffic. For example, the malware could communicate using alternative channels (e.g., Bluetooth [8]) or simply remain dormant for extended periods of time. Signature-based solutions also have severe shortcomings in industrial control system environments, including the inability to detect zero-day attacks [7, 9, 14, 15], the consumption of valuable host resources that CPU-constrained platforms simply do not have [11, 16], and the lack of support for embedded systems [10].

Power fingerprinting (PFP) is a promising new technique that detects malicious software execution using physical side channel measurements. The technique involves the direct monitoring of systems with constrained resources and does not require the loading of third-party software artifacts on target platforms. As such, power fingerprinting is ideal for detecting malicious software execution in industrial control system environments and can provide an extra layer of protection that is not afforded by traditional intrusion detection approaches.

This paper demonstrates the feasibility of using power fingerprinting to directly monitor programmable logic controllers and detect malicious software execution. The experimental results demonstrate that power fingerprinting can successfully detect the execution of malware similar to Stuxnet in a Siemens S7 programmable logic controller.

2.   Power Fingerprinting

Power fingerprinting analyzes a processor side channel, such as power consumption or electromagnetic emissions, to determine whether or not it deviates from expected operation. A power fingerprinting monitor, shown in Figure 1, uses a physical sensor to capture electromagnetic signals containing small patterns that emerge during the transition from one instruction to another. In power fingerprinting, captured power traces are processed by an external device that implements signal detection and classification techniques. The observed traces are compared against baseline references to assess whether or not execution has deviated from its expected behavior, such as when malware alters normal operation.

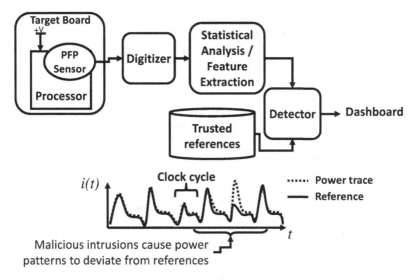

Figure 1. Power fingerprinting monitor.

Because monitoring is performed on an external device, memory and processing overhead on the target device are eliminated. Additionally, a power fingerprinting monitor can be built using commercial off-the-shelf components.

2.1 Basic Concepts

The concept behind power fingerprinting is relatively straightforward. It involves three main elements that are common to pattern recognition systems: (i) sensing; (ii) feature extraction; and (iii) classification. Sensing involves direct or indirect measurements of the instantaneous current drain. The measurements may be made using a variety of techniques, including current or electromagnetic probes.

During a runtime assessment, power fingerprinting compares the captured traces against baseline references and looks for deviations beyond what are characterized as normal execution. The baseline references uniquely identify the execution of software routines that are extracted in a controlled environment before the system is deployed. The power fingerprinting monitor uses the stored references to detect anomalous execution deviations at runtime.

The level of expected deviation during normal operation is identified during a characterization process that determines the threshold between normal and anomalous execution. An intrusion is deemed to have occurred when the observed traces do not match the baseline references within a defined tolerance.

2.2 Characterization

The baseline references contain the expected side channel signals and indicate the acceptable tolerance variation. Power fingerprinting baselines are determined by exercising a good sample in a controlled environment while capturing side channel signals. Note that this process is similar to automated software testing; thus, power fingerprinting can leverage existing tools to facilitate the baseline extraction process. Indeed, while references are unique to a target system, the process for extracting them is general and can be applied across platforms and applications.

Ideally, a reference is extracted for every execution path in the target. Programmable logic controllers are ideal candidates for complete characterization because their execution is limited in functionality. In cases where extracting a reference for every execution path is not feasible due to complexity, the characterization may focus on critical system modules (e.g., kernel and bootloader).

2.3   Advantages and Limitations

Power fingerprinting enables the continuous, real-time and direct monitoring of industrial control devices that currently lack commercial solutions for detecting malicious software execution. Power fingerprinting can detect malware that induces the slightest anomalies in execution, even when the malware remains dormant or mimics legitimate network traffic. This enhanced detection capability enables the implementation of immediate responses to neutralize a threat. Furthermore, power fingerprinting does not interfere with the operation of critical industrial control systems, allowing the monitoring of the most sensitive components.

While power fingerprinting is a powerful mechanism for detecting malicious software execution, it provides limited support for forensic analysis and attack attribution. Specifically, power fingerprinting can identify the modules that have been tampered with, but not the modifications made to the system or the attacker's intentions. Power fingerprinting is intended to be applied in a defense-in-depth approach as part of a comprehensive security solution.

2.4   Related Work

Power fingerprinting has been demonstrated in a number of experiments on a variety of target platforms [1–5]. Aguayo Gonzalez and Reed [4] have detected unauthorized software modifications in a basic commercial radio platform (PICDEM Z Evaluation Board with a PIC18 processor). The unauthorized modifications had a physical impact on the behavior of the system that could trigger regulatory certification violations. In a different experiment using the same platform, Aguayo Gonzalez and Reed [3] used a power fingerprinting monitor to detect execution deviations that affect the encryption process of radio transmissions.

Other researchers (e.g., [17, 18]) have used techniques similar to power fingerprinting for industrial control system security. In particular, they have used electromagnetic emissions to detect anomalies in Allen Bradley SLC-500 programmable logic controllers using a correlation-based approach.

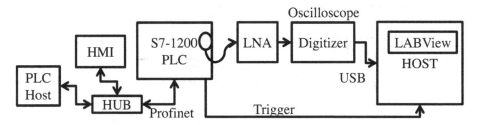

Figure 2. Power fingerprinting monitor setup.

3. Experimental Setup and Methodology

This section demonstrates the ability of power fingerprinting to monitor industrial control systems and identify malicious software execution. A reference system was implemented using a Siemens SIMATIC S7-1200 micro programmable logic controller to extract its power fingerprinting baseline references. A malicious modification, similar in structure and operation to Stuxnet, was introduced in the programmable logic controller and the baseline references were used to detect the resulting anomalous execution. The following sections describe the experimental setup and methodology.

3.1 Target Platform

The Siemens SIMATIC S7-1200 micro programmable logic controller used in the experiments had a 1212C CPU; a scalable and flexible design for compact solutions; an integrated Industrial Ethernet/PROFINET interface for programming, I/O and HMI connections, and CPU-to-CPU communications; and integrated technology functions for counting, measurement, closed-loop control and motion control.

3.2 Measurement Setup

The power fingerprinting monitor was implemented using commercial off-the-shelf components. The target programmable logic controller was first instrumented with a near-field sensor for electromagnetic compatibility testing to capture the side channel signal. The near-field sensor employed was a commercial probe from Beehive Electronics with fine spatial resolution that reduced interference from other subsystems on the board. The increased spatial resolution resulted in reduced sensitivity, which was compensated for by a wide-band amplifier with 30 dB gain. The power fingerprinting monitor setup is presented in Figure 2.

The signal captured by the sensor was digitized using a Tektronix oscilloscope. The oscilloscope was configured with a sampling rate of 2.5 GSPS; a total of 100K samples were collected in each trace. A triggering signal was provided by an I/O pin in the programmable logic controller for synchronization

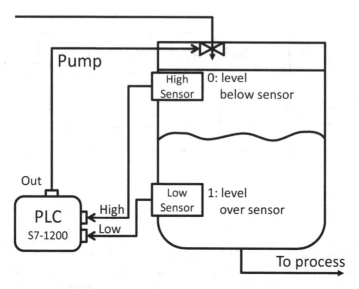

Figure 3.   Tank level control system.

purposes. The captured signals were transferred via a USB drive and processed by the power fingerprinting host using custom software tools and scripts.

3.3   Control System Logic

The experiment involved a simple tank level control system shown in Figure 3. In the experiment, the S7-1200 programmable logic controller was used to control the tank level using two sensors to determine when to turn the pump on and off.

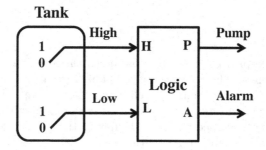

Figure 4.   Control system operation.

Figure 4 shows a simplified model of the control logic. The sensors were configured to provide a logical one when the tank water level was at or above the sensor level and a logical zero when the water level was below the sensor level.

Table 1. Control system logic table.

High Sensor	Low Sensor	Pump	Alarm
0	0	1 (On)	0 (Off)
0	1	*	0 (Off)
1	0	0 (Off)	1 (On)
1	1	0 (Off)	0 (Off)

According to the control system logic shown in Table 1, the programmable logic controller turns the pump on when the tank level drops below the low sensor and turns the pump off when the level reaches the high sensor. When the level is between both sensors (low sensor = 1 and high sensor = 0), there is no change in the pump state. The remaining combination of input values (low sensor = 0 and high sensor = 1) is a faulty condition and raises an alarm.

The control system logic was implemented in the S7-1200 programmable logic controller as a SCL program in block OB1. The following pseudocode specifies the control system logic:

```
// Power Fingerprinting Trigger
if L = 0 && H = 0 then
     pump = On
     alarm = Off
else if L = 1 && H = 1 then
     pump = Off
     alarm = Off
else if L = 0 && H = 1 then
     alarm = On
     pump = Off
     increase alarm counter
else
     outputs unchanged
end
// Power Fingerprinting Trigger
```

The control system logic has four execution paths. An execution path is selected based on the combination of input values at the beginning of the logic cycle. To facilitate synchronization, the logic incorporates a physical trigger, an electric signal sent to the digitizer via the output port of the programmable logic controller to indicate when the logic cycle is started.

3.4 Modified Control System Logic

In order to test the ability of power fingerprinting to detect malicious software execution, the control system logic was modified to incorporate a malicious

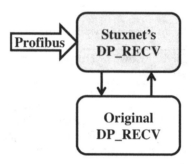

Figure 5. Functional representation of the attack.

attack. The alteration resembles the Stuxnet modification to Siemens S7-315 programmable logic controllers that hooked DP_RECV to collect information about normal uranium hexafluoride centrifuge operations.

The attack, which is shown in Figure 5, moves the original DP_RECV routine to a different logic block and replaces it with an infected block that monitors inputs and forwards requests to the original DP_RECV routine. The attack causes the pump to be turned on regardless of the sensor inputs while disabling the alarm.

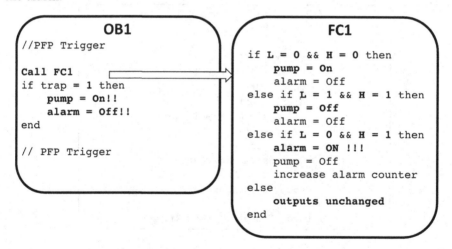

Figure 6. Modified control system logic SCL OB1.

Figure 6 shows how the original logic block is moved in the tampered version. After the original logic is executed, the tampered block post-processes the results to change the system behavior. The most important element of the tampering, however, is the fact that behavioral modifications only take place under specific conditions. Similar to Stuxnet, the attack remains dormant and the system exhibits normal behavior until the triggering condition is encountered.

The triggering condition is induced by another digital input pin that controls the sabotage routine. Note that the triggering mechanism is arbitrary; selecting

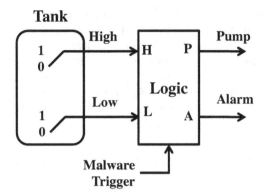

Figure 7. Tampered control system operation.

a different triggering mechanism would have no impact on power fingerprinting. Figure 7 shows a simplified model of the tampered control system logic.

Table 2. Tampered control system logic table.

High Sensor	Low Sensor	Malware Trigger	Pump	Alarm
x	x	1	1 (On)	0 (Off)
0	0	0	1 (On)	0 (Off)
0	1	0	*	0 (Off)
1	0	0	0 (Off)	1 (On)
1	1	0	0 (Off)	0 (Off)

Table 2 shows the tampered control system logic. When the triggering condition is induced, the programmable logic controller turns the pump on regardless of the sensor inputs, causing the water in the tank to overflow. When the triggering condition is absent, the observed behavior matches the original logic.

4. Experimental Results

After characterizing the original control logic and extracting the power fingerprinting references for all the execution paths, the power fingerprinting monitor was able to effectively monitor the integrity of the Siemens S7-1200 programmable logic controller. Furthermore, power fingerprinting successfully detected malicious software execution even when the triggering condition was absent.

4.1 Baseline Reference Extraction

In order to perform the runtime assessment of the original programmable logic controller, it was necessary to extract the baseline references for all the execution paths during the characterization process. Training traces were captured in a controlled environment in which input vectors were provided to exhaustively exercise all the possible execution paths.

A total of 100 training traces were captured for each execution path and processed using a spectral periodogram (spectrogram) to extract the frequency components of each training trace at different time segments. The spectrogram, which corresponds to the squared magnitude of the discrete-time short-time Fourier transform ($X(\tau, \omega)$), is given by:

$$\texttt{spectrogram}\{x\left(t\right)\}\left(\tau, \omega\right) = \left|X\left(\tau, \omega\right)\right|^2$$

where

$$X\left(m, \omega\right) = \sum_{n=-\infty}^{\infty} x[n]w[n-m]e^{-j\omega n}.$$

Note that $x[n]$ is the captured power fingerprinting trace and $w[n]$ is a Gaussian window. The power fingerprinting references were constructed by averaging the spectrograms of the 100 training traces for each execution path. For Path 0, the power fingerprinting reference is denoted by S_0; for Path 1, the power fingerprinting reference is denoted by S_1; and so on.

After the references for each execution path were computed, the power fingerprinting monitor captured a new runtime test trace $r[n]$, and compared it against the references to determine if $r[n]$ corresponded to an authorized execution path or if it should be flagged as an anomaly. In order to match $r[n]$ to a specific path reference S_i, the spectrogram of $r[n]$ was computed and subtracted from each baseline reference over selected time segments and frequency bands. The difference was then smoothed and summed across the selected time segments and frequency bands to determine the final distance for each path reference y_i.

The reference that produced the minimum distance from the test trace, $y_f = \min_i\{y_i\}$, was selected as the likely execution path that generated the test trace $r[n]$. If y_f is within the normal range as determined during the characterization, the power fingerprinting monitor classifies the trace as belonging to the corresponding execution path. If the test trace does not match any reference within the predefined tolerance, then the power fingerprinting monitor determines that an anomaly exists and raises an alarm.

4.2   Detection Performance

The ability of power fingerprinting to detect malicious software execution was tested by capturing 100 traces from the tampered programmable logic controller with the malware in a dormant state (i.e., the triggering condition was absent and the tampered version displayed the same observable behavior as the original logic).

Figure 8 shows the sample distribution (histogram) of the differences (y_f) between the original execution traces and the traces during the execution of

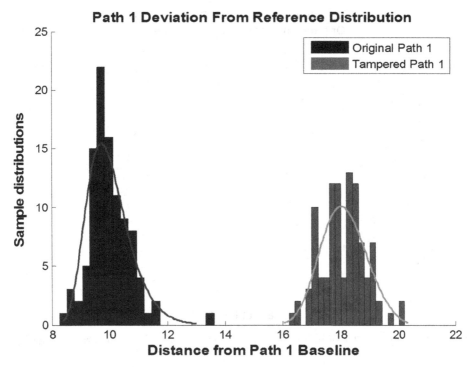

Figure 8. Deviation of Path 1 from the baseline sample distribution.

the tampered control system logic. Note that the closer y_f is to zero, the more similar the tampered execution trace is to the baseline reference trace. A clear separation can be seen between the distributions, which demonstrates the ability of power fingerprinting to detect malicious software execution.

Similar results were obtained for the other execution paths. Figure 9 presents a boxplot of an aggregated view of the execution paths. The boxplot shows that the separation between the original and tampered distributions is maintained for all possible execution paths. The results demonstrate the ability of power fingerprinting to detect malicious software in an industrial control system by directly monitoring programmable logic controller execution.

5.   Conclusions

Power fingerprinting is a novel technique for directly monitoring the execution of systems with constrained resources. The technique, which has been successfully demonstrated on a variety of platforms, does not require software artifacts to be loaded on the target platforms.

The experimental results demonstrate that power fingerprinting can directly monitor programmable logic controller execution and detect the presence of malware. Because of its zero-day detection capability and negligible overhead,

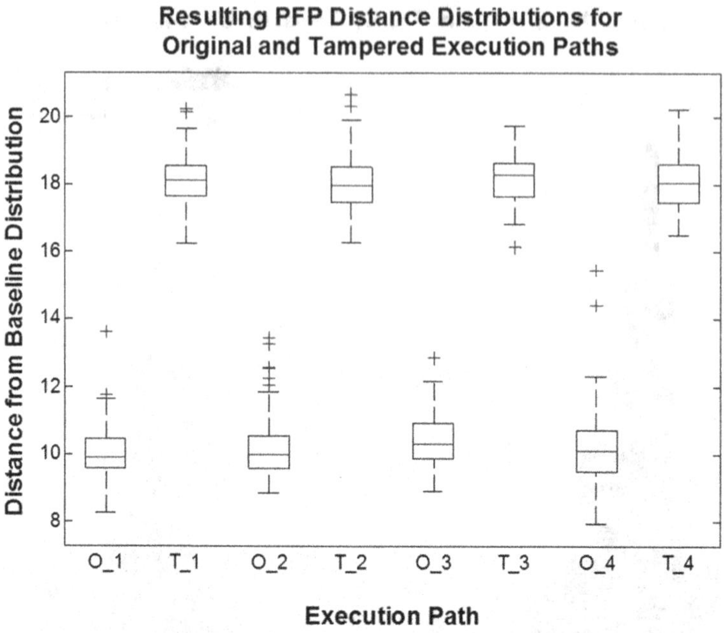

Figure 9. Anomaly detection performance for execution paths in the original logic.

power fingerprinting can potentially transform cyber security by enabling malware detection in industrial control systems as well as in other critical systems.

References

[1] C. Aguayo Gonzalez and J. Reed, Dynamic power consumption monitoring in SDR and CR regulatory compliance, *Proceedings of the Software Defined Radio Technical Conference and Product Exposition*, 2009.

[2] C. Aguayo Gonzalez and J. Reed, Power fingerprinting in SDR and CR integrity assessment, *Proceedings of the IEEE Military Communications Conference*, 2009.

[3] C. Aguayo Gonzalez and J. Reed, Detecting unauthorized software execution in SDR using power fingerprinting, *Proceedings of the IEEE Military Communications Conference*, pp. 2211–2216, 2010.

[4] C. Aguayo Gonzalez and J. Reed, Power fingerprinting in unauthorized software execution detection for SDR regulatory compliance, *Proceedings of the Software Defined Radio Technical Conference and Product Exposition*, pp. 689–694, 2010.

[5] C. Aguayo Gonzalez and J. Reed, Power fingerprinting in SDR integrity assessment for security and regulatory compliance, *Analog Integrated Circuits and Signal Processing*, vol. 69(2-3), pp. 307–327, 2011.

[6] S. Axelsson, The base-rate fallacy and the difficulty of intrusion detection, *ACM Transactions on Information and System Security*, vol. 3(3), pp. 186–205, 2000.

[7] A. Bose, X. Hu, K. Shin and T. Park, Behavioral detection of malware on mobile handsets, *Proceedings of the Sixth International Conference on Mobile Systems, Applications and Services*, pp. 225–238, 2008.

[8] A. Bose and K. Shin, On mobile viruses exploiting messaging and Bluetooth services, *Proceedings of the Second International Conference on Security and Privacy in Communications Networks and the Securecomm Workshops*, 2006.

[9] M. Christodorescu, S. Jha, S. Seshia, D. Song and R. Bryant, Semantics-aware malware detection, *Proceedings of the IEEE Symposium on Security and Privacy*, pp. 32–46, 2005.

[10] A. Cui and S. Stolfo, Defending embedded systems with software symbiotes, *Proceedings of the Fourteenth International Symposium on Recent Advances in Intrusion Detection*, pp. 358–377, 2011.

[11] S. Das, K. Kant and N. Zhang, *Handbook on Securing Cyber-Physical Critical Infrastructure: Foundations and Challenges*, Morgan Kaufmann, Waltham, Massachusetts, 2012.

[12] H. Erbacher and S. Hutchinson, Distributed sensor objects for intrusion detection systems, *Proceedings of the Ninth International Conference on Information Technology*, pp. 417–424, 2012.

[13] N. Falliere, L. O'Murchu and E. Chien, W32.Stuxnet Dossier, Version 1.4, Symantec, Mountain View, California, 2011.

[14] J. Oberheide, E. Cooke and F. Jahanian, CloudAV: N-version antivirus in the network cloud, *Proceedings of the Seventeenth USENIX Security Symposium*, pp. 91–106, 2008.

[15] M. Rajab, L. Ballard, N. Jagpal, P. Mavrommatis, D. Nojiri, N. Provos and L. Schmidt, Trends in Circumventing Web-Malware Detection, Google Technical Report rajab-2011a, Google, Mountain View, California, 2011.

[16] J. Reeves, A. Ramaswamy, M. Locasto, S. Bratus and S. Smith, Lightweight intrusion detection for resource-constrained embedded control systems, in *Critical Infrastructure Protection V*, J. Butts and S. Shenoi (Eds.), Springer, Heidelberg, Germany, pp. 31–46, 2011.

[17] S. Stone, Radio-Frequency-Based Programmable Logic Controller Anomaly Detection, Ph.D. Dissertation, Department of Electrical and Computer Engineering, Air Force Institute of Technology, Wright-Patterson Air Force Base, Ohio, 2013.

[18] S. Stone and M. Temple, Radio-frequency-based anomaly detection for programmable logic controllers in the critical infrastructure, *International Journal of Critical Infrastructure Protection*, vol. 5(2), pp. 66–73, 2012.

[19] C. Tankard, Advanced persistent threats and how to monitor and deter them, *Network Security*, vol. 2011(8), pp. 16–19, 2011.

Chapter 3

TIMING OF CYBER-PHYSICAL ATTACKS ON PROCESS CONTROL SYSTEMS

Marina Krotofil, Alvaro Cardenas, and Kishore Angrishi

Abstract   This paper introduces a new problem formulation for assessing the vulnerabilities of process control systems. In particular, it considers an adversary who has compromised sensor signals and has to decide on the best time to launch an attack. The task of selecting the best time to attack is formulated as an optimal stopping problem that the adversary has to solve in real time. The theory underlying the best choice problem is used to identify an optimal stopping criterion, and a low-pass filter is subsequently used to identify when the time series of a process variable has reached the state desired by the attacker (i.e., its peak). The complexities associated with the problem are also discussed, along with directions for future research.

Keywords: Cyber-physical attacks, optimal stopping, secretary problem

1.   Introduction

One of the growing research areas related to cyber-physical system security is developing threat models that consider an adversary who can manipulate sensor or actuator signals in order to drive a physical process to an undesired state. While many researchers have focused on the implications of manipulating signals, little work has attempted to understand the complexity and uncertainties associated with launching successful attacks and, in particular, finding the "best time" to launch an attack.

Attempting to disrupt a physical process without clearly understanding the consequences of the attack actions on the process is likely to result in a minor nuisance instead of an actual disruption – after all, breaking into a system is not the same a breaking a system.

This paper considers an attacker who can read a sensor signal for a given process variable and has to decide on a time to launch a denial-of-service (DoS) attack in order to "freeze" a certain process value above or below the setpoint stored in controller memory [5]. In doing so, the attacker deceives the controller

J. Butts and S. Shenoi (Eds.): Critical Infrastructure Protection VIII, IFIP AICT 441, pp. 29–45, 2014.
© IFIP International Federation for Information Processing 2014

about the current state of the process and evokes compensating reactions that could bring the process into the state desired by the attacker (e.g., unsafe state). In order to achieve the attack goal faster, the attacker may opt to freeze one of the peak values of a process variable (low or high) to expedite process dynamics. Typical sensor signals in a process control environment fluctuate around the setpoint or track dynamic changes in the process. In both cases, the process variable exhibits a time series of low and high peaks. The attacker neither knows how high nor how low the process variable can span, nor which of the peak values should be chosen from among all the possible boundary states.

This paper formulates the challenge as an optimal stopping time problem for the attacker. In particular, it is formulated as a best choice problem (also known as the secretary problem), in which the adversary is presented with a time series of system states provided by sensor measurements and has to decide on the optimal time to attack. Because the best choice problem assumes non-correlated time measurements, it is necessary to discern upward or downward trends in process measurements (time correlations) and then identify when a local optimum has been reached. This is a non-trivial task in many real-world environments because sensor measurements can be noisy and can have sudden fluctuations.

2.   Timing and Cyber-Physical Security

The miniaturization of processors has enabled them to replace analog components in many electronic products. The further integration of microprocessors with input and output system components has led to the evolution of microcontrollers. Microcontrollers are ubiquitous in applications ranging from consumer electronics to complex industrial systems. Microcontrollers are embedded in purpose-built computing systems used for myriad applications in the physical world. Collaborative environments comprising computational and communications elements that control physical entities with the help of sensors and actuators are called cyber-physical systems. Cyber abuses in the information technology domain do not generally depend on timing aspects. In certain instances, such as during race conditions, time-of-check to time-of-use vulnerabilities and cross-site scripting attacks that rely on gaining access to session cookies before they expire, the attacker has to ensure that the attack occurs within a tight window of time. In cyber-physical systems, however, timing is more critical because the physical state of a system changes continuously, and during the system evolution over time, some states might be more vulnerable to attacks than others. Timing plays an important role in cyber-physical systems because it characterizes the vulnerability of a system. For example, it may take minutes to observe a process change realized by an actuator action, hours to heat a tank of water or burn out a motor, and days to destroy centrifuges [6]. Understanding the timing parameters of a physical process enables an attacker to construct a successful attack as well as to maximize its impact (damage).

This paper focuses on industrial control systems, an aggregated term covering architectures, mechanisms and algorithms, that enable the processing of physical substances and the manufacturing of end products. Over the past few decades, industrial plants have undergone tremendous modernization. Technology has become an enabler of efficiency as well as a source of problems. Panels of relays are now embedded computers and simple analog sensors are now IP-enabled smart transmitters [8] with multiple wired and wireless communications modes, numerous configuration modes and even web-servers, so that maintenance staff can calibrate and manage the devices from remote locations. Thus, the possibility of remote exploitation of industrial control systems and the physical processes they manage has become a reality.

3. Optimal Stopping Problem

The adversary's goal is to cause a tangible impact on the targeted process. In the physical domain, the attacker can either tamper with the sensor signals or modify the manipulated variables issued by the controller. This paper focuses exclusively on sensor signals. In particular, it is assumed that an attacker intends to drive the process to an unsafe state by deceiving a controller about the current state of the process and thus forcing it to take harmful compensating actions. To accomplish this, the attacker can force the controller to believe that a process variable is below or above its setpoint. One way to achieve this is to forge the process variable by means of an integrity attack that subverts a sensor-controller communications channel and manipulates messages.

If the sensor-controller communications channel is secured (e.g., using message authentication codes), then the attacker might opt to jam the channel to prevent the controller from receiving process measurement updates. This type of attack is referred to as a DoS attack on the sensor signal. As a rule, controllers store sensor signals in dedicated memory registers that are updated when a new value is received. During the DoS attack, the input register designed to store measurements from a particular sensor are overwritten by fresh values. Therefore, the last process value that reached the controller before the attack is used for system control over the duration of the attack. As a result, the controller would generate control commands based on the last measurement received. In a general sense, a DoS attack is similar to an integrity attack, the only difference being that the adversary does not wield direct influence on the "attack value." Instead, the adversary may take advantage of the timing parameters of an attack, such as the starting time t_a and the duration T_a.

In previous work [4, 5], we have shown that the impact of an industrial control system attack is sensitive to the specific state of the targeted system. In particular, an attack may only be effective if the process variable is above (or below) a certain threshold. The higher (or lower) the attack process variable is beyond the threshold, the greater the impact. Moreover, since a DoS attack is easy to detect, the attacker must achieve the disruption objective as soon as possible after the attack is launched. Therefore, the attacker should aim at launching a DoS attack at the time the process variable of interest reaches a more vulnerable state, i.e., a local maximum (or minimum).

The attacker faces the following problem: given a time series that exhibits a sequence of peaks and valleys of different amplitudes, select one of the peaks to launch a DoS attack in real time. If the attacker strikes too soon, the opportunity to have a greater impact on the system is lost (compared with if the attacker waits until the process variable reaches a higher (or lower) value). However, if the attacker waits too long, the process variable may not reach a more vulnerable state than previously observed and the attacker could miss the opportunity to cause maximal damage and even have the implanted attack tools (e.g., communications jammers and sensor malware) detected before the attack is launched.

The problem of selecting an opportune time to attack can be framed as an optimal stopping problem. This problem focuses on choosing the time to take a particular action based on sequentially-observed random variables in order to maximize an expected payoff. The optimal stopping decision task, in which the binary decision to stop or continue the search depends only on the relative ranks, is modeled as the best choice problem, which is also known as the secretary problem [2].

3.1   Secretary Problem

In the standard version of the secretary problem, a finite and known number of items (or alternatives) n are presented to a decision maker sequentially and one-at-a-time in random order. Time is assumed to be discrete. At any period, the decision maker can rank all the items that have been observed in terms of their desirability or quality. For each item inspected, the decision maker must either accept the item, in which case the search process is terminated (reject), the next item in the random order is presented and the decision maker faces the same problem as before. The decision maker's objective is to maximize the probability of selecting the best item from among the n items available.

The classical secretary problem, which seeks to choose the best secretary from among all the applicants, has six assumptions:

- There is only one position available.

- The number of applicants n is finite and known to the decision maker.

- The n applicants are interviewed sequentially, one-at-a-time and in random order. Consequently, each of the $n!$ orders is equally likely.

- The decision maker can rank all n applicants from best to worst without ties. The decision to accept or reject an applicant in a given period is based only on the relative ranks of the applicants interviewed to that point.

- An applicant who is rejected cannot be recalled later.

- The decision maker is satisfied with nothing but the best. The payoff is one if the best applicant of the n applicants is selected; otherwise, the payoff is zero.

Note that an applicant is accepted only if the applicant is relatively the best among the applicants who have already been observed. A relatively best applicant is called a candidate.

The optimal stopping rule suggests that the best candidate can be selected with maximum probability $1/e$ using the rule: do not make an offer to the first n/e candidates and after that make an offer to the first candidate whose value exceeds the values of all the candidates seen thus far (or proceed to the last applicant if this never occurs). In other words, the algorithm starts with a learning phase in which the decision maker sees n/e candidates and sets an aspiration level equal to the highest value seen during the learning phase. After that, the decision maker hires the first candidate who exceeds the aspiration level.

The secretary problem assumptions impose more constraints on observation and selection than generally apply in practice [3]. Relaxing one or more assumptions to produce a more realistic formulation of the standard secretary problem has attracted the attention of the research community. This paper considers the classical solution along with a recent result that assumes the order in which the candidates arrive is not completely random, but has a probability distribution satisfying a hazard rate condition [7]. This assumption is commonly used in engineering applications – specifically, given that the value of a candidate is not less than y, the likelihood that it is equal to y increases as y increases. Gaussian, uniform and exponential distributions satisfy this property. Under these assumptions, it has been shown that the learning period falls from n/e to $n/log(n)$, meaning that it is enough to observe a much smaller number of candidates to set the optimal aspiration level. In a process control environment, the probability of detecting an intrusion increases with time, therefore, having a shorter learning phase is beneficial to the attacker.

3.2 Dealing with Correlated Time Series

While the secretary problem matches the problem that an attacker faces in our scenario, an additional condition that an attacker of a physical process encounters is that sensor signal samples do not arrive in random order. Instead, their time series represent continuous real-time measurements of physical phenomena and each sample X_i is heavily correlated with the next sample X_{i+1}. Thus, if a process variable (e.g., temperature) is increasing, it cannot drop radically in the next time instance.

Recall that the attacker sets the aspiration level to a value equal to the highest sample seen during the learning phase. According to the optimal solution algorithm for the secretary problem, upon completing the learning phase the attacker should select the first sample whose value exceeds the aspiration level. By doing so, the attacker would miss the opportunity to select an even higher value as in the case of an upward trend, where the process measurements keep increasing until a local peak is reached. Hence, unlike the static choice rule discussed above, the attacker may incorporate expectations about the future in the decision process. In this case, the choice between stopping and continuing to search at sample X_i is determined not only by the aspiration value but also by the difference between the stopping value and the continuation value X_{i+1}. The problem of identifying a signal peak is exacerbated by the fact that process variables are noisy and, therefore, an upward trend might be followed by a quick drop, followed again by an even higher gain.

To solve this problem, a low-pass filter is incorporated to smooth out short-term signal fluctuations and highlight the longer-term trends. This enables a peak to be identified as soon as a downward trend in a smoothed signal is detected (e.g., three consecutive measurement drops).

4.   Simulation Setup

The empirical analysis employed a Matlab model of the Tennessee Eastman challenge process [1] developed by Ricker [9]. It is implemented as a C-based MEX S-function with a Simulink model.

4.1   Tennessee Eastman Challenge Process

The Tennessee Eastman challenge process [1] is a modified model of a real plant-wide industrial process. The process produces two liquid (l) products from four gaseous (g) reactants involving two irreversible exothermic reactions:

$$A(g) + C(g) + D(g) \rightarrow G(l) \qquad \text{Product 1}$$
$$A(g) + C(g) + E(g) \rightarrow H(l) \qquad \text{Product 2.}$$

Figure 1 shows the Tennessee Eastman challenge process. It incorporates five major units: reactor, condenser, vapor-liquid separator, recycle compressor and stripper. The gaseous reactant and products are not specifically identified. Feed C is not pure and consists of 48.5% A and 51% C. The gas phase reactions are catalyzed by a substance dissolved in the liquid phase in the reactor. The products and unreacted ingredients leave the reactor in the vapor phase, pass through the condenser and then proceed to the vapor-liquid separator. Non-condensed components cycle back to the reactor via the recycle compressor. Condensed components are sent to the stripper that removes the remaining reactants. The byproducts and inerts are purged from the system in the vapor phase using the vapor-liquid separator whereas products G and H exit the stripper base and are separated in the downstream refining section.

The plant has eleven valves for manipulation and 41 measurements for process monitoring. In the simulation model, the control configuration involves eighteen proportional-integral (PI) controllers, sixteen process measurements XMEAS{1; 2; 3; 4; 5; 7; 8; 9; 10; 11; 12; 14; 15; 17; 31; 40} and nine setpoints that form eight multivariable control loops and one single feedback control loop [5]. All the process measurements include Gaussian noise with standard deviations typical of the types of measurements. The default simulation time for a single experiment is 72 hours with a sampling frequency of 100 measurement samples per hour. Timestamps of the simulated data sets are stored in the designated variable tout.

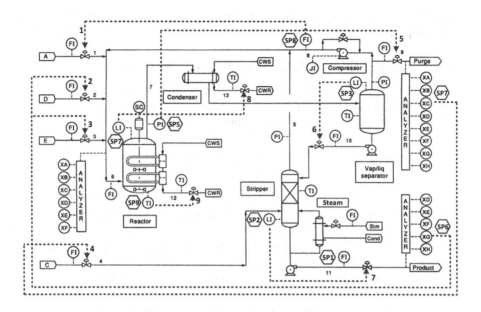

Figure 1. Tennessee Eastman challenge process [9].

In order to obtain statistically significant results, the original code was modified by generating a new seed for the random number generator for each run. In addition, higher sampling rates for the process variables – 2,000 sensor samples per hour (per sensor) – were incorporated in the Matlab workspace.

4.2   DoS Attack Modeling

Let $X_i(t)$ be the measurement by sensor i at time t where $0 \leq t \leq T$ and T be the duration of the simulation. The attack interval T_a is arbitrary and is limited to the simulation run time. The manipulated sensor readings X_i' are simulated as follows:

$$X_i'(t) = \begin{cases} X_i(t), & \text{for } t \notin T_a \\ X_i^a(t), & \text{for } t \in T_a \end{cases}$$

where $X_i^a(t)$ is the modified reading (attack value).

During a DoS attack, sensor signals do not reach the controller. If the attack starts at time t_a, we have:

$$X_i^a(t) = X_i(t_a - 1).$$

This is translated to the attacker's goal as follows: as soon as the peak is identified and the process value starts decreasing again, the attacker should immediately launch a DoS attack to freeze the peak value from the previous control loop cycle in the controller memory.

4.3   Low-Pass Filter for Sensor Signals

The simplest form of signal smoothing is the moving average, which corresponds to the mean of the previous N data points. If μ is the smoothing interval, then the moving mean is given by:

$$\hat{x}_n = \begin{cases} \hat{x}_{n-1} - \frac{x_{\mu-n}}{n} + \frac{x_\mu}{n} & \text{for } n > \mu \\ \frac{n-1}{n} \cdot \hat{x}_{n-1} + \frac{x_n}{n} & \text{for } n < \mu. \end{cases}$$

One of the side-effects of signal smoothing is the delay of the smoothed signal with respect to the original signal by $(\mu - 1)/2$ samples. To avoid shifting data in financial applications, it is recommended to average the same number of values before and after the average is calculated. However, this is not possible during real-time analysis. As a result, when the smoothed signal reaches its peak, the real measurement is already decaying. Another factor to consider is signal amplitude reduction. Increasing the smoothed signal width improves the signal-to-noise ratio but reduces the peak height. Because the aspiration value is determined based on the smoothed signal, it is not optimal.

Figure 2 shows the smoothing results for a sensor signal smoothed over different smoothing intervals. As can be seen, when μ is too small, smoothing does not sufficiently remove the noise (Figure 2(a)). As a result, stopping decisions are taken before the state reaches its local peak (Figure 2(b)).

To mitigate this problem, we introduce a retry parameter r. If $r = 0$, the search stops if the current sample is smaller than the previous sample because this could indicate that the peak has been determined and the process value is falling. Correspondingly, if $r = 3$, the search is stopped if three consecutive samples are smaller than the last "peak" sample. As discussed in the next section, the retry parameter plays an important role in the success of an attack.

In the Tennessee Eastman process, sensor signals can be roughly divided into four groups (Figure 3). A Type 1 sensor signal has large variations with low noise levels (XMEAS{1; 10; 11}). A Type 2 signal measures a variable that is at steady-state but has high frequency noise (XMEAS{2; 3; 9; 17}). A Type 3 signal is a noisy variation of a Type 1 signal (XMEAS{4; 5; 8; 12; 14; 15}). A Type 4 signal has multiple noisy signal peaks (XMEAS7). The next section shows that, in order for an attacker to successfully conduct an attack, it is necessary to consider the type of signal that will be exploited.

5.   Experimental Results

The experiments assume the presence of an attacker whose goal is to force the physical process to shut down. The result of such an attack is evaluated using the shutdown time (SDT), the time that the process is able to run before being shut down because it has exceeded the safety constraints. First, the

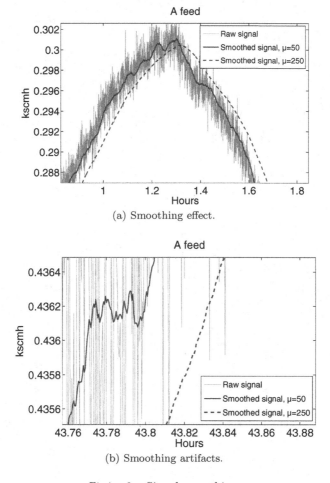

(a) Smoothing effect.

(b) Smoothing artifacts.

Figure 2. Signal smoothing.

shortest SDT that can be achieved using a DoS attack on each sensor signal is determined. Following this, to justify the importance of the strategic selection of the attack time, evidence of the ineffectiveness of DoS attacks conducted at random times is provided. In particular, it is shown that random selection not only significantly increases the time required to bring the process to the critical state, but in some cases, it could be completely ineffective. Also, the experiments evaluate the effects of the length of the learning phase and parameter smoothing on the attacker's prospects of selecting the highest (or lowest) possible process value in real time.

5.1   Shortest Shutdown Time

To find a reference value for the worst-case attacks, the lowest and highest possible process values based on the results of 20 simulations were determined.

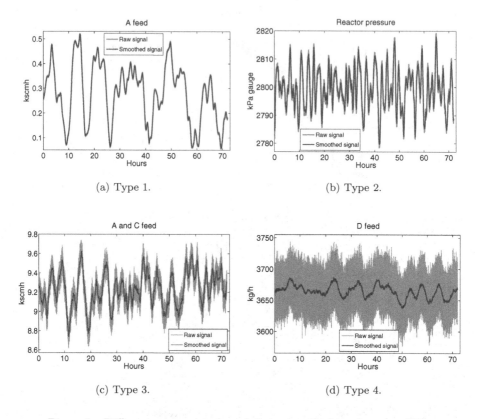

Figure 3. Different sensor signals and their smoothed versions (μ=250).

These can be considered to be the optimal attacks (but practically infeasible because the attacker has to analyze the signals and launch the attacks in real time). As $X_i^a(t)$, we use:

$$X_i^{min}(t) = \min_{t \in T} X_i(t) \quad \text{and} \quad X_i^{max}(t) = \max_{t \in T} X_i(t).$$

The mean times to shutdown for the attacks on different sensors were determined based on the results of 50 simulations. Table 1 summarizes the results. The 95% confidence intervals are calculated using the Student's t-distribution. The table does not include results for XMEAS{10; 11} because no attack on these sensors drives the system to an unsafe state.

Due to the variability of process measurement noise, the process is never in the same state. However, as the results indicate, the Tennessee Eastman process is, in general, resilient to noise variations and the SDT does not exhibit significant variations, with the exception of the attacks $F_{recycle}^{max}$ and F_A^{min}.

Table 1. Simulation results for the process-aware attack strategy.

XMEAS	Variable	Units	Min/Max	SDT (h)	Confidence Interval (95%)
(1)	A-Feed Rate	kscmh	0.0487/ 0.7466	12.116 –	(4.919; 19.310) –
(2)	D-Feed Rate	kg h^{-1}	3,556/ 3,750	3.840 3.489	(3.641; 4.040) (3.387; 3.590)
(3)	E-Feed Rate	kg h^{-1}	4,322/ 4,553	4.120 2.672	(3.916; 4.427) (2.517; 2.879)
(4)	C-Feed Rate	kscmh	8.524/ 9.825	0.284 0.920	(0.263; 0.305) (0.826; 1.026)
(5)	Recycle Flow	kscmh	29.32/ 35.17	3.824 7.324	(3.384; 4.153) (6.358; 8.773)
(7)	Reactor Pressure	kPa	2,771/ 2,829	8.300 –	(7.811; 8.638) –
(8)	Reactor Level	%	60.73/ 68.27	1.877 2.363	(1.778; 1.976) (2.100; 2.482)
(9)	Reactor Temperature	°C	122.86/ 123	1.310 0.374	(1.265; 1.346) (0.370; 0.381)
(12)	Separator Level	%	38.49/ 61.2	4.913 3.277	(4.726; 5.184) (3.168; 3.397)
(14)	Separator Underflow	m^3 h^{-1}	24.12/ 26.87	7.241 5.584	(6.847; 7.672) (5.168; 5.930)
(15)	Stripper Level	%	29.17/ 72.96	5.189 4.990	(4.900; 5.375) (4.880; 5.120)
(17)	Stripper Underflow	m^3 h^{-1}	22.37/ 23.5	1.287 0.932	(1.020; 1.634) (0.910; 0.960)

Attack F_A^{min} on the A-feed is of special interest. Not all attack instances trigger process shutdowns. Thus, the result for the F_A^{min} attack is based on 43 out of 50 cases where the process reaches an unsafe state. At the same time, attacks $P_{pressure}^{max}$ and F_A^{max} do not drive the process to an unsafe state. This means that an attacker who intends to launch an attack on reactor pressure should only strike at the minimum peaks.

5.2 Random Attack Strategy

The outcome of a DoS attack at a random time results in an arbitrary value being stored in controller memory. The closer the attack value to the setpoint, the more time it takes for the process to reach an unsafe state. To evaluate

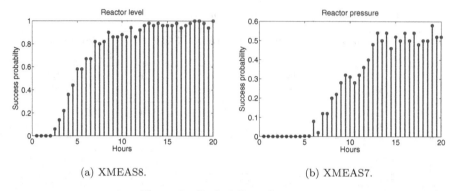

(a) XMEAS8.   (b) XMEAS7.

Figure 4.   Probability of success.

the effectiveness of launching a DoS attack at a random time, we compute the probability of the process reaching the safety limits based on 100 simulations for different DoS attack durations T_a.

The previous section noted that both the process-aware attacks $L^{max}_{reactor}$ and $L^{max}_{reactor}$ on XMEAS8 take about two hours to bring the process to an unsafe state. For purposes of comparison, Figure 4(a) shows the time taken to move the process to an unsafe state by striking randomly. Note that the attack would have to continue for at least seven hours to achieve reliable results (e.g., 75% probability). Furthermore, Figure 4(b) shows that, without process knowledge, the attacker cannot reliably succeed in launching an attack on XMEAS7.

Notably, it is almost impossible to execute a successful attack on XMEAS1 by conducting a random DoS attack. This is because the susceptibility of the process to an attack on the A-feed depends greatly on the attack value as well as the overall system state. Because a fresh stream of C contains 48.5% of A, the control scheme carefully maintains a stoichiometric balance of A and C in the system. As a result, certain attacks on XMEAS1 would be compensated for by the system.

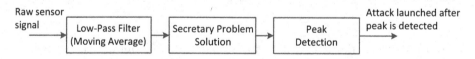

Figure 5.   Generalized approach.

5.3   Optimal Stopping Attack Strategy

The results in the preceding section demonstrate that the adversary cannot achieve the attack goal fast and/or reliably enough without strategic decision making with respect to the attack time. This section analyzes the attacker's prospects of selecting the highest possible process value in real time by applying the strategies described in the previous sections (Figure 5).

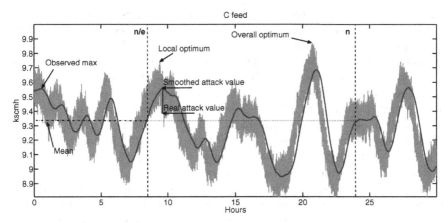

Figure 6. Educated guess approach.

Figure 6 shows the implementation of our approach. To begin, the attacker has to decide on the two parameters of the secretary problem, namely the number of samples or alternatives to consider (n) and the duration of the learning phase. For simplicity, n is measured in hours. For a time frame of 24 hours, the number of alternatives is equal to $24 \times f_s$ where f_s is the sampling rate of the sensor signal ($f_s = 2,000$). Next, the attacker must choose the smoothing parameter μ and retry parameter r. Experiments were conducted to decide on the appropriate smoothing interval; they yielded three values for the analysis: $\mu = \{50; 150; 250\}$. Similarly, reasonable values for the retry parameter were found to be in range $r = \{0; 1; 2; 3\}$.

The attacker begins the smoothing of the signal and conducts the selection process in real time. The aspiration level (reference value) is set based on the greatest value of the smoothed signal observed during the learning period. Upon completing the learning phase, the attacker sequentially inspects every sample of the smoothed signal until a sample is found whose value exceeds the reference value. Following this, the attacker applies the forward-looking strategy described in Section 3.2. Next, the value of the sample $\hat{x}_i$ is checked to see if it exceeds the previous one $\hat{x}_{i-1}$. If not, the search continues until the condition $\hat{x}_i > \hat{x}_{i-1}$ is met, because this may indicate that the process measurement has reached its peak and has started to decay. The value of the retry parameter determines how many times the latter condition should be met before making the final stopping decision. In this case, the real attack value is equal to the value of the raw signal sample X_i^a at time ($t_a - 1$).

Next, we evaluate the performance of the approach based on three metrics: (i) fractional error in identifying the peak (as a percentage) to measure the effectiveness of the low-pass filter and retry parameter r; (ii) fractional error in selecting the highest possible value in the time series (as a percentage) to measure the effectiveness of the stopping problem solution; and (iii) number of non-selections (last sample in the series is taken) evaluated as the average fractional error in selecting the largest possible sample.

Table 2 summarizes the results of applying the strategies to XMEAS1 (Type 1 signal) based on 50 simulations. The simulation results confirm that the learning period can be indeed cut down to $n/log(n)$ while producing results comparable with the n/e strategy. Due to the short learning period, the number of non-selections is reduced substantially (almost to zero). For the same reason, the fractional error in selecting the highest possible process value increases because the attacker has less time to achieve a sufficient aspiration level. Since the classic secretary problem solution results in an average of 25% non-selections, it can be a decisive factor to favor the $n/log(n)$ strategy.

The results also indicate that the appropriate selection of the smoothing factor significantly reduces the fractional error in selecting the highest possible alternative. Meanwhile, the retry parameter has a similar influence on the reduction of the fractional error in identifying the peak. The conclusion from the simulation results is that when planning an attack on a sensor signal of Type 1, the attacker should opt for the attack parameters $\mu = 250$ and $r = \{1; 2\}$ with learning window $n/log(n)$.

Finally, we demonstrate the performance for different types of sensor signals using histograms of the fractional errors in selecting the highest possible values in the corresponding time series (Figure 7). Note that the best results are obtained for sensor signals of Types 1 and 4. In contrast, the methodology proposed in this paper is not well suited to conducting attacks on sensor signals of Types 2 and 3 because of their noise levels. While applying a low-pass filter yields good results for attacks on low-noise signals, an alternative approach is required for dealing with noisy process variables. One possible approach, which we will examine in our future research, involves the use of non-parametric change detection statistics.

6.   Conclusions

This paper demonstrates that sensor signal characteristics must be considered carefully when developing attacks that target process measurements. Moreover, finding the appropriate values of parameters such as optimal signal smoothing (μ) and stopping decision (r) are not straightforward and the parameters are best determined experimentally.

An attacker may do extensive homework and proactively design portions of attacks, but the attacks would have to be tuned through reconnaissance activities such as changing configuration parameters, manipulating process variables and turning components on and off while observing the effects on the process system. From the defensive perspective, short-term process deviations arising from such "testing" can be detected by process-aware anomaly detection methods. Furthermore, in order to hinder the attacker's ability to disrupt a process system, plant administrators should strategically place misleading or false technical documentation to influence the attacker's strategy selection.

Overall, a better understanding of the complexities and uncertainties faced by an attacker when designing targeted cyber-physical attacks in the physical domain allows for better judgment regarding the efforts required to design

Table 2. Simulation results for the educated guess approach for XMEAS1.

	μ	r = 0	r = 1	r = 2	r = 3
N/e	μ = 50	• 1.06 (0.82; 1.32) • 49.46 (31.8; 67.11) • 7 (79.07)	• 0.7 (0.45; 0.96) • 44.86 (29.91; 59.81) • 4 (96.17)	• 0.62 (0.25; 0.98) • 35.78 (20.36; 51.20) • 6 (98.46)	• 0.82 (0.53; 1.11) • 54.08 (36.67; 73.04) • 8 (47.87)
24h	μ = 150	• 1.35 (1.03; 1.67) • 33.98 (11.14; 56.83) • 8 (112.56)	• 0.74 (0.48; 1.00) • 26.56 (8.06; 45.50) • 5 (61.35)	• 0.84 (0.55; 1.14) • 22.47 (9.73; 35.20) • 5 (35.39)	• 0.75 (0.35; 1.16) • 21.39 (7.01; 35.76) • 5 (89.16)
	μ = 250	• 1.42 (0.78; 2.07) • 26.87 (7.59; 46.04) • 7 (60.87)	• 0.73 (0.18; 1.29) • 8.56 (0.34; 16.78) • 3 (93.19)	• 0.80 (0.22; 1.38) • 6.33 (0.18; 12.49) • 7 (90.38)	• 0.69 (0.40; 0.98) • 27.96 (6.88; 49.03) • 5 (32.93)
N/log(N)	μ = 50	• 1.31 (0.98; 1.69) • 72.63 (57.62; 87.66) • 0	• 0.75 (0.46; 1.04) • 65.48 (51.79; 79.16) • 0	• 0.84 (0.58; 1.09) • 66.16 (50.76; 81.55) • 0	• 0.69 (0.47; 0.84) • 74.56 (59.88; 89.23) • 1 (91.32)
24h	μ = 150	• 1.04 (1.21; 1.59) • 49.73 (32.81; 66.65) • 0	• 1.03 (0.62; 1.45) • 48.26 (34.72; 61.35) • 1 (164.46)	• 1.00 (0.52; 1.47) • 33.6 (18.77; 48.42) • 0	• 0.96 (0.51; 1.43) • 27.85 (12.22; 43.49) • 0
	μ = 250	• 1.49 (1.01; 1.98) • 37.57 (20.98; 54.7) • 0	• 0.71 (0.27; 1.15) • 40.44 (23.00; 57.86) • 1 (53.81)	• 0.78 (0.43; 1.12) • 28.33 (13.42; 43.25) • 0	• 0.84 (0.52; 1.16) • 46.74 (32.18; 61.29) • 0

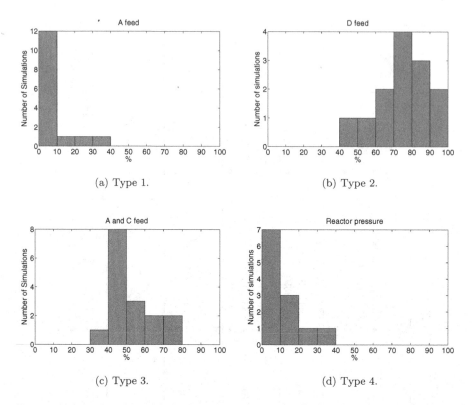

Figure 7. Distributions of fractional errors for sensor signals ($\mu = 250$, $r = 2$).

and conduct cyber-physical attacks with surgical precision (as in the case of Stuxnet). Clearly, developing sophisticated and effective cyber-physical attacks requires extensive experimentation with the same specialized industrial equipment as that installed at the targeted site.

References

[1] J. Downs and E. Vogel, A plant-wide industrial process control problem, *Computers and Chemical Engineering*, vol. 17(3), pp. 245–255, 1993.

[2] P. Freeman, The secretary problem and its extensions: A review, *Revue Internationale de Statistique*, vol. 51(2), pp. 189–206, 1983.

[3] J. Gilbert and F. Mosteller, Recognizing the maximum of a sequence, *Journal of the American Statistical Association*, vol. 61(313), pp. 35–73, 1966.

[4] Y. Huang, A. Cardenas, S. Amin, Z. Lin, H. Tsai and S. Sastry, Understanding the physical and economic consequences of attacks on control systems, *International Journal of Critical Infrastructure Protection*, vol. 2(3), pp. 73–83, 2009.

[5] M. Krotofil and A. Cardenas, Resilience of process control systems to cyber-physical attacks, *Proceedings of the Eighteenth Nordic Conference on Secure IT Systems*, pp. 166–182, 2013.

[6] R. Langner, To Kill a Centrifuge: A Technical Analysis of What Stuxnet's Creators Tried to Achieve, The Langner Group, Arlington, Virginia, 2013.

[7] M. Mahdian, R. McAfee and D. Pennock, The secretary problem with a hazard rate condition, *Proceedings of the Fourth International Workshop on Internet and Network Economics*, pp. 708–715, 2008.

[8] C. McIntyre, Using smart instrumentation, *Control Engineering* (`www.controleng.com/single-article/using-smart-instrumentation/a0ec350155bb86c8f65377ba66e59df8.html`), April 8, 2011.

[9] N. Ricker, Tennessee Eastman Challenge Archive, Department of Chemical Engineering, University of Washington, Seattle, Washington (`depts.washington.edu/control/LARRY/TE/download.html`), 2014.

Chapter 4

RECOVERY OF STRUCTURAL CONTROLLABILITY FOR CONTROL SYSTEMS

Cristina Alcaraz and Stephen Wolthusen

Abstract   Fundamental problems in control systems theory are controllability and observability, and designing control systems so that these properties are satisfied or approximated sufficiently. However, it is prudent to assume that an attacker will not only be able to subvert measurements but also control the system. Moreover, an advanced adversary with an understanding of the control system may seek to take over control of the entire system or parts thereof, or deny the legitimate operator this capability. The effectiveness of such attacks has been demonstrated in previous work. Indeed, these attacks cannot be ruled out given the likely existence of unknown vulnerabilities, increasing connectivity of nominally air-gapped systems and supply chain issues. The ability to rapidly recover control after an attack has been initiated and to detect an adversary's presence is, therefore, critical. This paper focuses on the problem of structural controllability, which has recently attracted substantial attention through the equivalent problem of the power dominating set introduced in the context of electrical power network control. However, these problems are known to be $\mathcal{NP}$-hard with poor approximability. Given their relevance to many networks, especially power networks, this paper studies strategies for the efficient restoration of controllability following attacks and attacker-defender interactions in power-law networks.

Keywords: Control systems, structural controllability, power domination, resilience

1.   Introduction

Domination, a central topic in graph theory, is a relevant theme in the design and analysis of control systems because it is an equivalent problem to that of (Kalman) controllability. The motivation comes from the concept

J. Butts and S. Shenoi (Eds.): Critical Infrastructure Protection VIII, IFIP AICT 441, pp. 47–63, 2014.

of structural controllability introduced by Lin [15], which is based on control
theory as defined by Kalman [13]:

$$\dot{x}(t) = \mathbf{A}x(t) + \mathbf{B}u(t), \; x(t_0) \; = \; x_0. \tag{1}$$

In this formulation, $x(t)$ is a vector $(x_1(t), \ldots, x_n(t))^T$ representing the current state of a system with n nodes at time t; $\mathbf{A}$ is an $n \times n$ adjacency matrix
specifying the network topology that identifies interaction between nodes; and
$\mathbf{B}$ is an $n \times m$ input matrix, where $m \leq n$, identifies the set of nodes controlled
by a time-dependent input vector $u(t) = (u_1(t), \ldots, u_m(t))$ that forces the system to a desired state in a finite number of steps. According to Kalman's rank
criterion, the system in Equation (1) is controllable if and only if:

$$\text{rank}[\mathbf{B}, \mathbf{A}\mathbf{B}, \mathbf{A}^2\mathbf{B}, \ldots, \mathbf{A}^{n-1}\mathbf{B}] = n. \tag{2}$$

However, this formulation is quite restrictive for large networks (e.g., power
networks or similarly large control systems) where there exists an exponential
growth of input values as a function of nodes. This is the main reason that
our investigations concentrate on structural controllability, where matrix $\mathbf{A}$ in
Equation (1) represents the network topology and matrix $\mathbf{B}$ contains the set of
nodes with the capacity to drive control [16].

Lin [15] defines $\mathcal{G}(\mathbf{A}, \mathbf{B}) = (V, E)$ as a digraph where $V = V_{\mathbf{A}} \cup V_{\mathbf{B}}$ is the set
of vertices and $E = E_{\mathbf{A}} \cup E_{\mathbf{B}}$ is the set of edges. In this representation,
$V_{\mathbf{B}}$ comprises the nodes capable of injecting control signals into the entire
network, also known as driver nodes (denoted as n_d) corresponding to input
vector u in Equation (1). The identification of these nodes has so far been
studied in relation to general networks. This paper concentrates on power-law
networks, most pertinent to a number of large-scale infrastructure networks. To
identify the minimum driver node subsets $\mathbf{N}_D$, we follow the approach based
on the power dominating set (PDS) problem, which is described in more detail
in [1, 2]. This interest is primarily because PDS-based networks have similar
logical structures as real-world monitoring systems, where driver nodes can
represent, for example, remote terminal units that control industrial sensors and
actuators. In fact, the PDS problem was originally introduced as an extension
of the dominating set (DS) by Haynes, et al. [12], mainly motivated by the
structure of electric power networks and the need to efficiently monitor the
networks.

Building on previous work [1, 2], this paper proposes several restoration
strategies for controlling a network after $\mathbf{N}_D$ has been perturbed. Different
attack patterns that compromise nodes and the effects of the attacks have been
considered extensively in [1, 2], in particular, the analysis and evaluation of
interactive and non-interactive attacks, including multiple rounds between attackers and defenders, respectively. However, it is clearly undesirable to restore
overall controllability through complete re-computation if the PDS properties
are only partially violated – where this is possible given the constraints imposed by compromised nodes – because the PDS problem is known to be $\mathcal{NP}$-

complete for general graphs as well as for bipartite and chordal graphs as shown by Haynes, *et al.* [12].

Subsequent research by Guo, *et al.* [11] extended $\mathcal{NP}$-completeness proofs to planar, circle and split graphs, with the exception of partial k-tree graphs with $k \geq 1$ and parameterized using $\mathbf{N}_D$, in which the DS and PDS problems can become tractable in linear-time, while the parameterized intractability can result in $W[2]$-hardness [8]. Pai, *et al.* [17] have provided results for grid graphs while Atkins, *et al.* [3] have studied block graphs. There are other approaches that address PDS for specific cases [5, 6], but none of them focus on efficient solutions for the restoration of the PDS problem following perturbations, i.e., where a PDS of the original graph $\mathcal{G}$ is known along with the changes induced on $\mathcal{G}$.

The restoration strategies defined in this paper center on general power-law and scale-free distributions by offering similar characteristics to real power networks. In particular, three strategies are defined to determine the complexity of restoration. To evaluate the complexity, this paper considers: (i) a strategy without any type of constraint for restoration; (ii) a strategy based on the graph diameter to minimize the intrinsic problem of the non-locality of PDS; and (iii) a strategy based on backup instances of driver nodes. The paper shows that this offers a gain in efficiency over re-computation while resulting in acceptable deviations from an optimal (i.e., minimal $|\mathbf{N}_D|$) PDS. Because many critical infrastructures require timely or even real-time bounded restoration to ensure resilience and continued operation, the ability to restore controllability rapidly is essential and, of course, highly desirable.

2. Conditions for the Analysis

This section discusses the initial assumptions and conditions used to restore the structural controllability when nodes are attacked from within a network. Let $G(V, E)$ be a directed acyclic graph (DAG) based on an arbitrary set of nodes V and a set of edges E, where each vertex $v_i \in V$ can be linked to other $v_j \in V$ such that $(v_i, v_j) \in E$, without producing loops or self-loops (i.e., $v_i \neq v_j$).

2.1 Assumptions for Perturbation

The first assumption we consider here is that one or several vertices can be targeted by one or several attackers, knowing the structure or probability distribution of edges of the graph, its topology, and the identities of the current driver nodes $\mathbf{N}_D$ (note that $\mathbf{N}_D$ is not necessarily unique). These driver nodes that also belong to V satisfy the two observation rules for controllability, which were simplified by Kneis, *et al.* [14] from the original formulation specified by Haynes, *et al.* [12]. The two rules and their algorithms are detailed in [1, 2] and below:

- **OR1:** A vertex in $\mathbf{N}_D$ observes itself and all its neighbors.

- **OR2:** If an observed vertex v of degree $d \geq 2$ is adjacent to $d-1$ observed vertices, the remaining unobserved vertex becomes observed as well.

Note that the omission of OR2 already results in the $\mathcal{NP}$-complete DS problem with a polynomial-time approximation factor of $\Theta(\log n)$ [9]. The following condition is that the construction of $\mathbf{N}_D$ is arbitrary and depends on the selection of vertices satisfying OR1, allowing the customizable selection of controllability generation strategies as specified in [1]. After $\mathbf{N}_D$ has been obtained, we evaluate two different scenarios concentrating on attacks against either node or edge (communications link) availability [1, 2]:

- **SCN-1:** Randomly remove some (not all) edges of one or several vertices, which may compromise the controllability of dependent nodes or disconnect parts of the control graph and underlying network.

- **SCN-2:** Randomly isolate one or several vertices from the network by intentionally deleting all their links (i.e., this attack may result in the complete isolation of nodes from the network).

As detailed in [1, 2], either attack scenario may result in a degradation of the control of a network and a significant reduction in observability (including partial observability). To address this aspect, we identify two classes of nodes:

- **U-1:** The node u is not observed by an n_d, but belongs to $\mathbf{N}_D$ and is part of the control node set.

- **U-2:** The node u is not observed by an n_d and does not belong to $\mathbf{N}_D$. This means that u is part of the set of observed nodes, denoted as O, such that $O = V - \mathbf{N}_D$.

When such a node is not being observed by a member of $\mathbf{N}_D$, the set of unobserved nodes U has to be updated so that each node $u \in U$ can be again observed by at least one member of $\mathbf{N}_D$.

2.2 Assumptions for Restoration

We assume that the restoration of structural controllability $\mathbf{N}_D$ is initially based on searching driver nodes in $\mathbf{N}_D$ that offer the coverage of unobserved nodes in U with dependence on attacked nodes in A. The term coverage refers to the ability of a new link to be established between the best candidate in $\mathbf{N}_D$ and an unobserved node in U such that the two observation rules OR1 and OR2 specified above are satisfied. For this, the candidates for restoring the controllability must have the following properties:

- Satisfy the conditions of OR1, i.e., select an $n_d \in \mathbf{N}_D$ capable of observing itself and an unobserved $u \in U$ through a new link $(n_d, u) \in E$ such that $|\mathbf{N}_D| \geq 1$.

- None of the new restoration links must violate the out-degree distribution of a power-law network and must not introduce cycles.

- Satisfy the conditions of OR2, i.e., verify that $\forall\, n_d \in \mathbf{N}_D$ of degree $d \geq 2$, OR2 is not infringed. This can involve the inclusion of one or several new members in $\mathbf{N}_D$ such that $|\,\mathbf{N}_D\,| \leq |\,V\,|$.

At the end of the algorithm, the restored set $\mathbf{N}_D$ can increase the initial number of driver nodes such that $U = \oslash$ (note that $|\,\mathbf{N}_D\,| = |\,V\,|$ in degenerate cases). However, and unfortunately, we must also consider the handicap of non-locality of PDS and the $\mathcal{NP}$-complete property demonstrated by Haynes, *et al.* [12].

Our heuristic approach is based on ensuring that the hard constraints, i.e., observation rules, are satisfied primarily and that, as a secondary constraint, the out-degree distribution property of the underlying power-law network remains unaltered. This strategy also depends on the approaches taken for each restoration strategy defined in the remainder of the paper. In this case, the study is based on two main approaches:

- **APPR-1:** Find an $n_d \in \mathbf{N}_D$ to re-link it to an unobserved node $u \in U$.

- **APPR-2:** Find an $n_{d_{bl}}$ belonging to a backup list of driver nodes such that there is an edge between $n_{d_{bl}}$ and unobserved node $u \in U$.

Likewise, each restoration strategy has to consider some of the following "restoration rules" (heuristics):

- **RR1:** If u is a U-1, then it is necessary to ensure that u still satisfies OR1.

- **RR2:** If u is a U-2, and the restoration strategy follows the APPR-1 approach, it is necessary to first find the driver node $n_d \in \mathbf{N}_D$ with out-degree equal to zero, or find a vertex $n_d \in \mathbf{N}_D$ of out-degree $d \geq 2$ such that $|\,children(n_d) - \mathbf{N}_D\,| \geq 1$ where $children(n_d)$ is a function that obtains the set of child nodes corresponding to the out-degree of n_d. In this way, the violation of OR2 after the link is avoided.

- **RR3:** If u is a U-2 and the restoration strategy follows the APPR-2 approach, it is necessary to first find the driver node $n_{d_{bl}}$ of a given backup list with out-degree equal to one (pointing out to itself), or find an $n_{d_{bl}}$ in the backup list of out-degree $d \geq 2$ such that $|\,children(n_{d_{bl}}) - \mathbf{N}_D\,| > 1$ to avoid violating OR2.

3. Restoration of Structural Controllability

The three restoration rules given in Section 2.1 are the basic constraints to address the following three restoration strategies:

Algorithm 1 : Basic_Re-Link($\mathcal{G}(V, E), \mathbf{N}_D, U, A$).

---
output $\mathbf{N}_D$
local $S_1, u, n_d, or2$;
$or2 \leftarrow false$;
while $U \neq \oslash$ **do**
   ($\star$) *Randomly choose a vertex* $u \in U$;
   if $u \notin \mathbf{N}_D$ **then**
      ($\star$) ($S_1 \leftarrow \forall n_d \in \mathbf{N}_D - A$ *with maximum in_degree*)
      and ((n_d, u) $\in E$ *is DAG*);
      ($\star$) *Common_Relink*($\mathcal{G}(V, E), \mathbf{N}_D, S_1, u, U, A, or2$);
   end if
   $U \leftarrow U \setminus \{u\}$;
end while
return ($\star$) *verifyOR2*($\mathcal{G}(V, E), \mathbf{N}_D, A, or2$);

- **STG-1:** No constraints through APPR-1.

- **STG-2:** Parameterization using the network diameter and APPR-1.

- **STG-3:** A backup list of driver nodes through APPR-2.

This section develops and analyzes the three associated algorithms, considering in addition the parameters and functions described above.

3.1   STG-1: Restoration Algorithm and Analysis

For any attack scenario (SCN-1 and SCN-2), the approach involves finding the candidates in $\mathbf{N}_D$ that can provide coverage to each vertex contained in U through a new edge. This approach is specified by Algorithm 1, where the symbol ($\star$) is an indication for the complexity analysis given in Section 4.

We briefly outline the semantics of Algorithm 1. For each unobserved node, the first step is to verify that it is part of $\mathbf{N}_D$. If a vertex $u \in U$ is an n_d by itself (U-1), then it is not necessary to find a member of $\mathbf{N}_D$ to establish the link because such a node observes itself, satisfying the first restoration condition (RR1) given in Section 2.2. Otherwise, a non-attacked n_d is randomly chosen to proceed with link restoration. However, because this new link (generated by Algorithm 2) can change the power-law distribution given in $\mathcal{G}(V, E)$, only the candidates with the highest in-degree (≥ 0) are chosen so as not to skew the degree distribution, effectively obtaining a preferential attachment process [4]. From these candidates, those that do not produce cycles after the attachment are selected in order to comply with the second assumption given in Section 2.2.

Regardless of the type of restoration strategy (STG-1, STG-2, STG-3) and the state of U, the verification of the existence of nodes in $\mathcal{G}(V, E)$ that violate OR2 after a perturbation is always required. To be more concise, the analysis is reduced to a subset of nodes instead of the entire graph; this subset contains the nodes related to the set of A. Moreover, depending on the target (TG) that is attacked, the analysis can vary:

Algorithm 2 : Common_Re-Link($\mathcal{G}(V, E), \mathbf{N}_D, S_1, u, U, A, or2$).

---

output $\mathcal{G}(V, E), \mathbf{N}_D, or2$
local S_2, n_d;
if $S_1 \neq \oslash$ then
    ($\star$) $S_2 \leftarrow \forall\, n_d \in S_1 / (out\_degree == 0)$ or $(|\, children(n_d) - \mathbf{N}_D\, | \geq 1)$;
    if $S_2 \neq \oslash$ then
        Randomly choose a $n_d \in S_2$;
    else
        ($\star$) *Randomly choose a* $n_d \in S_1$;
        ($\star$) $\mathbf{N}_D \leftarrow \mathbf{N}_D \cup \{n_d\}$; ($\star$) $or2 \leftarrow true$;
    end if
    Establish a link between n_d *and* u, *such that* $(n_d, u) \in E$;
else
    $\mathbf{N}_D \leftarrow \mathbf{N}_D \cup \{u\}$; $or2 \leftarrow true$;
end if

- **TG-1:** An n_d has been attacked, so OR2 is performed for each n_d in A. However, the verification process is only effective for scenarios SCN-1 in which the state of each child of an affected node has to be evaluated. This process is disrupted when there is an $n_d \in A$ of degree ≥ 2 with $|\, children(n_d) - \mathbf{N}_D\, |= 1$.

- **TG-2:** A node $v \in O$ has been attacked, so OR2 is applied for each $v \in A$. However, the analysis is only effective for scenarios SCN-1 where the algorithm is applied to the father nodes $n_{d_{f_v}}$ related to v and $n_{d_{f_v}} \in \mathbf{N}_D$. Because of TG-1, the proof may be interrupted when there is an $n_{d_{f_v}}$ of degree ≥ 2 with $|\, children(n_{d_{f_v}}) - \mathbf{N}_D\, |= 1$. The set of driver fathers is obtained through the function *fathers(v)* corresponding to the in-degree of v.

As stated in Algorithm 3, the breach of OR2 involves an update of $\mathbf{N}_D$ and the execution of Algorithm OR2, which is detailed in [1]. On the other hand, the correctness proof of STG-1 involves induction:

- **Precondition:** $A \neq \oslash$ such that $|\, \mathbf{N}_D - A\, | \geq 1$.

- **Postcondition:** $U = \oslash$, and OR1 and OR2 are fulfilled.

- **Case 1:** $U = \oslash$ after perturbation (SCN-1 or SCN-2). Although the while loop in Algorithm 1 is not processed, Algorithm 3 must be executed to verify the fulfillment of OR2. Depending on the attack scenario, the resolution of Algorithm 3 changes. For scenarios SCN-1, the loops for the sets *attacked_N_D* and *attacked_O* must be launched to detect the existence of one driver node ($\in attacked\_N_D$) or parent drivers ($\in attacked\_O$) that violate the second controllability rule. In contrast, such sets are not considered for SCN-2 scenarios because the affected nodes are completely isolated, without children and parent vertices, satisfying OR2 through *out_degree* $= 0$.

Algorithm 3 : Common_VerifyOR2($\mathcal{G}(V, E), \mathbf{N}_D, A, or2$).

---

output $\mathbf{N}_D$
local $n_d, attacked\_N_D, attacked\_O, or2, i$;
$attacked\_N_D \leftarrow N_D \cap A$; $attacked\_O \leftarrow A - N_D$;
if $(attacked\_N_D \notin \oslash)$ and $(or2 == false)$ then
   if $\exists$ a $n_d \in attacked\_N_D$ that breaks OR2 then
      $\mathbf{N}_D \leftarrow \mathbf{N}_D \cup \{children(n_d) - \mathbf{N}_D\}$; $or2 \leftarrow true$;
   end if
end if
if $(attacked\_O \notin \oslash)$ and $(or2 == false)$ then
   $i \leftarrow 1$;
   while $(i \leq | attacked\_O |)$ and $(or2 == false)$ do
      $S_1 \leftarrow fathers(attacked\_O[i])$;
      if $\exists$ a $s_1 \in S_1$ that breaks OR2 then
         $\mathbf{N}_D \leftarrow \mathbf{N}_D \cup \{children(s_1) - \mathbf{N}_D\}$; $or2 \leftarrow true$;
      end if
      $i \leftarrow i + 1$;
   end while
end if
if $or2$ then
   Execute OR2 defined in [1];
end if
return $(\star)$ $\mathbf{N}_D$;

- **Case 2:** $U \neq \oslash$ after perturbation, being $| U | = 1$. In these circumstances, two cases must be distinguished:

  (i) If u is U-1, the condition RR is met.

  (ii) If u is U-2, it is necessary to explore the existence of one or several candidates $\{n_{d_1}, \ldots, n_{d_n}\}$ with maximum in-degree (≥ 0) and with the capability to cover u without producing cycles and complying with RR2. If this is the case, we ensure that $\exists$ an $n_d \in \mathbf{N}_D$ for coverage, and u therefore becomes part of O, guaranteeing that U is null for next iteration. If not, $\mathbf{N}_D$ is updated with $\mathbf{N}_D \cup \{u\}$ to be observed at least by itself, where $U = \oslash$ in the next iteration. However, this updating involves performing a verification process of OR2 [1] to determine the observation degree of the entire network after the loop of Algorithm 1.

- **Induction:** Assuming that we are in step k ($k > 1$) with $U \neq \oslash$, $k = | U |$ and $| \mathbf{N}_D | \geq 1$, we randomly select a node $u \in U$ in each iteration of the while loop. When selecting a node, two cases can arise depending on u (U-1 or U-2), which pursue the same goals as Case 2 (but with $| U | > 1$). At the end of Algorithm 1, the set U and k are always updated through $U = U \setminus \{u\}$ (see Case 2). In the next state, with $k - 1$, the procedure adopted is still valid, which means that the postcondition $U = \oslash$ is not met and the loop must be run again for the next state k until $k = 0$.

Algorithm 4 : Diameter-Based Relinking($\mathcal{G}(V,E), \mathbf{N}_D, U, A$).

---

output $\mathbf{N}_D$
local $S_{d_1}, S_{d_2}, S_1, u, n_d, or2$;
$or2 \leftarrow false$;
while $U \neq \oslash$ do
    ($\star$) *Randomly choose a vertex $u \in U$*;
    if $u \notin \mathbf{N}_D$ then
        ($\star$) $S_{d_1} \leftarrow BFS(\mathcal{G}(V,E))$;
        ($\star$) $S_{d_2} \leftarrow \forall\, n_d \in \mathbf{N}_D - A$ *with minimum diameter* $\in S_{d_1}$
        and $(n_d, u) \in E$ *is DAG*;
        if $S_{d_2} \neq \oslash$ then
            ($\star$) $S_1 \leftarrow \forall\, n_d \in S_{d_2}$ *with maximum in_degree(n_d)*;
            ($\star$) *Common_Relink*($\mathcal{G}(V,E), \mathbf{N}_D, S_1, u, U, A, or2$);
        else
            $\mathbf{N}_D \leftarrow \mathbf{N}_D \cup \{u\}$; $or2 \leftarrow true$;
        end if
    end if
    $U \leftarrow U \setminus \{u\}$;
end while
return ($\star$) *verifyOR2*($\mathcal{G}(V,E), \mathbf{N}_D, A, or2$);

When $k = 0$, Case 1 occurs, and therefore the postcondition is true and Algorithm 1 terminates.

3.2   STG-2: Restoration Algorithm and Analysis

One extension of STG-1 is to consider the network diameter as described in Algorithm 4. By induction, the proof of STG-1 can be expanded by taking into account the initial and final conditions and base cases. For each iteration k ($k > 1$) with $U \neq \oslash$ and $\mid \mathbf{N}_D \mid \geq 1$, a node $u \in U$ is selected randomly. As in the previous proof, we distinguish two types of affected nodes. If the node is U-1, then RR1 is still satisfied. However, if the node is U-2, then $\forall\, n_d \in \mathbf{N}_D - A$ nodes with the minimum diameter are selected to ensure acyclic graphs after repair. Because the graph is unweighted, breadth-first search is used to obtain a list of nodes together with their diameters, and through this list the n_d with minimum diameter (≥ 0) with respect to the entire graph are obtained.

In the case where there does not exist a candidate node that satisfies all the constraints, the unobserved node becomes part of the $\mathbf{N}_D$ to guarantee at least OR1; otherwise, the inductive proof of STG-1 can be employed. At the end of the loop, the precondition $\mid U \mid = k$ is updated in each stage k by computing $U = U \setminus \{u\}$ until $k = 0$. As a result of the proof of STG-1, the postcondition is true and Algorithm 4 terminates when Case 1 as defined in STG-1 is finally reached.

3.3   STG-3: Restoration Algorithm and Analysis

This strategy requires initial pre-processing before the generation of backup instances composed of driver nodes in $\mathcal{G}(V, E)$. These instances have to be organized into a tree-like structure based on the concept of "nice tree decomposition." To do this, a previous construction of a tree decomposition must be built, taking into account the network diameter for later transformation into a nice tree decomposition. A tree decomposition is a tree T of $\mathcal{G}(V, E)$ with I nodes, where each node in T is a bag containing a set of $n_d \subseteq \mathbf{N}_D$ satisfying the following properties [11]:

- **Property 1:** $\bigcup_{i \in T} bag_i = \mathbf{N}_D$.

- **Property 2:** $\forall (n_{d_{bl_w}}, n_{d_{bl_z}}) \in E$ with diameter ≥ 0, there exists a bag_i in T such that $(n_{d_{bl_w}}, n_{d_{bl_z}}) \subseteq bag_i$.

- **Property 3:** $\forall bag_i, bag_j, bag_z \in T$, if bag_j is on the path from bag_i to bag_z in T, then $bag_i \cap bag_z \subseteq bag_j$.

The tree width corresponds to the minimum width w over all tree decompositions of $\mathcal{G}(V, E)$, where $w = max_{i \in I}(| bag_i | \in T) - 1$ and $w \geq 1$. This means that a tree decomposition T of width w with $| \mathbf{N}_D |$ driver nodes can be turned into a nice tree decomposition of width w, but subject to the diameter associated with each driver node within the network [7]. In this way, bags containing driver nodes with smaller diameters are the leaves of T while driver nodes with higher diameters are located closer to the root.

For transformation to a nice tree decomposition, each node i in the tree T has at most two children (j, z) complying with two additional conditions: (i) nodes with two children bag_j and bag_z, $bag_i = bag_j = bag_z$ (bag_i as a join node); and (ii) nodes with a single child bag_j such that $bag_i = bag_j \cup \{n_d\}$ (bag_i as an introduce node) or $bag_i = bag_j - \{n_d\}$ (bag_i as a forget node). In practice, these trees are constructed using tables with at least three columns (i, j, z), where each entry i contains those subsets of n_d in relation to i. However, this data structure also takes into account the maximum diameter associated with each bag because the approach does not focus on re-linking (APPR-1), the value of which remains constant throughout the restoration process. Therefore, the spatial overhead for such a table may become $3 \times 2^{w+1} = O(2^{w+1})$ entries [10].

Algorithm 5 describes the behavior of the restoration strategy with one or several nice tree decompositions T_{bk} as the main input parameter with a storage cost of $O(\sum_{bk=1}^{M} 2^{w+1})$. The idea is to process this parameter in a bottom-up fashion to find the driver nodes with minimum diameter that ensure the fulfillment of RR3 specified in Section 2.2. The inductive proof begins by defining the initial and final conditions, and the base cases:

- **Precondition:** $A \neq \oslash$ with at least one T_{bk_j} with $M \geq j \geq 1$.

- **Postcondition:** $U = \oslash$, and OR1 and OR2 are fulfilled.

Algorithm 5 : Backup Instance-Based Scheme($\mathcal{G}(V,E), N_D, A, U, T_{bk}, M$).

---

output $\mathbf{N}_D$

local *current_diam*, $S_1, S_2, u, n_d, or2, bk$;

$or2 \leftarrow false$;

while $U \neq \oslash$ do

 Randomly choose a vertex $u \in U$;

 if $u \notin N_D$ then

  for $bk \leftarrow 1 \; to \; M$ do

   current_diam $\leftarrow \infty$;

   while ($maximun(diameter \; in \; bag_i) \leq current\_diam$) and

    (! *visited the whole* T_{bk}) do

    if ($\exists$ a $n_{d_{bl}} \in (bag_i - A)$ such that $(n_{d_{bl}}, u) \in E$) and

    $((out\_degree == 1)$ or $(\mid children(n_{d_{bl}}) - \mathbf{N}_D \mid > 1))$ then

     ($\star$) *current_diam* $\leftarrow maximum(diameter \; in \; bag_i)$;

     if $n_{d_{bl}} \in \mathbf{N}_D$ then

      $S_1 \leftarrow S_1 \cup \{n_{d_{bl}}\}$;

     else

      ($\star$) $S_2 \leftarrow S_2 \cup \{n_{d_{bl}}\}$;

     end if

    end if

   end while

  end for

  if $S_1 = \oslash$ then

   if $S_2 \neq \oslash$ then

    ($\star$) *Randomly choose a vertex* $s_i \in S_2$; ($\star$) $N_D \leftarrow N_D \cup \{s_i\}$;

   else

    ($\star$) $N_D \leftarrow N_D \cup \{u\}$; ($\star$) $or2 \leftarrow true$;

   end if

  end if

 end if

 $U \leftarrow U \setminus \{u\}$;

end while

return ($\star$) $verifyOR2(\mathcal{G}(V,E), \mathbf{N}_D, A, or2)$;

- **Case 1:** Analogous to Case 1 of the STG-1 proof in Section 3.1.

- **Case 2:** $U \neq \oslash$ after perturbation, being $\mid U \mid = 1$. As in Case 2 of the STG-1 proof, two sub-cases must be distinguished:

 (i) If u is **U-1**, then the condition RR1 is satisfied.

 (ii) If u is **U-2**, then Algorithm 5 needs to traverse all trees T_{bk_j} from the bottom to locate the bags in T_{bk_j} that contain the best driver candidates to cover u. This process involves the verification of the existence of an $n_{d_{bl}} \in bags_i - A$ such that $(n_{d_{bl}}, u) \in E$ with minimum diameter in which RR3 is fulfilled. During this process, we also explore if such an $n_{d_{bl}}$ belongs to $\mathbf{N}_D$ to avoid increasing $\mathbf{N}_D$. If so, the set S_1 is updated through $S_1 \cup \{n_{d_{bl}}\}$; otherwise, S_2 is updated. In the case where $S_1 \neq \oslash$, we ensure that u is covered by at least one member in $\mathbf{N}_D$ and the set O is updated, guaranteeing that U is empty in the next iteration. In contrast, if there is no perfect candidate (as above) in $\mathbf{N}_D$ and $S2 \neq \oslash$, we also guarantee the existence of an $n_{d_{bl}} \in T_{bk_j}$ with the ability to cover u, and hence $O = O \cup \{u\}$ and $U = \oslash$ for the next iteration. However, $\mathbf{N}_D$ must be updated with $\mathbf{N}_D \cup \{n_{d_{bl}}\}$, requiring Algorithm 5 to verify the observation degree of the entire network when the loop finishes.

This verification process, described in detail in Section 3.1, may also be performed when there is no perfect candidate ($S_1 = \oslash$ and $S_2 = \oslash$) to cover u. In this case, u becomes part of $\mathbf{N}_D$ to comply with OR1, and hence $U = \oslash$ in the next iteration. When $U = \oslash$ and the rule OR2 is satisfied, the postcondition is true.

- **Induction:** In step k ($k > 1$) with $U \neq \oslash$, $k = |U|$ and $|\mathbf{N}_D| \geq 1$, we randomly select a node $u \in U$ in each iteration of the loop. When selecting a node, two situations can occur depending on u: U-1 or U-2, and both following the same goals set out for Case 2 (of this proof), but with $|U| > 1$. At the end of the algorithm, the set U and k are always updated through $U = U \setminus \{u\}$. In the next state, with $k - 1$, the procedure adopted is still valid, which means that the postcondition $U = \oslash$ is not met and the loop must be run up again for the next state k until $k = 0$. When this happens, Case 1 of the STG-1 proof must be verified to conclude that the postcondition is true, and therefore Algorithm 4 terminates.

4.   Complexity Analysis and Discussion

This section analyzes the computational complexity of the three restoration algorithms, Algorithm 1, Algorithm 4 and Algorithm 5. In the case of STG-1, it is required to process the entire U set k times where $k = |U|$. For these k iterations, the algorithm must also find the best candidates in $\mathbf{N}_D - A$ with the highest in-degree to ensure the fulfillment of RR2 in the best scenario, or increase $\mathbf{N}_D$, at least, by one unit in the worst case.

For simplicity, we denote $|V| = n$, $|E| = e$, $|A| = a$ $(= 1)$, $|\mathbf{N}_D| = nd$ and $f = fathers(n_d)$; and we study the upper bounds for SCN-1 and SCN-2. To evaluate the worst scenario of each SCN-x ($x = \{1, 2\}$), we assume that $nd \approx n$ and the adversarial scenario is non-interactive (a single target TG-x ($x = \{1, 2\}$)), so that if $A \subseteq \mathbf{N}_D$, then $nd - a \approx n$ as well. In addition, we must also select the longest trace of Algorithm 1 that includes Algorithm 3, following the indication given by $\star$ – note that both the assignment and if instructions have constant complexity $O(i)$ and can be neglected. To address this aspect, we first evaluate the upper bound needed to find the non-attacked driver nodes $(\mathbf{N}_D - A)$ with maximum in-degree (≥ 0) that satisfy the directed acyclic test after repair and RR2. The computation time of this entire process may become $O(kn^2)$ if $nd \approx n$.

Depending on SCN-x and the targeted node TG-x, the computational complexity of Algorithm 3 can become variable as described in Section 3.1:

- **TG-1 in SCN-1:** In this case, it is necessary to verify OR2 for each attacked driver node in *attacked_N$_D$* with a cost of $O(a + e)$. As we are evaluating the worst scenario, we must observe that after computing all the nodes in *attacked_N$_D$*, there exists an n_d that infringes OR2, which forces Algorithm 3 to compute Algorithm OR2 given in [1] with an overhead of $O(nd(nd + e)) = O(n^2)$. Therefore, the total complexity for this scenario is $O(kn^2 + ((a + e) + n^2)) = O(kn^2)$.

- **TG-1 in SCN-2:** The verification of OR2 is not possible because of the complete isolation of the nodes in *attacked_N$_D$*; hence $O(kn^2 + (a+e)) = O(kn^2)$.

- **TG-2 in SCN-1:** This attack scenario requires Algorithm 3 to explore the existence of a parent $n_{d_{f_v}}$ related to $v \in$ *attacked_O* that does not comply with OR2. This entails an upper bound of $O(kn^2 + (a(f + e) + n^2)) = O(kn^2)$.

- **TG-2 in SCN-2:** This case is similar to TG-1 in the SCN-2 proof.

The extension of $\mathbf{N}_D$ can be influenced according to:

- **TG-x in SCN-1:** An increase of at least two new n_d in $\mathbf{N}_D$.

- **TG-x in SCN-2:** An increase of one unit in $\mathbf{N}_D$ in the worst case.

The computational cost of Algorithm 4 is analogous to that of restoration strategy STG-1 (Algorithm 1), but this time it is necessary to consider the overhead involved in the best-first search ($O(n + e)$) to compute the diameter of the entire network. After the list with diameter values is obtained, the driver nodes related to $\mathbf{N}_D - A$ are extracted in order to validate them with an acyclicity test ($O((nd - a)(n + e)) = O(n^2)$) and to subsequently obtain the driver nodes with the highest in-degree ($O(nd - a) = O(n)$) that comply with RR2 ($O((nd - a) + e) = O(n + e)$). The overhead of the first part is so far $O(k((n + e) + n^2 + n + (n + e))) = O(kn^2)$ if $nd \approx n$. The rest of the analysis follows the same steps as for SCN-x and TG-x stated above, with the results summarized in Table 1.

With regard to strategy STG-3, we simplify the study considering $b = w + 1$ (largest bag in T_{bk_j}) and the worst case with $n_d \approx n$. To compute a bag bag_i of T_{bk_j} with $j \leq M$, Algorithm 5 must identify the existence of an $n_{d_{bl}}$ that complies with RR3, which yields a cost of $O(b + e)$. To obtain the best candidates of each backup instance T_{bk_j} stored in memory, the algorithm needs to process each tree with a computational cost of $O(\sum_{bk=1}^{M} 2^{w+1}(b + e))$. The second part of the approach follows the same approach described above for Algorithm 3, which is summarized below and in Table 1:

Table 1.   Complexity of the three restoration strategies.

	Threat Scenarios			
	SCN-1 – TG-x		**SCN-2 – TG-x**	
	Time	$\mathbf{N}_D$	Time	$\mathbf{N}_D$
STG-1	$O(kn^2)$	$nd+2$	$O(kn^2)$	$nd+1$
STG-2	$O(kn^2)$	$nd+2$	$O(kn^2)$	$nd+1$
STG-3	$O(k(\sum\limits_{bk=1}^{M}(2^{w+1}(b+e))))$	$nd+2$	$O(k(\sum\limits_{bk=1}^{M}(2^{w+1}(b+e))))$	$nd+1$

- **TG-x in SCN-1:** $O(k(\sum\limits_{bk=1}^{M}(2^{w+1}(b+e)))) + O((a+e)+n^2)$, resulting in $O(k(\sum\limits_{bk=1}^{M}(2^{w+1}(b+e))))$, where $\mathbf{N}_D$ increases its value at least in two nodes in the worst case.

- **TG-x in SCN-2:** $O(k(\sum\limits_{bk=1}^{M}(2^{w+1}(b+e)))) + O(n^2) = O(k(\sum\limits_{bk=1}^{M}(2^{w+1}(b+e))))$, where $\mathbf{N}_D$ increases its value at least in one node.

Therefore, the computational cost of STG-3 depends on the width $w+1$ of T_{bk_j}, whose cost can become undesirable for critical scenarios where the control has to be resolved in linear time. However, this study concentrates on the worst cases where $nd \approx n$, without considering the ability of the approach to prepare each backup instance using the diameter in the best cases. Similarly, STG-1 can also be an inadequate strategy with respect to STG-2 because the diameter computed in STG-2 benefits the fulfillment of RR2 ($out\_degree = 0$), reducing the computational costs and the expansion of $\mathbf{N}_D$ in each iteration. On the other hand, STG-1 and STG-2 have to transverse the entire network to search for the best candidates that satisfy conditions RR1 and RR2 (explicitly taking into account non-locality); while STG-3 must go over each backup instance to obtain the best candidates that satisfy condition RR3. Nevertheless, the dynamic computation of the diameter in STG-2 again highlights the benefit of the strategy to mitigate the non-locality problem of PDS inherent in the strategies by pre-computation.

On the other hand, we have implemented the three strategies over a power-law distribution called PLOD [18], which is analyzed in [1]. The developments are based on Matlab with a low connectivity probability to produce a more realistic critical scenario with sparse distributions, using y^{α} with $\alpha = 0.2$ and networks with medium ($\leq 1{,}000$) and large ($\leq 3{,}100$) numbers of nodes. For each network produced, we have analyzed the resulting effect that can cause an attack of the types SCN-1 and SCN-2 in one arbitrary node (either a TG-1 or a TG-2) or in a subset of "nodes/2" arbitrary nodes that are either TG-1 or TG-2. The results of the simulations are shown in Table 2, which depicts

Table 2. Changes in $\mathbf{N}_D$ when one or $n/2$ random nodes are targeted.

n	$\mathbf{N}_D^{bef}$	$\mathbf{N}_D^{STG-1}$	$\mathbf{N}_D^{STG-2}$	$\mathbf{N}_D^{STG-3}$
SCN-1: One Target				
100	92	=	=	=
1,100	1,073	=	=	=
2,100	2,036	=	=	=
3,100	3,000	=	=	=
SCN-1: n/2 Random Targets				
100	95	=	=	=
1,100	1,072	1,074	=	1,073
2,100	2,029	2,034	2,030	2,030
3,100	3,022	3,026	=	3,030
SCN-2: One Target				
100	94	=	=	=
1,100	1,066	=	=	=
2,100	2,010	=	=	=
3,100	3,000	=	=	=
SCN-2: n/2 Random Targets				
100	99	100	=	100
1,100	1,049	1,052	1,051	1,052
2,100	2,053	2,059	=	2,056
3,100	3,013	3,019	3,014	3,036

the efficiency of the three strategies with regard to the changes caused on the size of $\mathbf{N}_D$ after perturbation. It can be deduced from the table that the variation of the set of driver nodes does not become significant with respect to the number of attacked nodes. In addition, it is important to note that 99% of the observation rate (for U-1 and U-2 nodes) were completely lost for all cases after perturbation. Despite this, we also observed that the networks were equally able to retake 100% of the control after recovery without significant changes in the majority of the cases, and especially for STG-2 partly due to the use of the network diameter.

5.   Conclusions

Structural controllability offers a powerful abstraction for understanding the properties of critical nodes in a control network, which is vital to restoring control following node or link failures and, in particular, deliberate attacks.

This helps minimize the period during which a control system is held by an adversary. Also, it helps minimize the period during which the system may reach undesirable states – in the case of electrical power systems and networks, this period can be in the order of seconds or less before severe effects occur.

The main contributions of this paper are the three repair strategies for controllability in control graphs using the structural controllability abstraction, and relying on the PDS formulation to gain a clearer understanding of the effects of topology constraints on the repair strategies. These include re-linking without restrictions, re-linking with constrained network diameter and the use of pre-computed instances of driver nodes. In this way, controllability power-law networks can be restored more efficiently than by re-computing the controlling nodes when their links have been perturbed by attacks on availability. The three strategies have been analyzed formally and subjected to a complexity analysis. The results highlight that the use of a network diameter can be a suitable option to establish control with low computational and storage costs.

Our future work will focus on extending the analysis to explore the possibility of restoring control subgraphs instead of the entire network while retaining acceptable control graph parameters (primarily the number of nodes, maximum out-degree and diameter), thereby improving the respective approaches and their complexity. Another topic involves the renewed study of power-law networks and optimizing approximation mechanisms for controllability that give satisfactory average-time complexity. Finally, our research will also investigate new attack models, especially those involving interactions between attackers and defenders.

Acknowledgements

This research was partially funded by the Marie Curie COFUND Programme U-Mobility supported by the University of Malaga, by the EC FP7 Project under GA No. 246550, and by the Ministerio de Economia y Competitividad (COFUND2013-40259). This research was also partially funded by the EU FP7 ARTEMIS Project under GA No. 269374 and by the Spanish Ministry of Science and Innovation under the ARES Project (CSD2007-00004).

References

[1] C. Alcaraz, E. Miciolino and S. Wolthusen, Structural controllability of networks for non-interactive adversarial vertex removal, *Proceedings of the Eighth International Conference on Critical Information Infrastructures Security*, pp. 129–132, 2013.

[2] C. Alcaraz, E. Miciolino and S. Wolthusen, Multi-round attacks on structural controllability properties for non-complete random graphs, *Proceedings of the Sixteenth Information Security Conference*, 2014.

[3] D. Atkins, T. Haynes and M. Henning, Placing monitoring devices in electric power networks modeled by block graphs, *Ars Combinatorica*, vol. 79, 2006.

[4] A. Barabasi, R. Albert and H. Jeong, Scale-free characteristics of random networks: The topology of the world-wide web, *Physica A: Statistical Mechanics and its Applications*, vol. 281(1-4), pp. 60–77, 2000.

[5] J. Brueni and L. Heath, The PMU placement problem, *SIAM Journal on Discrete Mathematics*, vol. 19(3), pp. 744–761, 2005.

[6] M. Dorfling and M. Henning, A note on power domination in grid graphs, *Discrete Applied Mathematics*, vol. 154(6), pp. 1023–1027, 2006.

[7] Y. Dourisboure and C. Gavoille, Tree-decompositions with bags of small diameter, *Discrete Mathematics*, vol. 307(16), pp. 2008–2029, 2008.

[8] R. Downey and M. Fellows, *Parameterized Complexity*, Springer-Verlag, New York, 1999.

[9] U. Feige, A threshold of $\ln n$ for approximating set cover, *Journal of the ACM*, vol. 45(4), pp. 634–652, 1998.

[10] J. Guo and R. Niedermeier, Exact algorithms and applications for tree-like weighted set cover, *Journal of Discrete Mathematics*, vol. 4(4), pp. 608–622, 2006.

[11] J. Guo, R. Niedermeier and D. Raible, Improved algorithms and complexity results for power domination in graphs, *Algorithmica*, vol. 52(2), pp. 177–202, 2008.

[12] T. Haynes, S. Hedetniemi, S. Hedetniemi and M. Henning, Domination in graphs applied to electric power networks, *SIAM Journal on Discrete Mathematics*, vol. 15(4), pp. 519–529, 2002.

[13] R. Kalman, Mathematical description of linear dynamical systems, *Journal of the Society of Industrial and Applied Mathematics, Series A, Control*, vol. 1(2), pp. 152–192, 1963.

[14] J. Kneis, D. Molle, S. Richter and P. Rossmanith, Parameterized power domination complexity, *Information Processing Letters*, vol. 98(4), pp. 145–149, 2006.

[15] C. Lin, Structual controllability, *IEEE Transactions on Automatic Control*, vol. 19(3), pp. 201–208, 1974.

[16] H. Mayeda, On structural controllability theorem, *IEEE Transactions on Automatic Control*, vol. 26(3), pp. 795–798, 1981.

[17] K. Pai, J. Chang and Y. Wang, Restricted power domination and fault-tolerant power domination on grids, *Discrete Applied Mathematics*, vol. 158(10), pp. 1079–1089, 2010.

[18] C. Palmer and J. Steffan, Generating network topologies that obey power laws, *Proceedings of the IEEE Global Telecommunications Conference*, vol. 1, pp. 434–438, 2000.

Chapter 5

INDUSTRIAL CONTROL SYSTEM TRAFFIC DATA SETS FOR INTRUSION DETECTION RESEARCH

Thomas Morris and Wei Gao

Abstract   Supervisory control and data acquisition (SCADA) systems monitor and control physical processes associated with the critical infrastructure. Weaknesses in the application layer protocols, however, leave SCADA networks vulnerable to attack. In response, cyber security researchers have developed myriad intrusion detection systems. Researchers primarily rely on unique threat models and the corresponding network traffic data sets to train and validate their intrusion detection systems. This leads to a situation in which researchers cannot independently verify the results, cannot compare the effectiveness of different intrusion detection systems, and cannot adequately validate the ability of intrusion detection systems to detect various classes of attacks. Indeed, a common data set is needed that can be used by researchers to compare intrusion detection approaches and implementations. This paper describes four data sets, which include network traffic, process control and process measurement features from a set of 28 attacks against two laboratory-scale industrial control systems that use the MODBUS application layer protocol. The data sets, which are freely available, enable effective comparisons of intrusion detection solutions for SCADA systems.

Keywords: Industrial control systems, SCADA, intrusion detection, MODBUS

1.   Introduction

Supervisory control and data acquisition (SCADA) systems are computer-based process control systems that control and monitor remote physical processes. SCADA systems are strategically important because they are widely used in the critical infrastructure. Several incidents and cyber attacks affecting SCADA systems have been documented; these clearly illustrate the vulnerability of critical infrastructure assets. The reported incidents demonstrate that cyber attacks against SCADA systems can have severe financial impact

J. Butts and S. Shenoi (Eds.): Critical Infrastructure Protection VIII, IFIP AICT 441, pp. 65–78, 2014.

Table 1. Intrusion detection systems by threat model and network protocol.

System	Threat Model	Protocol
SRI Modbus [2]	Access, reconnaissance and attack	MODBUS
NNIDSCI [8]	Traffic from Nmap, Nessus, Metasploit	–
AKKR-SPRT [16]	DoS attacks simulated by Sun servers	SNMP
IDAEM [10]	RTU attacks	–
Multidimensional CSA [1]	Simulated attacks on critical states	MODBUS
SGDIDS [17]	KDD 99 Cup Data Set	–
Pattern Detection [15]	Reconnaissance	MODBUS
KSSM [7]	False data injection	–
Statistical Estimation [12]	Overflow exploits	MODBUS
RAIM [14]	File system and status modification	C37.118

and can result in damage that is harmful to humans and the environment. In 2000, a disgruntled engineer compromised a sewage control system in Maroochy Shire, Australia, causing approximately 264,000 gallons of raw sewage to leak into a nearby river [13]. In 2003, the Slammer worm caused a safety monitoring system at the Davis-Besse nuclear plant in Oak Harbor, Ohio to go offline for approximately five hours [11]. The insidious Stuxnet worm [3], which was discovered in 2010, targeted nuclear centrifuge system controllers, modifying system behavior by distorting monitored process information and altering control actions.

Cyber security researchers have developed numerous intrusion detection systems to detect attacks against SCADA systems. Much of the research uses training and validation data sets created by the same researchers who developed the intrusion detection systems. Indeed, no standardized data set containing normal SCADA network traffic and attack traffic is currently available to researchers. In order to evaluate the performance of data mining and machine learning algorithms for SCADA intrusion detection systems, a network data set used for benchmarking intrusion detection system performance is sorely needed. This paper describes four data sets, which include network traffic, process control and process measurement features from a set of 28 attacks against two laboratory-scale industrial control systems that use the MODBUS application layer protocol. The data sets, which are freely available, enable effective comparisons of intrusion detection solutions for SCADA systems.

2. Related Work

Several SCADA security researchers have developed intrusion detection systems that monitor network traffic and detect attacks against SCADA systems. Table 1 lists example intrusion detection systems, the threat models they use and the network protocols they analyze. Note that each intrusion detection system uses a unique threat model. Some threat models are based on attacks executed against SCADA laboratory testbeds while others are based on manipulated data sets drawn from other domains. The network protocols also differ; MODBUS is the most common protocol (used in three systems) while the IEEE C37.118 protocol is used in just one system. The remaining systems use threat models with attacks implemented at different network layers.

A noticeable drawback of the research identified in Table 1 is that the threat models only include subsets of attack classes. Not surprisingly, exploit coverage is limited for each of the data sets. Only a few of the threat models consider reconnaissance attacks while some models only include response injection attacks. Indeed, the malicious behavior captured in the data sets is neither consistent nor comprehensive in terms of normal operations and attacks. For this reason, it is difficult to judge the effectiveness of an intrusion detection system against sophisticated attacks. This also leads to a situation in which researchers cannot independently verify intrusion detection results and cannot compare the performance of intrusion detection systems.

3.   Test Bed Description

The data sets described in this paper were captured using a network data logger, which monitored and stored MODBUS traffic from a RS-232 connection. Two laboratory-scale SCADA systems were used: a gas pipeline and water storage tank.

Figure 1 shows the gas pipeline and water storage tank systems along with the associated human machine interfaces (HMIs). The gas pipeline system includes a small airtight pipeline connected to a compressor, a pressure meter and a solenoid-controlled relief valve. The pipeline system attempts to maintain the air pressure in the pipeline using a proportional integral derivative (PID) control scheme.

The water storage tank system includes a tank that holds approximately two liters of water, a manually-operated relief valve to deplete water from the tank, a pump to add water to the tank from an external water source and a meter to measure the water level as percentage of tank capacity. The water storage tank uses an on/off control scheme to maintain the water level between the high (H) and low (L) setpoints. The water storage tank activates an alarm when the water level is above the high alarm setpoint (HH) or below the low alarm setpoint (LL). Detailed descriptions of the functionality of the two systems and their respective components are provided in a separate paper [9].

A bump-in-the-wire approach was used to capture data logs and to inject attacks. The device was implemented via a C program running on a VMware virtual machine. The virtual machine included two RS-232 serial ports connected to a USB-to-serial converter. The C program monitored each serial port for traffic. Detected traffic was timestamped and recorded in a log file. To facilitate attacks, the C program incorporated hooks to inject, delay, drop and alter network traffic.

(a) Gas pipeline.   (b) Gas pipeline HMI.

(c) Water storage tank.   (d) Water storage tank HMI.

Figure 1.   Gas pipeline and water storage tank systems.

4.   Description of Attacks

The data sets presented in this paper include network traffic, process control and process measurement features from normal operations and attacks against the two SCADA systems. The attacks are grouped into four classes: (i) reconnaissance; (ii) response injection; (iii) command injection; and (iv) denial-of-service (DoS).

4.1   Reconnaissance Attacks

Reconnaissance attacks gather SCADA system information, map the network architecture and identify device characteristics (e.g., manufacturer, model number, supported network protocols, device address and device memory map). The reconnaissance class of attacks in the data set includes four attacks against MODBUS servers: address scan, function code scan, device identification attack and points scan. The address scan discovers SCADA servers connected to a network by polling for responses from different MODBUS addresses. The function code scan identifies supported MODBUS function codes that can be used by an identified server. The device identification attack allows an attacker to obtain device vendor information, product code and major and minor firmware revisions. The points scan allows the attacker to build a memory map of MODBUS coils, discrete inputs, holding registers and input registers.

4.2 Response Injection Attacks

SCADA systems commonly use polling techniques to continuously monitor the state of a remote process. Polling takes the form of a query transmitted from the client to the server followed by a response packet transmitted from the server to the client. State information is provided to a human machine interface for monitoring the process, storing process measurements in a data historian and providing feedback to control loops that measure process parameters and take the appropriate control actions based on the process state. Response injection attacks alter responses from the server to client, providing false system state information.

Response injection attacks are divided into naive malicious response injection (NMRI) attacks and complex malicious response injection (CMRI) attacks. NMRI attacks leverage the ability to inject or alter response packets in a network; however, they lack the ability to obtain information about the underlying process being monitored and controlled. Eight NRMI attacks were used in creating the data sets described in this paper. The naive read payload size attack returns a malicious response with the correct payload size but sets the payload to all zeros, ones or random bits. The invalid read payload size attack returns a malicious response with a length that does not conform to the requested length. The invalid exception code attack returns false error responses to the client after a read command. The negative sensor measurements attack injects negative process measurements; this is problematic because many systems use floating point numbers to represent values that can only be positive. The sensor measurements grossly out-of-bounds attack injects process measurements that are significantly outside the bounds of alarm setpoints. The sporadic sensor measurement injection attack sends false process measurements outside the bounds of the H and L control setpoints while staying within the alarm setpoint range specified by HH and LL. The random sensor measurement injection attack sends random process measurements of gas pipeline pressure or water tank water level.

CMRI attacks attempt to mask the actual state of the physical process and negatively affect feedback control loops. They are more sophisticated than NMRI attacks because they require an in-depth understanding of the targeted system. As such, CMRI attacks are designed to appear like normal process functionality. These attacks can be used to mask alterations to process state perpetrated by malicious command injection attacks. CMRI attacks are more difficult to detect because they project a state of normalcy.

Five CMRI attacks were used to create the data sets. The constant sensor measurement injection attack repeatedly sends malicious packets containing the same measurement to mask the real state of the system. The calculated sensor measurement injection attack sends pre-calculated process measurements. The high frequency measurement injection attack increases the rate of change of a process measurement beyond its normal range. The low frequency measurement injection attack decreases the rate of change of a process measurement below its normal range. A replayed measurement injection attack resends process measurements that were previously sent from the server to a client.

4.3　Command Injection Attacks

Command injection attacks inject false control and configuration commands to alter system behavior. The potential impacts of malicious command injections include loss of process control, interruption of device communications, unauthorized modification of device configurations and unauthorized modification of process setpoints. Command injection attacks are divided into malicious state command injection (MSCI) attacks, malicious parameter command injection (MPCI) attacks and malicious function code command injection (MFCI) attacks. Comprehensive descriptions of these attacks are provided in [4].

MSCI attacks change the state of the process control system to drive the system from a safe state to a critical state by sending malicious commands to remote field devices. MSCI attacks may involve a single injected command or multiple injected commands. Three MSCI attacks were used to create the data sets. The altered system control scheme attack changes the control mode from automatic to manual and then turns on the compressor or pump to increase the pressure in the pipeline or raise the water level in the water storage tank, respectively. The altered actuator state attack changes the state of an actuator in a system. In the case of the gas pipeline system, this attack includes command injections that turn the compressor on or off, and those that open or close the relief valve; in the case of the water storage tank system, the altered actuator state attack turns the pump on or off. The continuous altered actuator state attack repeatedly changes the actuator states in a system. For example, command packets could be continually transmitted to switch the state of the compressor and pump in the pipeline and storage tank systems, respectively. Additionally, a continuous altered actuator state attack may be used to repeatedly transmit MODBUS write register commands to invert the state of the solenoid that controls the relief valve in the gas pipeline system.

MPCI attacks alter programmable logic controller (PLC) field device setpoints. The data sets include two MPCI attacks. The altered control setpoint attack changes the H and L setpoints for the water storage tank while disabling the liquid level alarms. A proportional integral derivative (PID) controller is commonly used in SCADA systems to maintain a desired setpoint by calculating and adjusting for system error; the altered proportional integral derivative parameter attack changes the PID parameters used in the gas pipeline system.

MFCI attacks use built-in protocol functions in a manner different from what was intended. The data sets include four MFCI attacks. The force listen only mode attack causes a MODBUS server to stop transmitting on the network. The restart communications attack sends a command that causes the MODBUS server to restart, leading to a temporary loss of communications. The clear communications event log attack erases the communications event log of the

MODBUS server. Finally, the change ASCII input delimiter attack changes the delimiter used for MODBUS ASCII devices.

4.4 Denial-of-Service Attacks

Denial-of-service attacks target communications links and system programs in an attempt to exhaust resources. The data sets include two denial-of-service attacks. The invalid cyclic redundancy code (CRC) attack injects a large number of MODBUS packets with incorrect CRC values into a network. The MODBUS master traffic jamming attack uses a non-addressed slave address to continually transmit random data to random destination addresses.

5. SCADA Traffic and Payload Data Sets

The KDD Cup 1999 Data Set [6] was developed to train and validate intrusion detection systems associated with traditional information technology systems. The use of this common data set by numerous researchers facilitated the independent validation of research results and the comparison of many intrusion detection system approaches. In the area of SCADA security, however, researchers develop their own data sets to test intrusion detection systems because there is a lack of availability and access to SCADA network traffic. Indeed, no standard data set is available that includes normal and attack traffic for a SCADA network that can serve as a benchmark to evaluate and compare SCADA intrusion detection system performance. This section describes a data set that is intended to provide researchers with a common platform to evaluate the performance of data mining and machine learning algorithms designed for SCADA intrusion detection systems. The data set includes different classes of attacks that cover a variety of SCADA system attack scenarios.

The common data set described in this paper has three primary benefits. First, not all researchers have access to SCADA equipment to generate their own data sets; a common data set would enable more researchers to work in the area of SCADA security. Second, a common data set would allow researchers to independently validate the results of other researchers. Third, a common data set would enable the comparison of the performance of different algorithms, leading to better intrusion detection systems.

5.1 Data Set Organization

The data sets created as a result of this research effort are stored in the Attribute Relationship File Format (ARFF) for use with the WEKA software [5]. WEKA is a comprehensive framework that enables researchers to compare and verify machine learning algorithms.

The organization of the MODBUS data set is similar to that of the KDD Cup 1999 Data Set [6]. Each instance in the data set represents one captured network transaction pair (e.g., merged MODBUS query and response). An instance includes network traffic information and the current state of the process

Table 2.　Data sets.

Data Set	Index
Data Set I	Gas pipeline system complete data set
Data Set II	Water storage tank system complete data set
Data Set III	Gas pipeline system reduced (10%) data set
Data Set IV	Water storage tank system reduced (10%) data set

control system based on payload content. Note that each instance contains a label identifying it as normal MODBUS traffic or as attack traffic with the designated attack class.

Four data sets were created as part of this research. Table 2 provides the descriptions of the four data sets. Data Set I contains transactions from the gas pipeline system. Data Set II contains transactions from the water storage tank system. The two data sets were generated from network flow records captured with a serial port data logger.

Two reduced size data sets were also created. Data Set III is a gas pipeline system data set, which was created by randomly selecting 10% of the instances in Data Set I. Likewise, Data Set IV is a water storage tank system data set, which was created by randomly selecting 10% of the instances in Data Set II. The two reduced data sets minimize memory requirements and processing time when validating classification algorithms. They are intended for applications for which quick feedback is desired.

Two categories of features are present in the data sets: network traffic features and payload content features. Network traffic features describe the communications patterns in SCADA systems. Compared with traditional enterprise networks, SCADA network topologies and services are relatively static. Note that some attacks against SCADA systems may change network communications patterns. As such, network traffic features are used to describe normal traffic patterns in order to detect malicious activity. Network traffic features include the device address, function code, length of packet, packet error checking information and time intervals between packets. Payload content features describe the current state of the SCADA system; they are useful for detecting attacks that cause devices (e.g., PLCs) to behave abnormally. Payload content features include sensor measurements, supervisory control inputs and distributed control states.

5.2　Network Traffic Features

Table 3 lists the ten attributes that comprise the network traffic features. The first and second attributes are the command device address and response device address. Note that the MODBUS serial command address is one byte long, with each server having a unique device address. As such, the command and response device addresses should match during normal operations. An address mismatch is an indicator of a reconnaissance attack. MODBUS serial

Table 3. Attacks on MODBUS systems.

Attribute	Description
command_address	Device ID in command packet
response_address	Device ID in response packet
command_memory	Memory start position in command packet
response_memory	Memory start position in response packet
command_memory_count	Number of memory bytes for R/W command
response_memory_count	Number of memory bytes for R/W response
command_length	Total length of command packet
response_length	Total length of response packet
time	Time interval between two packets
crc_rate	CRC error rate

systems are configured so that all the slave devices (servers) see all the master transactions. Each slave must check the device address to discern the intended recipient before acting on a packet. Based on the system configuration, the set of device addresses that a slave device should encounter is fixed; device addresses not specified in the configuration are anomalous.

The command memory, response memory, command memory count and response memory count include internal memory addresses and field sizes for read and write commands. The memory of a MODBUS server is grouped into data blocks called coils, discrete inputs, holding registers and input registers. Coils and discrete inputs represent a single, read-only Boolean bit with authorized values of 0x00 and 0xFF. Holding and input registers are 16-bit words; holding registers are read/write capable while input registers are read only. Each data block may have its own set of contiguous address space or the data blocks may share a common memory address space based on vendor implementation. The command memory and response memory features are coil or register read/write start addresses taken from command and response packets, respectively. The command and response memory count features are the numbers of objects to be read and written, respectively.

The command and response packet length features provide the lengths of the MODBUS query and response frames, respectively. The MODBUS protocol data unit (PDU) is limited to 253 bytes with an additional three bytes for device ID and CRC fields, resulting in a 256-byte packet. In the gas pipeline and water storage tank systems, the master repeatedly performs a block write to a fixed memory address followed by a block read from a fixed memory address. The read and write commands have fixed lengths for each system, and the read and write responses have fixed lengths for each system. Note, however, that many of the described attacks have different packet lengths. As such, the packet length feature provides a means to detect many attacks.

The time interval attribute is a measurement of the time between a MODBUS query and its response. The MODBUS protocol is a request-response protocol and the time interval varies only slightly during normal operations.

Table 4. List of common payload attributes.

Feature Name	Description
comm_fun	Value of command function code
response_fun	Value of response function code
sub_function	Value of sub-function code in the command/response
measurement	Pipeline pressure or water level
control_mode	Automatic, manual or shutdown
pump_state	Compressor/pump state
manual_pump_setting	Manual mode compressor/pump setting
label	Manual classification of the instance

The malicious command injection, malicious response injection and DOS attacks often result in significantly different time interval measurements due to the nature of the attacks.

The last attribute is the command/response CRC error rate. This attribute measures the rates of CRC errors identified in command and response packets. Because SCADA network traffic patterns are relatively static, the normal command and response CRC error rates are expected to stay somewhat constant. In a normal system, the error rates should be low; however, the rates are expected to increase when a system is subjected to a denial-of-service attack such as the invalid CRC attack.

5.3   Payload Content Features

The payload content features differ for the gas pipeline and water storage system data sets due to different control schemes and different measured variables. The attributes common to both systems are listed in Table 4. During normal operations, the response function code matches the command function code if there is no error. If there is an error, the response sub-function code is the command function code value plus 0x80. The measurement attribute provides the current value of the gas pipeline pressure or water tank level. The naive malicious response injection attack and the complex malicious response injection attack influence process measurements by manipulating the expected values. The system control mode is determined based on data in a command packet. The system control mode can place the system in the shutdown, manual or automatic modes; zero represents the shutdown mode, one represents the manual mode and two represents the automatic mode. A malicious state command injection attack can attempt to modify the system operating mode or shut down the system. The gas pipeline system/water storage tank system use a compressor/pump to add air/water, respectively, to maintain the desired setpoint. If the compressor/pump state has a value of one, then the compressor/pump is on; if it is zero, the compressor/pump is off. When a system is in the automatic mode, the PLC logic controls the compressor/pump state. A malicious complex response injection attack may modify this value in

Table 5. Unique features of the gas pipeline system data sets.

Feature Name	Description
set_point	Target pressure in the gas pipeline
control_scheme	Control scheme of the gas pipeline
solenoid_state	State of solenoid used to open the gas relief valve
gain	Gain parameter value of the PID controller
reset	Reset parameter value of the PID controller
dead_band	Dead band parameter value of the PID controller
rate	Rate parameter value of the PID controller
cycletime	Cycle time parameter value of the PID controller

order to mask the actual compressor/pump working state. Note that, in the manual mode, the compressor/pump state is controlled by the manual compressor/pump setting value. A malicious state command injection attack may change the compressor/pump mode continually or intermittently.

Table 5 shows the eight attributes that are specific to the gas pipeline system. The initial attribute identifies the setpoint for the nominal gas pressure. The second attribute identifies the operating mode of the system. In the automatic mode, the PLC logic attempts to maintain the gas pressure in the pipeline using a PID control scheme by selecting if the compressor or the relief valve is activated. If the control scheme is zero, then the compressor is activated to increase pressure; if the control scheme is one, then the relief valve is activated using a solenoid to decrease the pressure. In the manual mode, the operator controls the pressure by sending commands to start the compressor or open the relief valve. Additionally, there are five attributes related to the PID controller. The gain, reset, dead band, rate and cycle time impact PID controller behavior and should be fixed during system operation. A malicious parameter command injection attack tries to modify these parameters to interrupt normal control operations.

Table 6. Unique features of the water storage system data sets.

Feature Name	Description
HH	Value of HH setpoint
H	Value of H setpoint
L	Value of L setpoint
LL	Value of LL setpoint

Table 6 shows the four attributes that are specific to the water storage tank system: HH, H, L and LL. In the automatic mode, the PLC logic maintains the water level between the L and H setpoints using an on/off controller scheme. When the sensors detect that the water level has reached the L level, the PLC logic turns the water pump on. Alternatively, when the sensors determine that

Table 7.   Instance classification values.

Label Name	Label Value	Label Description
Normal	0	Instance is not part of an attack
NMRI	1	Naive malicious response injection attack
CMRI	2	Complex malicious response injection attack
MSCI	3	Malicious state command injection attack
MPCI	4	Malicious parameter command injection attack
MFCI	5	Malicious function command injection attack
DoS	6	Denial-of-service attack
Reconnaissance	7	Reconnaissance attack

the water level has reached the H level, the PLC logic turns the water pump off. Note that the water storage tank includes a manual drainage valve that allows water to drain out of the tank when the valve is open. If the manual drainage valve is open, the water level in the tank oscillates between the H and L setpoints continuously as the pump cycles on and off to compensate. When the manual drainage valve is closed, the pump stays on until the water level reaches the H setpoint, at which point it turns off and maintains a constant level. Due to a system fault, if the water level rises to the HH setpoint or falls to the LL setpoint, then an alarm is triggered at the human machine interface that monitors the water storage tank. In the manual mode, the pump state is controlled manually by the human machine interface (i.e., an operator can manually activate and deactivate the pump).

Table 7 lists the eight possible label values. Recall that each data set instance is labeled as normal or according to its attack class. The labeling scheme was chosen to match the KDD Cup 1999 Data Set [6], which identified attacks by class. Note that specific attacks in each attack class have similar exploit methods and similar impact on the SCADA system.

5.4   Discussion

The data sets described in this paper are relevant to other SCADA systems – systems that use protocols other than MODBUS as well as systems other than gas pipelines and water storage tanks. The features in the data sets are divided into two groups in a similar manner as SCADA protocols divide packets into network traffic related fields and content fields. Indeed, other protocols include similar, albeit not identical, network traffic information such as addresses, function codes, payloads and checksums. Additionally, most SCADA protocols tend to adhere to query-response traffic patterns similar to MODBUS. The content features in the data sets include remote commands and system states similar to how other types of systems monitor and update system settings. As such, the data sets provide a framework to measure the accuracy of intrusion detection approaches designed for a variety of SCADA systems.

6.   Conclusions

Researchers have developed numerous intrusion detection approaches for detecting attacks against SCADA systems. To date, researchers have generally engaged unique threat models and the associated network traffic data sets to train and validate their intrusion detection systems. This leads to a situation where researchers cannot independently verify the results of other research efforts, cannot compare the effectiveness of intrusion detection systems against each other and ultimately cannot adequately judge the quality of intrusion detection systems.

The four data sets developed in this research include network traffic, process control and process measurement features from two laboratory-scale SCADA systems. Data Set I contains transactions from a gas pipeline system while Data Set II contains transactions from a water storage tank system. The data sets were generated from network flow records captured with a serial port data logger in a laboratory environment. A set of 28 attacks was used to create the data sets; the attacks were grouped into four categories: reconnaissance, response injection, command injection and denial-of-service attacks. Reduced size data sets corresponding to Data Sets I and II were also created. Data Set III is a gas pipeline system data set containing 10% of the instances in Data Set I while Data Set IV is a water storage tank system data set containing 10% of the instances in Data Set II. The four data sets comprising normal and attack traffic can be used by security researchers to compare different SCADA intrusion detection approaches and implementations.

References

[1] A. Carcano, A. Coletta, M. Guglielmi, M. Masera, I. Fovino and A. Trombetta, A multidimensional critical state analysis for detecting intrusions in SCADA systems, *IEEE Transactions on Industrial Informatics*, vol. 7(2), pp. 179–186, 2011.

[2] S. Cheung, B. Dutertre, M. Fong, U. Lindqvist, K. Skinner and A. Valdes, Using model-based intrusion detection for SCADA networks, *Proceedings of the SCADA Security Scientific Symposium*, 2007.

[3] N. Falliere, L. O'Murchu and E. Chien, W32.Stuxnet Dossier, Version 1.4, Symantec, Mountain View, California, 2011.

[4] W. Gao, Cyber Threats, Attacks and Intrusion Detection in Supervisory Control and Data Acquisition Networks, Ph.D. Dissertation, Department of Electrical and Computer Engineering, Mississippi State University, Mississippi State, Mississippi, 2014.

[5] M. Hall, E. Frank, G. Holmes, B. Pfahringer, P. Reutemann and I. Witten, The WEKA data mining software: An update, *ACM SIGKDD Explorations*, vol. 11(1), pp. 10–18, 2009.

[6] S. Hettich and S. Bay, The UCI KDD Archive, Department of Information and Computer Science, University of California at Irvine, Irvine, California (kdd.ics.uci.edu), 1999.

[7] O. Linda, M. Manic and M. McQueen, Improving control system cyber-state awareness using known secure sensor measurements, *Proceedings of the Seventh International Conference on Critical Information Infrastructures Security*, pp. 46–58, 2012.

[8] O. Linda, T. Vollmer and M. Manic, Neural network based intrusion detection system for critical infrastructures, *Proceedings of the International Joint Conference on Neural Networks*, pp. 1827–1834, 2009.

[9] T. Morris, A. Srivastava, B. Reaves, W. Gao, K. Pavurapu and R. Reddi, A control system testbed to validate critical infrastructure protection concepts, *International Journal of Critical Infrastructure Protection*, vol. 4(2), pp. 88–103, 2011.

[10] P. Oman and M. Phillips, Intrusion detection and event monitoring in SCADA networks, in *Critical Infrastructure Protection*, E. Goetz and S. Shenoi (Eds.), Springer, Boston, Massachusetts, pp. 161–173, 2008.

[11] K. Poulsen, Slammer worm crashed Ohio nuke plant network, *Security-Focus*, Symantec, Mountain View, California (www.securityfocus.com/news/6767), August 19, 2003.

[12] J. Rrushi and K. Kang, Detecting anomalies in process control networks, in *Critical Infrastructure Protection III*, C. Palmer and S. Shenoi (Eds.), Springer, Heidelberg, Germany, pp. 151–165, 2009.

[13] J. Slay and M. Miller, Lessons learned from the Maroochy water breach, in *Critical Infrastructure Protection*, E. Goetz and S. Shenoi (Eds.), Springer, Boston, Massachusetts, pp. 73–82, 2008.

[14] C. Ten, J. Hong and C. Liu, Anomaly detection for cybersecurity of substations, *IEEE Transactions on Smart Grid*, vol. 2(4), pp. 865–873, 2011.

[15] A. Valdes and S. Cheung, Communication pattern anomaly detection in process control systems, *Proceedings of the IEEE Conference on Technologies for Homeland Security*, pp. 22–29, 2009.

[16] D. Yang, A. Usynin and J. Hines, Anomaly-based intrusion detection for SCADA systems, presented at the *IAEA Technical Meeting on Cyber Security of Nuclear Power Plant Instrumentation and Control and Information Systems*, 2006.

[17] Y. Zhang, L. Wang, W. Sun, R. Green and M. Alam, Distributed intrusion detection system in a multi-layer network architecture of smart grids, *IEEE Transactions on Smart Grid*, vol. 2(4), pp. 796–808, 2011.

Chapter 6

AN INDUSTRIAL CONTROL SYSTEM TESTBED BASED ON EMULATION, PHYSICAL DEVICES AND SIMULATION

Haihui Gao, Yong Peng, Zhonghua Dai, Ting Wang, Xuefeng Han, and Hanjing Li

Abstract   This paper demonstrates the utility of an industrial control system testbed that incorporates a universal, realistic, measurable, controllable and reusable experimental platform for cyber security research and testing. The testbed has a layered architecture that leverages physical devices and emulation and simulation technologies. The testbed enables researchers to create experiments of varying levels of fidelity for vulnerability discovery, product evaluation and system certification. The utility of the testbed is demonstrated via a case study involving an industrial boiler control system.

Keywords: Industrial control systems, cyber security, testbed, simulation

1.   Introduction

Industrial control systems (ICSs) monitor and control processes in critical infrastructure assets [12]. Due to their increased connectivity with corporate networks and the Internet, industrial control systems are no longer immune to cyber attacks. Indeed, in 2010, the Stuxnet worm demonstrated to the world the seriousness of industrial control system vulnerabilities and the potential threats [9].

In order to protect industrial control systems, it is important to conduct cyber security research and testing to identify and mitigate existing vulnerabilities [1, 7]. However, testing and evaluation of actual industrial control systems are difficult to perform due to the uptime requirements and the risk of damage to operational systems. Therefore, it is necessary to build suitable experimental platforms to develop and test cyber security solutions for industrial control systems [9].

J. Butts and S. Shenoi (Eds.): Critical Infrastructure Protection VIII, IFIP AICT 441, pp. 79–91, 2014.
© IFIP International Federation for Information Processing 2014

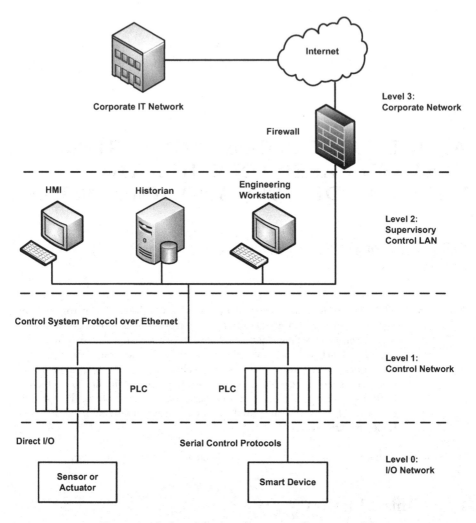

Figure 1. Industrial control system reference model.

The emulation, physical devices and simulation for industrial control systems (EPS-ICS) testbed presented in this paper seeks to address this problem. The testbed provides configurable fidelity using physical devices for core system components, while emulating or simulating the other components. The proposed solution is an inexpensive, albeit useful, approximation of an industrial control system environment. Indeed, the EPS-ICS testbed strikes the right balance between research requirements and construction costs.

2. Architecture

Figure 1 shows an example industrial control system reference model that conforms to the ANSI/ISA-99 standard [5]. The architecture is segmented into four levels: (i) corporate network; (ii) supervisory control local area network (LAN); (iii) control network; and (iv) input/output (I/O) network.

In the ANSI/ISA-99 standard, the corporate network level (Level 3) is responsible for management and related activities (e.g., production scheduling, operations management and financial transactions) [11]. This level is consistent with traditional information technology, including the general deployment of services and systems such as FTP, websites, mail servers, enterprise resource planning (ERP) systems and office automation systems. The supervisory control LAN level (Level 2) includes the functions involved in monitoring and controlling physical processes and the general deployment of systems such as human-machine interfaces (HMIs), engineering workstations and historians. The control network level (Level 1) includes the functions involved in sensing and manipulating physical processes. Typical devices at this level are programmable logic controllers (PLCs), distributed control systems, safety instrumented systems and remote terminal units (RTUs). The I/O network level (Level 0) includes the actual physical processes and sensors and actuators that are directly connected to process equipment.

3. Testbed Construction

Industrial control system testbeds may be categorized as:

- Physical testbeds that are constructed using replication methodologies.

- Software (virtual) testbeds that are constructed using modeling methodologies.

- Hybrid testbeds that are constructed using replication and modeling methodologies.

A replicated testbed is a copy of a real system with the same physical devices and information systems. An example is the National SCADA Testbed (NSTB) of the U.S. Department of Energy [8]. Although a replicated architecture provides the highest fidelity, building an identical replica of a real-world system is usually cost prohibitive.

A software testbed uses modeling methodologies instead of actual physical devices; it typically includes a physical process simulator, network simulator and attack simulator. Such a testbed is a low cost solution for research focused on attacks on industrial control systems and the development of security strategies. However, due to the absence of real components and devices, the architecture provides low fidelity.

A hybrid testbed incorporates replicated devices and systems as well as software models. The architecture provides a high degree of fidelity and is also cost effective. The EPS-ICS testbed described in this paper is based on a hybrid architecture.

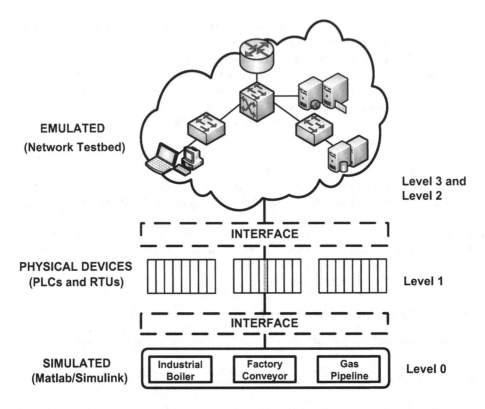

Figure 2. EPS-ICS testbed architecture.

4.   EPS-ICS Testbed Architecture

Figure 2 shows the EPS-ICS testbed architecture. The architecture has four types of components: (i) emulated components; (ii) physical components; (iii) simulated components; and (iv) interface components. The industrial control system of interest is modeled as a single testbed comprising emulated, physical and simulated devices. Levels 2 and 3 of the ANSI/ISA-99 industrial control system reference model are implemented using emulation technologies similar to Emulab [2]. Level 1 of the reference model is implemented by replicating physical devices while Level 0 is implemented using simulated mathematical models of controlled processes developed with Matlab/Simulink.

Figure 3 shows the EPS-ICS network architecture. It is a dynamically controlled construct, consisting of a measurable and reusable experimental environment with switches, servers and other physical resources. The hardware includes wired and wireless nodes. Note that the testbed effectively models a corporate network (Level 3) and supervisory control LAN (Level 2).

The Level 1 control network is the core of the industrial control system reference model. The EPS-ICS testbed incorporates physical devices in Level 1 to achieve high fidelity for research and testing requirements.

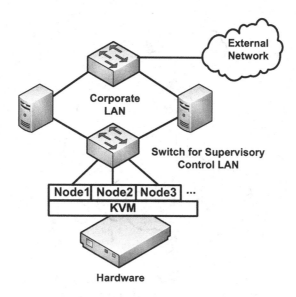

Figure 3. EPS-ICS network architecture.

The testbed uses Matlab/Simulink to construct Level 0 models in order to reduce costs and reuse I/O layer components. This flexibility enables the testbed to model a variety of controlled processes (e.g., steam boiler, storage tank and heat exchanger).

The EPS-ICS testbed effectively replicates the interactions between industrial control system components. Industrial control system components, such as the corporate network and supervisory control LAN, may be implemented as emulations or as physical components using the testbed interface. Thus, the EPS-ICS testbed can provide varying levels of fidelity to meet diverse research and testing objectives.

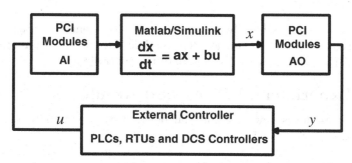

Figure 4. Interfaces between physical and simulated devices.

Interfaces between emulated and physical devices implement communications using IP routing (e.g., routers, layer-three switches and wired/wireless networks). Figure 4 shows interface communications between physical and

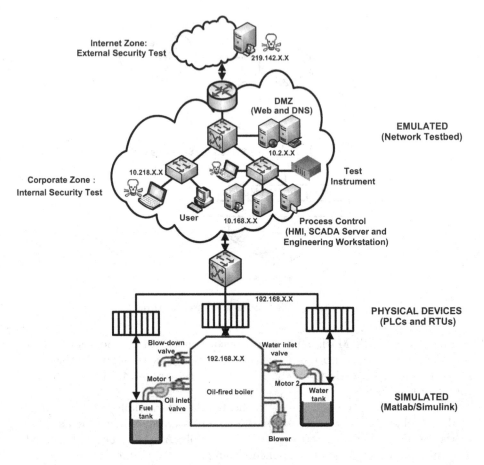

Figure 5.   Industrial boiler control system based on the EPS-ICS testbed.

simulated devices; special hardware between the devices enables data exchange.
Peripheral component interconnect (PCI) modules support full communications
between Matlab/Simulink models and external controllers.

5.   Experimental Setup and Results

This section shows how an industrial boiler control system is constructed
using the EPS-ICS testbed.

5.1   Corporate and Control Networks

Figure 5 shows the experimental industrial boiler control system. The computers in the corporate zone are used to simulate daily office activities and internal security testing. The Internet zone is used for external security testing.
Web servers and external DNS servers are deployed in the demilitarized zone

(DMZ) for external communications (e.g., Internet connectivity). HMI servers, SCADA servers and other production systems are deployed in the process control zone; they interact with field devices (e.g., PLCs). The process control functionality is represented by physical and simulated devices corresponding to the boiler system.

5.2 Industrial Boiler Control System Model

A Matlab/Simulink simulation model was developed by performing a comprehensive engineering analysis of an industrial oil-fired boiler. The control of the oil-fired boiler simulation model is achieved by integrating PLCs and RTUs in the industrial control network. The following sections describe the mathematical models of the furnace, boiler drum, riser, downcomer and superheater [3, 4, 10].

Furnace Model. The mass balance, energy balance and furnace radiation heat transfer equations are:

$$\dot{m}_f + \dot{m}_a - \dot{m}_g = V_f \frac{d}{dt}(\rho_g) \tag{1}$$

$$\dot{m}_f Q_f + \dot{m}_a h_a - \dot{m}_g h_g - Q_{rht} = V_f \frac{d}{dt}(\rho_g h_g) \tag{2}$$

$$Q_{rht} = \alpha_{hd}\sigma\psi F_l T_g^4 \xi \tag{3}$$

where $\dot{m}_f$ is the fuel flow into the furnace, Q_f is the fuel heat, $\dot{m}_a$ is the air flow into the furnace, h_a is the air enthalpy, $\dot{m}_g$ is the gas flow out of the furnace, h_g is the gas enthalpy, Q_{rht} is the radiation heat transfer, V_f is the furnace volume, ρ_g is the gas density, σ is the Boltzmann black body radiation constant, α_{hd} is the furnace emissivity, ψ is the furnace water degree, ξ is the fouling factor, T_g is the gas temperature and F_l is the furnace area.

Boiler Drum Model. The upper section of the boiler drum contains steam and the bottom section contains water. The liquid zone mass conservation, vapor zone mass conservation, drum energy balance and drum liquid level equations are:

$$\dot{m}_w + (1-x)\dot{m}_{rc} - \dot{m}_{dcin} - \dot{m}_{pw} - \dot{m}_{ec} = \frac{d}{dt}(\rho_w V_d^w) \tag{4}$$

$$\dot{m}_{rc}x - \dot{m}_s + \dot{m}_{ec} = \frac{d}{dt}(\rho_s V_d^s) \tag{5}$$

$$\dot{m}_w h_w + (1-x)\dot{m}_{rc} h_w + x\dot{m}_{rc} h_s - \dot{m}_{dcin} h_w - \dot{m}_s h_s - \dot{m}_{pw} h_w$$
$$= \frac{d}{dt}(\rho_s V_d^s h_s + \rho_w V_d^s h_w + M_{dm} C_{dm} T_d) - JV_d \frac{d}{dt}(P_d) + \dot{m}_{ec} h_s \qquad (6)$$

$$V_d^w = \frac{1}{3}\pi L_v^2 (3r - L_v) + \frac{1}{2}(L - 2r)r^2(\theta - \sin\theta) \qquad (7)$$

$$\theta = 2\cos^{-1}(\frac{r-L}{r}) \qquad (8)$$

where $\dot{m}_w$ is the feed water flow from the economizer, x is the steam dryness, $\dot{m}_{rc}$ is the steam-water flow in the riser, $\dot{m}_{dcin}$ is the downcomer inlet flow, $\dot{m}_{pw}$ is the blow-down flow, $\dot{m}_{ec}$ is the dynamic evaporation flow, ρ_w is the saturated water density, V_d^w is the drum liquid zone volume, $\dot{m}_s$ is the steam discharge capacity, ρ_s is the steam density, V_d^s is the drum vapor zone volume, h_w is the feed water enthalpy from the economizer, h_s is the steam enthalpy, M_{dm} is the drum metal quality, C_{dm} is the drum metal specific heat capacity, T_d is the drum temperature, J is the unit conversion factor, V_d is the drum volume, P_d is the drum pressure, L is the drum length, r is the drum radius and $L_v = f^{-1}(V_d^w)$ is the drum liquid level.

Riser Model. The riser contains both liquid and vapor. The liquid zone mass conservation, vapor zone mass conservation, energy balance, metal energy balance, average ratio of vapor per cross-sectional area in the vapor zone, liquid zone accounted for in the riser length ratio, and steam volume in the riser equations are:

$$\dot{m}_{dcout} - (1-x)\dot{m}_{rc} - \dot{m}_{evp} - \dot{m}_{ecl} = \frac{d}{dt}(\rho_w V_{rc}^w) \qquad (9)$$

$$\dot{m}_{ecl} + \dot{m}_{evp} - x\dot{m}_{rc} = \frac{d}{dt}(\rho_s V_{rc}^s) \qquad (10)$$

$$\dot{m}_{dcout} h_{dcout} - (1-x)\dot{m}_{rc} h_w - x\dot{m}_{rc} h_s + Q_{rc} =$$
$$\frac{d}{dt}(\rho_s V_{rc}^s h_s + \rho_w V_{rc}^w h_w) - JV_{rc}\frac{d}{dt}(P_d) \qquad (11)$$

$$Q_{rht} - Q_{rc} = M_{mrc} C_{mrc} \frac{d}{dt}(T_{mrc}) \qquad (12)$$

$$\varphi_{rc} = \frac{k}{1 + \frac{\rho_s}{\rho_w}(\frac{1}{x_s} - 1)} \tag{13}$$

$$\gamma_{rc} = \frac{\dot{m}_{dcout}(h_w - h_{dcout})}{Q_{rc}} \tag{14}$$

$$V_{rc}^s = V_{rc}(1 - \gamma_{rc})\varphi_{rc} \tag{15}$$

where $\dot{m}_{dcout}$ is the downcomer outlet water flow, $\dot{m}_{evp}$ is the evaporation generated by heat absorption, $\dot{m}_{ecl}$ is the dynamic evaporation flow, V_{rc}^w is the water volume in the riser, Q_{rc} is the medium heat in the riser, h_{dcout} is the medium enthalpy at the downcomer outlet, V_{rc}^s is the steam volume in the riser, V_{rc} is the riser volume, M_{mrc} is the riser metal mass, C_{mrc} is the riser metal specific heat capacity, T_{mrc} is the riser metal temperature, φ_{rc} is the liquid zone steam section ratio in the ascending pipe and x_s is the average steam dryness in the vapor zone.

Downcomer Model. The downcomer preheats the water supply and returns cool water to the bottom of the drum. The energy balance equation is:

$$\dot{m}_{dcin}h_{dcin} - \dot{m}_{dcout}h_{dcout} = \frac{d}{dt}(\rho_w V_{dc}h_{dcout} + M_{mdc}C_{mdc}T_{mdc}) \tag{16}$$

where $\dot{m}_{dcin}$ is the inlet water flow, $\dot{m}_{dcout}$ is the outlet water flow, h_{dcin} is the inlet water enthalpy, h_{dcout} is the outlet water enthalpy, V_{dc} is the volume, M_{mdc} is the metal quality, C_{mdc} is the metal specific heat capacity and T_{mdc} is the metal temperature at the downcomer.

Superheater Model. The superheater increases the thermal energy. The mass balance and energy balance equations are:

$$\dot{m}_{sin} - \dot{m}_{sout} = V_{sh} \cdot \frac{d\bar{\rho}_s}{dt} \tag{17}$$

$$Q_g - M_{msh} \cdot C_{msh} \cdot \frac{dT_{msh}}{dt} + \dot{m}_{sin} \cdot h_{sin} - \dot{m}_{sout} \cdot h_{sout} = V_{sh} \cdot \frac{d(\bar{\rho}_s \cdot \bar{h}_s)}{dt} \tag{18}$$

where $\dot{m}_{sin}$ is the inlet steam flow, $\dot{m}_{sout}$ is the outlet steam flow, V_{sh} is the superheater volume, $\bar{\rho}_s$ is the inlet and outlet average steam density, Q_g is the heat release of the gas, M_{msh} is the superheater metal mass, C_{msh} is the superheater metal specific heat capacity, T_{msh} is the superheater metal

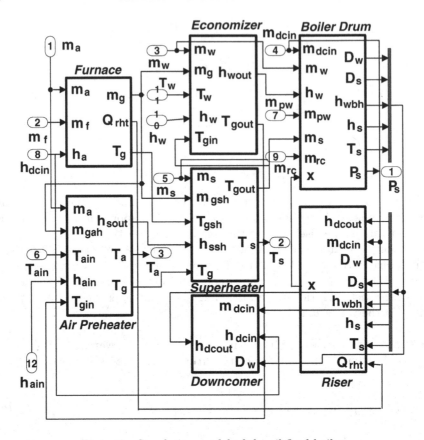

Figure 6. Simulation model of the oil-fired boiler.

temperature, h_{sin} is the inlet steam enthalpy, h_{sout} is the outlet steam enthalpy and $\bar{h}_s$ is the inlet and outlet average steam enthalpy.

Figure 6 shows the oil-fired boiler simulation model implemented using Matlab/Simulink. The boiler simulation model interacts with external controllers. The resulting EPS-ICS testbed can be used for cyber security research and testing.

5.3   Device Evaluation and Certification

Devices that are to be evaluated and certified interact with the EPS-ICS testbed via a network interface or TAP device using Layer 2 access. Table 1 shows some common testing devices that can interact with the EPS-ICS testbed [13].

Researchers can select three EPS-ICS access points for testing: (i) Internet zone; (ii) corporate zone; and (iii) process control zone. Figure 7 shows an example attack path that includes man-in-the-middle, denial-of-service and replay attacks. Table 2 lists the potential outcomes of and assessment [6].

Table 1. Common testing devices [13].

Tool	Availability	Certification	Critical Techniques
Achilles	Commercial	Achilles Certification	Fuzzing, Storm, Monitor
Mu-8000	Commercial	MUSIC Certification	Fuzzing, Monitor
Defensics	Commercial	None.	Fuzzing
BreakPoint	Commercial	None	Fuzzing, Storm
beSTORM	Commercial	None	Fuzzing
Sully	Free	None	Fuzzing

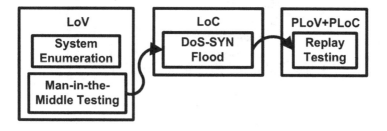

Figure 7. Test procedures and results.

Table 2. Description of vulnerabilities [6].

Terms	Device Under Test (DUT)
Loss of View (LoV)	DUT network stack no longer sends or processes legitimate network traffic
Loss of Control (LoC)	DUT process control functionality is disrupted
Permanent Loss of View (PLoV)	Loss of view persists; manual intervention is required to return DUT to normal state
Permanent Loss of Control (PLoC)	Loss of control persists; manual intervention is required to return DUT to normal state

The first step in the assessment is system discovery, which identifies information assets, operating system types, service ports and running applications. The second step involves a man-in-the-middle attack that tampers with the data transmitted between host computers and end devices. The third step involves a denial-of-service (SYN flood) attack that consumes end device resources. The fourth step involves a replay attack that bypasses password protection, uploads and modifies an end device program and disrupts system execution. Figure 8 shows the results of the assessment.

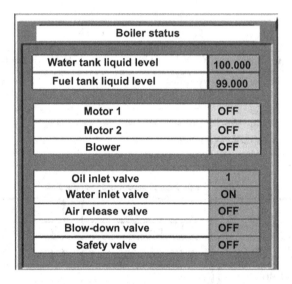

Figure 8.   Assessment results.

6.   Conclusions

The EPS-ICS testbed presented in this paper is designed specifically for industrial control system security research and testing. It seamlessly integrates emulation, physical device and simulation technologies to strike the right balance between fidelity and construction costs. The industrial boiler control system case study demonstrates the application and utility of the EPS-ICS testbed for industrial control system evaluation and certification. Future research will focus on the continued refinement of the EPS-ICS testbed, which will involve developing new monitoring and analysis techniques, expanding the applicability of the testbed and constructing a complementary cyber-physical testbed.

References

[1] M. Brandle and M. Naedele, Security for process control systems: An overview, *IEEE Security and Privacy*, vol. 6(6), pp. 24–29, 2008.

[2] Flux Research Group, Emulab, Total Network Testbed, School of Computing, University of Utah, Salt Lake City, Utah (www.emulab.net), 2014.

[3] M. Flynn and M. 0'Malley, A drum boiler model for long term power system dynamic simulation, *IEEE Transactions on Power Systems*, vol. 14(1), pp. 209–217, 1999.

[4] H. Gan, J. Zhang and H. Zeng, Development of main boiler simulation system for LNG ship, *International Journal of Advancements in Computing Technology*, vol. 4(17), pp. 466–475, 2012.

[5] International Society of Automation, Security for Industrial Automation and Control Systems, Part 1: Terminology, Concepts and Models, ANSI/ISA-62443-1-1 (99.01.01)-2007, Research Triangle Park, North Carolina, 2007.

[6] N. Kube, K. Yoo and D. Hoffman, Automated testing of industrial control devices: The Delphi database, *Proceedings of the Sixth International Workshop on Automation of Software Testing*, pp. 71–76, 2011.

[7] A. Neves Bessani, P. Sousa, M. Correia, N. Ferreira Neves and P. Verissimo, The CRUTIAL way of critical infrastructure protection, *IEEE Security and Privacy*, vol. 6(6), pp. 44–51, 2008.

[8] Office of Electricity Delivery and Energy Reliability, National SCADA Test Bed, Department of Energy, Washington, DC (`energy.gov/oe/tech nology-development/ energy-delivery-systems-cybersecurity/nat ional-scada-test-bed`), 2014.

[9] C. Queiroz, A. Mahmood, J. Hu, Z. Tari and X. Yu, Building a SCADA security testbed, *Proceedings of the Third International Conference on Network and System Security*, pp. 357–364, 2009.

[10] H. Rusinowski, M. Szega and A. Milejski, Mathematical model of the CFB boiler co-fired with coal and biomass, *Proceedings of the Thirteenth International Carpathian Control Conference*, pp. 604–607, 2012.

[11] M. Schwartz, J. Mulder, J. Trent and W. Atkins, Control System Devices: Architectures and Supply Channels Overview, Sandia Report SAND2010-5183, Sandia National Laboratories, Albuquerque, New Mexico, 2010.

[12] K. Stouffer, J. Falco and K. Scarfone, Guide to Industrial Control Systems (ICS) Security, NIST Special Publication 800-82, Revision 1, National Institute of Standards and Technology, Gaithersburg, Maryland, 2013.

[13] W. Zhao, Y. Peng, Y. Gao, X. Han, H. Gao and W. Wang, Security testing methods and techniques of industrial control devices, *Proceedings of the Ninth International Conference on Intelligent Information Hiding and Multimedia Signal Processing*, pp. 433–436, 2013.

II

INFRASTRUCTURE SECURITY

Chapter 7

EVIDENCE THEORY FOR CYBER-PHYSICAL SYSTEMS

Riccardo Santini, Chiara Foglietta and Stefano Panzieri

Abstract   Telecommunications networks are exposed to new vulnerabilities and threats due to interdependencies and links between the cyber and physical layers. Within the cyber-physical framework, data fusion methodologies such as evidence theory are useful for analyzing threats and faults. Unfortunately, the simple analysis of threats and faults can lead to contradictory situations that cannot be resolved by classical models.

Classical evidence theory extensions, such as the Dezert-Smarandache framework, are not well suited to large numbers of hypotheses due to their computational overhead. Therefore, a new approach is required to handle the complexity while minimizing the computational overhead. This paper proposes a hybrid knowledge model for evaluating the intersections among hypotheses. A hybrid frame of discernment is presented using a notional smart grid architecture that transforms the basic probability assignment values from the classical framework. Several analyses and simulations are conducted, with the goal of decreasing conflicts between two independent sources. A comparative analysis is performed using different frames of discernment and rules in order to identify the best knowledge model. Additionally, a computational time analysis is conducted.

Keywords: Cyber-physical systems, Dempster-Shafer evidence theory

1. Introduction

The pervasive growth of network technology has led to the integration of telecommunications technologies and physical processes to create cyber-physical systems. Cardenas, *et al.* [3] define a cyber-physical system as integrating computing, communications and storage capabilities with monitoring and/or control of entities in the physical world, which is done in a dependable, safe, secure and efficient manner under real-time constraints. A cyber-physical system is characterized by the tight connection and coordination between cyber and

J. Butts and S. Shenoi (Eds.): Critical Infrastructure Protection VIII, IFIP AICT 441, pp. 95–109, 2014.

physical resources. Poovendran [7] notes that the concept of a cyber-physical system changes the notion of a physical system to include humans, the infrastructure and the software platform in which the overall system is highly networked.

Examples of cyber-physical systems include supervisory control and data acquisition (SCADA) systems that monitor and control electric power grids, oil and gas pipelines, water supply networks and wastewater treatment systems [2]. Research activities related to these systems usually focus on reliability and resilience. Krishna and Koren [5] have proposed an adaptive control methodology for cyber-physical systems to handle failures of cyber and physical components. Cardenas, et al. [3] have studied integrity, confidentiality and denial-of-service attacks on cyber-physical systems. This paper considers cyber-physical systems in the context of evidence theory, with the goal of properly identifying the causes of faults and threats when a cyber attack compromises power grid operations. Evidence theory has been applied in multi-sensor fusion problems such as diagnosis [1]. Siaterlis and Genge [10] have proposed an evidence theory framework for anomaly detection. In contrast, this paper proposes a hybrid knowledge model for evaluating the intersections among hypotheses. The new approach handles complexity while reducing the computational overhead.

2.   Evidence Theory

Evidence theory is a mathematical formalism for handling uncertainty by combining evidence from different sources to converge to an accepted belief [9]. The basic concept is to reduce uncertainty in order to identify the set that contains the correct answer to a question.

2.1   Frame of Discernment

Let $\Omega = \{\omega_1, \cdots, \omega_n\}$ be the frame of discernment – the set of hypotheses that represents a possible value of the variable ω. In classical evidence theory, the hypotheses are assumed to be mutually exclusive [4, 9].

Given a frame of discernment Ω, it is possible to define the power set $\Gamma(\Omega) = \{\gamma_1, \cdots, \gamma_{2^{|\Omega|}}\}$ with cardinality $|\Gamma(\Omega)| = 2^{|\Omega|}$. This set contains all possible subsets of Ω, including the empty set $\gamma_1 = \emptyset$ and the universal set (frame of discernment) $\gamma_{2^{|\Omega|}} = \Omega$.

2.2   Basic Probability Assignment

Smets and Kennes [12] have defined a model for evidence theory called the transferable belief model. The model relies on a basic probability assignment (BPA) function: $m : \Gamma(\Omega) \to [0, 1]$. The BPA function assigns a value between 0 and 1 to each element of the power set subject to the constraint:

$$\sum_{\gamma_a \subseteq \Gamma(\Omega)} m(\gamma_a) = 1 \quad \text{with} \quad m(\emptyset) = 0. \tag{1}$$

Each element γ_a with $m(\gamma_a) \neq 0$ is called a focal set.

One of the key goals is to quantify the confidence of propositions of the form: "the true value of ω_i is in γ_a" where $\gamma_a \in \Gamma(\Omega)$. For $\gamma_a \in \Gamma(\Omega)$, $m(\gamma_a)$ is the portion of confidence that supports exactly γ_a. This means that the true value is in the set γ_a; however, due to the absence of additional information, it is not possible to better support any strict subset of γ_a. Note that this does not correspond to a probability function and it does not respect the property of additivity, i.e., $m(\gamma_a \cup \gamma_b) \neq m(\gamma_a) + m(\gamma_b)$.

Each BPA is an atomic element in the transferable belief model. In fact, each sensor, agent and node must be able to assign BPA values based on subjective assumptions or using algorithms that automatically determine the assignments.

2.3 Combination Rules

In the case of independent information sources, a rule that aggregates the data is required. Several combination rules have been proposed in the literature. The most commonly rules are Dempster's rule [4] and Smets' rule [12]. This paper considers an additional rule, called proportional conflict redistribution no. 6 (PCR-6), in order to obtain sufficient solutions in terms of a quality-conflict ratio.

Dempster's Rule. Dempster's rule of combination [4], which was the first to be formalized, is a purely conjunctive operation. This rule strongly emphasizes the agreement between multiple sources and ignores conflicting evidence through a normalization factor:

$$\text{Dempster}\{m_i, m_j\}(\emptyset) = 0 \tag{2}$$

$$\text{Dempster}\{m_i, m_j\}(\gamma_a) = \frac{\displaystyle\sum_{\gamma_b \cap \gamma_c = \gamma_a} m_i(\gamma_b) m_j(\gamma_c)}{1 - \displaystyle\sum_{\gamma_b \cap \gamma_c = \emptyset} m_i(\gamma_b) m_j(\gamma_c)} \qquad \forall \gamma_a \in \Gamma(\Omega). \tag{3}$$

Note that Dempster's rule assigns a null mass to the empty set, which has certain limitations when the conflict value is very high.

Smets' Rule. Smets' rule of combination [12] provides the ability to explicitly express contradictions in the transferable belief model by letting $m(\emptyset) \neq 0$. Smet's rule, unlike Dempster's rule, avoids normalization while preserving commutativity and associativity. The rule is formalized as follows:

$$\text{Smets}\{m_i, m_j\}(\gamma_a) = m_i(\gamma_a) \otimes m_j(\gamma_a) \qquad \forall \gamma_a \in \Gamma(\Omega) \tag{4}$$

where

$$m_i(\gamma_a) \otimes m_j(\gamma_a) = \sum_{\gamma_b \cap \gamma_c = \gamma_a} m_i(\gamma_b) m_j(\gamma_c) \qquad \forall \gamma_a \in \Gamma(\Omega). \tag{5}$$

The inequality $m(\emptyset) > 0$ can be explained in two ways. The first is the open world assumption of Dempster [4], which expresses the idea that the frame of discernment must contain the true value. Necessarily, if the open world assumption is true, then the set of hypotheses must contain all the possibilities. Under this interpretation, if $\emptyset$ is the complement of Ω, then mass $m(\emptyset) > 0$ represents the case where the truth is not contained in Ω.

The second interpretation of $m(\emptyset) > 0$ is that there is some underlying conflict between sources. Hence, the mass $m(\emptyset)$ represents the degree of conflict. In particular, the mass $m(\emptyset)$ is computed as:

$$m_i(\emptyset) \otimes m_j(\emptyset) = 1 - \sum_{\gamma_b \cap \gamma_c = \emptyset} (m_i(\gamma_b) \otimes m_j(\gamma_c)). \tag{6}$$

PCR-6 Rule. The proportional conflict redistribution rule no. 6 (PCR-6) [11] is a non-Bayesian rule for combining BPAs. PCR-6 considers two sources of information evaluated as $\text{PCR}_6(\emptyset) = 0$ and $\forall \gamma_a \in \Gamma(\Omega) \setminus \emptyset$ according to the following equation:

$$\text{PCR}_6\{m_i, m_j\}(\gamma_a) = \text{Smets}\{m_i, m_j\}(\gamma_a) +$$

$$\sum_{\substack{\gamma_b \in \Gamma(\Omega) \setminus \gamma_a, \\ \gamma_a \cap \gamma_b = \emptyset}} \left[\frac{m_i^2(\gamma_a) m_j(\gamma_b)}{m_i(\gamma_a) + m_j(\gamma_b)} + \frac{m_j^2(\gamma_a) m_i(\gamma_b)}{m_j(\gamma_a) + m_i(\gamma_b)} \right]. \tag{7}$$

The conflict is redistributed between the elements of the power set. In the case of high-conflict sources, only the focal sets that generate the conflict are involved in the redistribution (see the normalization factor in Equation (7)). Therefore, the solutions obtained after the combination are better in terms of the quality-conflict ratio.

3. Architecture for Smart Grid Diagnostics

A smart grid is an excellent example of a cyber-physical system – it comprises the physical electrical grid and an integrated telecommunications network that monitors and controls the energy flow. Figure 1 shows a simplified cyber-physical representation of a smart grid. Note that the EMS/DMS control system uses a telecommunications network to send and receive information from substations in the power grid.

Two assumptions are made about the smart grid architecture. The first assumption concerns the information exchanged by the equipment: under normal conditions, the cyber information can be represented by the timing and volume of four packet types (Command, Ack-Receive, Reply and Ack-Response). The second assumption concerns the sensors used for smart grid management: a packet-sniffing sensor is used in the cyber layer to detect the number of packets

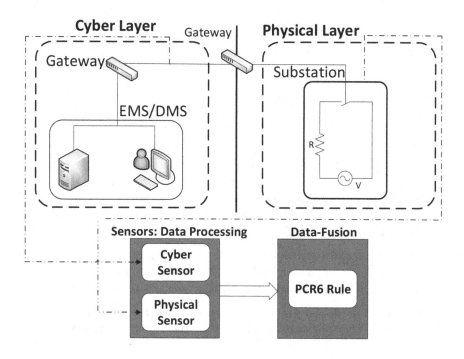

Figure 1. Cyber-physical representation of a smart grid.

in the network and a physical layer sensor is used to indicate whether a piece of equipment (e.g., circuit breaker) is working or not.

In order to apply evidence theory to determine the cause of a malfunction, it is necessary to define the appropriate frame of discernment Ω. In the the example under consideration, there are three hypotheses: normal behavior (N), physical fault (P) and cyber threat (C). The system has normal behavior when the breaker is working and the network packets conform to the operational timing and volume constraints. A physical fault exists when the sensors detect a breaker fault. A cyber threat exists when there is excess or low packet volume. As shown in Figure 2, in the classical evidence theory framework, the hypotheses are mutually exclusive with empty intersections.

A plausible scenario is simulated using the specified architecture and parameters. The scenario involves an attacker who compromises the operation of a piece of equipment (circuit breaker) via a telecommunication attacks (distributed denial-of-service attack). A simulation, which has a duration of 100 seconds, is divided into four different situations:

- **Situation 1 (0 to 27 seconds):** The smart grid behaves normally and no alarms are detected. The breaker is working and the number of network packets in the specified time window is normal.

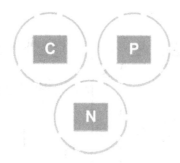

Figure 2. Representation of the frame of discernment.

- **Situation 2 (28 to 35 seconds):** The cyber sensor detects an increasing number of packets in the network (due to the attacker's intrusion), but the breaker is still working.

- **Situation 3 (36 to 95 seconds):** The cyber sensor and the physical sensor both detect anomalous behavior. The packet-sniffing sensor detects a high number of packets and the breaker does not respond to commands.

- **Situation 4 (96 to 100 seconds):** The smart grid is back to normal after the cyber-physical attack because the countermeasures were successful.

Table 1. Events during the simulation and the associated alarms.

Time (sec)	Events	Detecting Sensor
0 – 27	Normal State	–
28 – 35	Cyber Anomaly	Cyber Sensor
36 – 95	Cyber Anomaly + Physical Fault	Cyber + Physical Sensors
96 – 100	Normal State	–

Table 1 summarizes the simulation events, with a focus on the time and information sources.

The goal is to fuse all the data provided by the sensors during a simulation in order to detect a cyber-physical attack. As such, the relative frame of discernment Ω according to the classical evidence theory is:

$$\Omega = \{C, P, N\}. \tag{8}$$

Starting with Ω, the power set is:

$$\Gamma(\Omega) = \{\emptyset, C, P, N, C \cup P, C \cup N, P \cup N, C \cup P \cup N\}. \tag{9}$$

Each sensor has to distribute a unitary mass over specific focal sets during a simulation. Using a combination rule, a fusion result can then be obtained.

Specifically, the focal sets for the cyber sensor are $\{C, N, P \cup N, \Omega\}$. Note that a cyber security expert could identify a cyber anomaly, but is unlikely to discern a physical anomaly. Similarly, the focal sets for the physical sensor are $\{P, N, C \cup N, \Omega\}$.

Santini, *et al.* [8] have used the PCR-6 rule to develop metrics for identifying the effects of cyber attacks that are designed to inflict physical damage. A cyber-physical fault is detected in the presence of mutually exclusive hypotheses by noticing the existence of non-zero similar masses in the cyber cause set and the physical cause set. Such problems are primarily related to the BPA assignments for the sources, which are application dependent. Another problem relates to the interpretation of conflict values that is done in an *ad hoc* manner. The following exponential function (depending on the number of captured packets) is used as the BPA assignment to set the mass of $\{C\}$:

$$e^{-(a \cdot p)/x} \tag{10}$$

where a and p are positive tuning parameters and x is the number of packets. Equation (10) is used in the same manner to express the mass of $\{P\}$ after a physical fault, where x is the persistence of the fault.

When two information sources that have high conflict exist in the cyber and physical realms, the rough values obtained after fusion using the PCR-6 rule are unsuitable. The solution proposed in [8] is to evaluate at each fusion step the conflict value of the mass distribution over Ω using Smet's rule and compare it with the sum of the two masses in $\{C\}$ and $\{P\}$. The cyber-physical alarm triggering equation is given by:

$$\begin{cases} \max\left\{m_{\text{PCR-6}}(\gamma_a)\right\} \forall \gamma_a \in \Omega, & \text{if } m_{\text{Smets}}(\{\emptyset\}) \leq \rho \\ m_{\text{PCR-6}}(\{C\}) + m_{\text{PCR-6}}(\{P\}) \geq m_{\text{Smets}}(\{\emptyset\}), & \text{if } m_{\text{Smets}}(\{\emptyset\}) \geq \rho \end{cases} \tag{11}$$

where $\rho = 0.7$ is a pre-defined threshold for an admissible conflict value. Typically, the decision-making rule in evidence theory is set with the highest BPA value after combining the information from all the sources.

In the smart grid case study, Equation (11) is not always valid throughout the simulation: during the cyber-physical anomaly, the decision rule yields different sets for the same events (i.e., initially $\{C\}$ and then $\{P\}$).

As shown in Figure 3, the results are quite interesting. During the simulation, $m(\{C\})$ and $m(\{P\})$ converge to the same value even if they belong to two exclusive sets as the classical evidence theory assumes.

Using Equation (11), it is possible to transmit to the control center the current state of the system, underlying the occurrence of the cyber-physical attack. Upon analyzing the results, it is possible to confirm that an intersection exists among the sets in the frame of discernment.

Smarandache and Dezert [11] have proposed an extended version of evidence theory. The extended theory eliminates the constraint on the exclusivity of hypotheses and explicitly considers intersections among the elements of the power set. Although the theory appears to be useful in our case study,

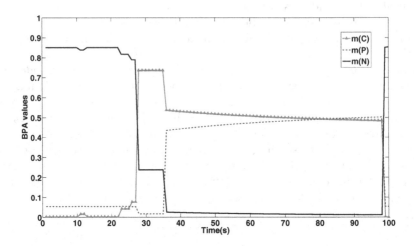

Figure 3.   Results using the PCR-6 rule for singletons.

the main problem is the intersection operator. In fact, after defining the frame of discernment Ω, it is necessary to define a special power set called the hyper power set D^Ω. The cardinality of D^Ω due to the intersection operator follows the Dedekind number sequence: 1, 2, 5, 19, 167, 7580, 7828353, 56130437228687557907787... [11, 13]. Note that only cases up to $n < 7$ are tractable with current computing technology. This paper resolves the problem by using a hybrid knowledge model based on classical evidence theory and Dezert-Smarandache theory, which is described in the following section.

4.   Exploring the Frame of Discernment

The computational overhead when using the Dezert-Smarandache theory is extremely high. To address this problem, the initial frame of discernment is modified by considering a hybrid knowledge model between classical evidence theory and Dezert-Smarandache theory. In particular, the intersection of $\{C\}$ and $\{P\}$ is explicitly evaluated as in the case of Dezert-Smarandache theory, but in the context of classical evidence theory.

The new frame of discernment, which is shown in Figure 4, is given by:

$$\Omega' = \{C', P', N, C \cap P\} \qquad (12)$$

where $\{C'\} \in \Omega'$ is equal to $\{C\} \setminus \{P\}$ in the initial frame of discernment Ω, and $\{P'\} \in \Omega'$ is $\{P\} \setminus \{C\} \in \Omega$. The intersection $\{C \cap P\}$ is added to the frame of discernment because most of the conflict is between the sets $\{C\}$ and $\{P\}$.

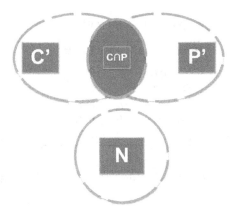

Figure 4. Representation of the new frame of discernment.

The new power set is given by:

$$\begin{aligned}
\Gamma(\Omega') = \{&\emptyset, C', P', N, C \cap P, C' \cup P', \\
&C' \cup N, C' \cup (C \cap P), P' \cup N, P' \cup (C \cap P), \\
&N \cup (C \cap P), C' \cup P' \cup N, C' \cup P' \cup (C \cap P), \\
&C' \cup N \cup (C \cap P), P' \cup N \cup (C \cap P), \Omega'\}
\end{aligned} \tag{13}$$

In the new approach, when the intersection $C \cap P$ is embedded as another hypothesis in Ω', the cardinality of $\Gamma(\Omega')$ is 16. In contrast, using the Dezert-Smarandache approach and the Dedekind sequence, the cardinality of $|\Gamma(\Omega')|$ is 19. Of course, it is possible to apply the new approach for a number of elements $n \geq 4$ to obtain a hybrid power set with cardinality $< D^\Omega$.

Table 2. BPA assignment for cyber sensor with the new frame ($a = 5$, $p = 2$).

	Percentage	Number of Packets
$\mathbf{m}(C')$	55% $m(\alpha)$	$0.55 \cdot e^{-(a \cdot p)/x}$
$\mathbf{m}(C \cap P)$	45% $m(\alpha)$	$0.45 \cdot e^{-(a \cdot p)/x}$
$\mathbf{m}(N)$	55% $(1 - m(\alpha))$	$0.55 \cdot (1 - e^{-(a \cdot p)/x})$
$\mathbf{m}(P' \cup N \cup (C \cap P))$	31.5% $(1 - m(\alpha))$	$0.315 \cdot (1 - e^{-(a \cdot p)/x})$
$\mathbf{m}(\Omega')$	13.5% $(1 - m(\alpha))$	$0.135 \cdot (1 - e^{-(a \cdot p)/x})$

Considering the results obtained in the case study above and the results obtained using the approach presented in [8], we selected the function defined in Equation (10) for the BPA assignment. The BPA values for the cyber sensor and physical sensor are summarized in Tables 2 and 3, respectively. Note that the only difference is related to the BPA assignment of the focal sets:

Table 3.　BPA assignment for physical sensor with the new frame ($a = 5$, $p = 2$).

	Percentage	Fault	No Fault
m(P')	55% m(β)	$0.55 \cdot e^{-(a \cdot p)/t}$	0.055
m$(C \cap P)$	45%i m(β)	$0.45 \cdot e^{-(a \cdot p)/t}$	0.045
m(N)	55% $(1 - \text{m}(\beta))$	$0.55 \cdot (1 - e^{-(a \cdot p)/t})$	0.495
m$(C' \cup N \cup (C \cap P))$	31.5% $(1 - \text{m}(\beta))$	$0.315 \cdot (1 - e^{-(a \cdot p)/t})$	0.2835
m(Ω')	13.5% $(1 - \text{m}(\beta))$	$0.135 \cdot (1 - e^{-(a \cdot p)/t})$	0.1215

- $m(N)$ has the same value because its intersection with the new set is empty and $\{N\} \cap \{C \cap P\} = \emptyset$.

- $m(C)$ is divided into the sets $\{C'\}$ and $\{C \cap P\}$ belonging to Ω', as reported in Table 2.

- $m(P)$ is divided between $m(\{P'\})$ and to $m(\{C \cap P\})$ of Ω', as reported in Table 3.

- $m(\{P \cup N\})$ is now assigned to $m(\{P' \cup N \cup (C \cap P)\})$ and $m(\{C' \cup N\})$ to $m(\{C' \cup N \cup (C \cap P)\})$, as reported in Tables 2 and 3.

As discussed above, the BPA assignment is still an open question in the context of evidence theory. Indeed, there is no consensus on how to assign the BPA values. Thus, the BPA functions are selected based on the application. Note that the values reported in Tables 2 and 3 were obtained after exhaustive tests on the system.

5.　　Hybrid Power Set: Simulations and Results

The hybrid power set was tested by fusing the information using the Dempster and PCR-6 rules. Figures 5(a) and 5(b) show comparisons of the evaluations of the conflict between the information sources. Note that the conflict value in Ω' is smaller than Ω and is reduced by approximately 11% during the simulation compared with the original case.

When Dempster's rule is used, the values are low and demonstrate contradictory behavior. Note that the set $P - C$ is set P' in Ω' and $C - P$ is C' in Ω'. As shown in Figure 6, during the cyber-physical anomaly, the values of $m(C)$ and $m(P)$ are approximately the same ($\simeq 0.05$). Note that $m(C \cap P)$ has a higher value ($\simeq 0.2$), but this is not relevant because the conflict value is high.

Figure 7 shows the values of the singletons after fusion using the PCR-6 rule. Note that the set $P - C$ is set P' in Ω' and $C - P$ is C' in Ω'. In this case, the dashed line (i.e., $m(C \cap P)$) is greater than the others during the cyber-physical anomaly. Upon examining Figure 6, it is seen that the values of $m(C \cap P)$ are comparable with $m(C)$ or $m(P)$ using Ω instead of Ω' as the frame of discernment. Therefore, with the hybrid power set, it is possible to manage the intersection between hypotheses to obtain good results.

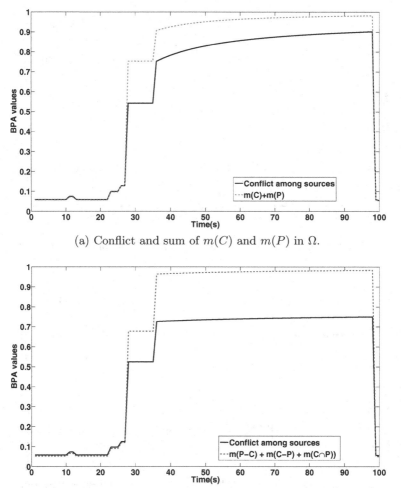

(a) Conflict and sum of $m(C)$ and $m(P)$ in Ω.

(b) Conflict and sum of $m(P - C)$, $m(C - P)$ and the intersection $m(C \cap P)$ in Ω'.

Figure 5. BPA trends in the power set Ω and hybrid power set Ω'.

Using the new frame of discernment and the PCR-6 rule, an operator is able to recognize, with the help of the fusion algorithm, a cyber-physical anomaly represented by $C \cap P$. With the hybrid frame of discernment, the results can be analyzed using a classical metric (see Equation (11)). Note that throughout the simulation there is one element of the power set with the highest value. As such, an operator does not need any other metrics to trigger a particular event (i.e., cyber-physical anomaly).

For the other elements of the power set $\Gamma(\Omega')$, the sets represented in Figure 8 are the only ones with non-zero masses. The values $m(C' \cup N \cup (C \cap P))$ (triangle-marked line) and $m(P' \cup N \cup (C \cap P))$ (dotted line) are the same.

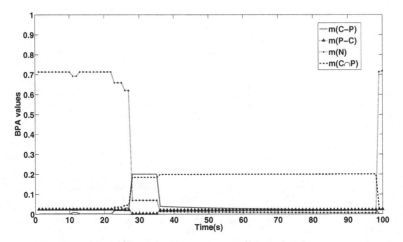

Figure 6.   Results using Dempster's rule for the new frame of discernment Ω'.

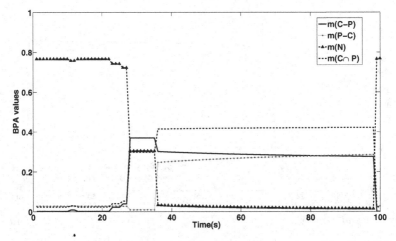

Figure 7.   Results using the PCR-6 rule for the frame of discernment Ω'.

Table 4.   Computational times for the power sets $\Gamma(\Omega)$ and $\Gamma(\Omega')$.

	Mean Time	Variance
$\Gamma(\Omega)$	4.1290 sec	0.1604
$\Gamma(\Omega')$	20.6636 sec	0.0373

Table 4 shows the computational times of the fusion script for the two frames of discernment Ω and Ω'. The script, which was written in Matlab [6], was tested on a laptop with a 2.6 GHz quad-core Intel Core i7 processor and 8 GB

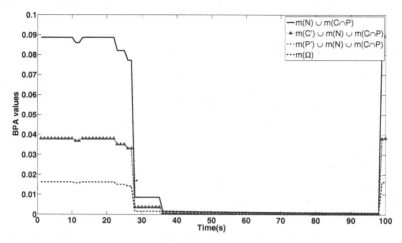

Figure 8. Results using the PCR-6 rule for the remaining meaningful elements of Ω'.

RAM. The script was executed 100 times. Table 4 reports the means and the variances. The frame of discernment with fewer elements (i.e., Ω) requires less time on the average than Ω', but the time required has greater variance. Note that the performance would improve if a non-interpreted programming language such as Java or C++ were to be used. Nevertheless, the results are encouraging with regard to the application of evidence theory in real-time environments.

6.   Conclusions

The application of evidence theory to diagnose faults in a cyber-physical system is an important topic in critical infrastructure protection. In certain situations, such as when cyber and physical faults are both present, the classical Dempster-Shafer evidence theory is somewhat restrictive. Therefore, it is necessary to redefine the frame of discernment to better represent the knowledge model due to non-empty intersections between hypotheses. The Dezert-Smarandache model explicitly considers the intersection, but it has a high computational overhead due to the cardinality of the hyper power set. The solution, as presented in this paper, is to use a hybrid knowledge model where the intersection is included in the frame of discernment. The results obtained are encouraging. The conflict value is lower and the situation is described by the singleton set $\{C \cap P\}$ as having the highest value among the elements of the hybrid power set during a cyber-physical anomaly.

Our research is currently focusing on generalizing evidence theory using different BPA values. An issue requiring further research is defining BPAs for different cyber attacks that seek to inflict physical damage. Another problem is to manage conflicts and understand the source of inconsistent results. Additionally, it is necessary to study of theoretical properties of the hybrid power set.

Acknowledgement

This research was partially supported by the 7th Framework Programme of the European Union STREP Project under Grant Agreement 285647 (COCK-PITCI – Cybersecurity of SCADA: Risk Prediction, Analysis and Reaction Tools for Critical Infrastructures (www.cockpitci.eu).

References

[1] O. Basir and X. Yuan, Engine fault diagnosis based on multi-sensor information fusion using Dempster-Shafer evidence theory, *Information Fusion*, vol. 8(4), pp. 379–386, 2007.

[2] M. Burmester, E. Magkos and V. Chrissikopoulos, Modeling security in cyber-physical systems, *International Journal of Critical Infrastructure Protection*, vol. 5(3-4), pp. 118–126, 2012.

[3] A. Cardenas, S. Amin and S. Sastry, Secure control: Towards survivable cyber-physical systems, *Proceedings of the Twenty-Eighth International Conference on Distributed Computing Systems Workshops*, pp. 495–500, 2008.

[4] A. Dempster, Upper and lower probabilities induced by a multivalued mapping, in *Classic Works of the Dempster-Shafer Theory of Belief Functions*, R. Yager and L. Liu (Eds.), Springer, Berlin-Heidelberg, Germany, pp. 57–72, 2008.

[5] C. Krishna and I. Koren, Adaptive fault-tolerance for cyber-physical systems, *Proceedings of the International Conference on Computing, Networking and Communications*, pp. 310–314, 2013.

[6] MathWorks, MATLAB version 8.0.0, Natick, Massachusetts (www.math works.com/products/matlab), 2014.

[7] R. Poovendran, Cyber-physical systems: Close encounters between two parallel worlds, *Proceedings of the IEEE*, vol. 98(8), pp. 1363–1366, 2010.

[8] R. Santini, C. Foglietta and S. Panzieri, Evidence theory for smart grid diagnostics, *Proceedings of the Fourth IEEE/PES Conference on Innovative Smart Grid Technologies Europe*, 2013.

[9] G. Shafer, *A Mathematical Theory of Evidence*, Princeton University Press, Princeton, New Jersey, 1976.

[10] C. Siaterlis and B. Genge, Theory of evidence-based automated decision making in cyber-physical systems, *Proceedings of the IEEE International Conference on Smart Measurements for Future Grids*, pp. 107–112, 2011.

[11] F. Smarandache and J. Dezert (Eds.), *Advances and Applications of DSmT for Information Fusion (Collected Works)*, American Research Press, Rehoboth, New Mexico, 2004.

[12] P. Smets and R. Kennes, The transferable belief model, *Artificial Intelligence*, vol. 66(2), pp. 191–234, 1994.

[13] D. Wiedemann, A computation of the eighth Dedekin number, *Order*, vol. 8(1), pp. 5–6, 1991.

Chapter 8

AN AUTOMATED DIALOG SYSTEM FOR CONDUCTING SECURITY INTERVIEWS FOR ACCESS CONTROL

Mohammad Ababneh, Malek Athamnah, Duminda Wijesekera, and Paulo Costa

Abstract   Visa, border entry and security clearance interviews are critical homeland security activities that provide access privileges to the geographical United States or to classified information. The person conducting such an interview may not be an expert in the subject area or could be deceived by a manipulative interviewee, resulting in negative security consequences. This paper demonstrates how an interactive voice response system can be used to generate context-sensitive, yet randomized, dialogs that provide confidence in the trustworthiness of an interviewee based on his/her ability to answer questions. The system uses contextual reasoning and ontological inference to derive new facts dynamically. Item response theory is employed to create relevant questions based on social, environmental, relational and historical attributes related to interviewees who seek access to controlled areas or sensitive information.

Keywords: Automated dialog system, security interviews, border control

1.   Introduction

Security mechanisms such as guarded gates, border control points and visa issuance counters are implemented to allow access to individuals upon proper authentication and authorization. Legitimacy is usually determined by rules, regulations and/or policies applied by entry control personnel who attempt to ensure that the entry requirements are enforced. Correctly identifying a person may require an examination of an electronic passport, identity card and paper documents in addition to asking the person questions about information contained in the documents.

J. Butts and S. Shenoi (Eds.): Critical Infrastructure Protection VIII, IFIP AICT 441, pp. 111–125, 2014.
© IFIP International Federation for Information Processing 2014

In order to perform authentication and authorization, an official often conducts an interview in which the aspiring entrant is asked a series of questions based on the specific situation. Ideally, these questions should be relevant, of a reasonable level of difficulty (i.e., neither too difficult nor common knowledge) and should not have been asked previously in similar venues.

The success of interactive voice response (IVR) in auto attendants, satellite navigation devices, personal assistants and mobile applications supported by Apple's Siri, Google Voice and Microsoft's Speech has motivated this research on using interactive voice response systems for access control in visa interviews, entry point interviews, biometric enrollment interviews, resetting passwords and granting access to sensitive resources. Indeed, the goal is to leverage voice technology in automating dialogs used for access control determination.

The use of interactive voice response systems for access control has some limitations. First, most interactive voice response systems have a finite number of pre-programmed conversations. Therefore, the set of questions generated by such a system is the same for every conversation. This may expose the set of questions so that aspiring entrants may arrive with prepared answers. A second limitation is that using a set of random questions from a large pool (typically done to prevent an individual from obtaining the entire knowledge set) may not have the adequate level of difficulty to challenge the aspiring entrant appropriately to determine his/her trustworthiness. A third limitation is that current interactive voice response systems are incapable of discriminating between an individual who knows the subject matter from an individual who correctly guesses the answers. Finally, current interactive voice response technology cannot generate a semantically-coherent sequence of questions that is relevant to the sub-domain that is the focus of the interrogation.

To address the above limitations, this paper proposes an ontological inference-based interactive voice response system that uses item response theory (IRT) to select relevant questions and evaluate trustworthiness. The system uses the access control markup language (XACML) to specify attributes of eligible subjects in the form of an access policy. The proposed system uses an ontology to generate the terms in the access control policy to produce questions. By using an inference engine, a large number of previously-unknown facts about the policy, its attributes and relevant facts are obtained; this provides a large random sample of potential questions [1]. Because the system does not need to store inferred information or save previous question-answer pairs, it can defend against the primary misuse case of human replay attacks. Item response theory is employed to overcome the limitation of selecting relevant questions with acceptable levels of difficulty by creating questions from a large number of attributes present in the policy and ontology.

2.   Background

This section describes the theory and technology underlying the interactive voice response system.

2.1 Semantic Web and Ontologies

Mature semantic web technologies, including the Ontology Web Language (OWL), reasoners, repositories and the Simple Protocol and RDF Query Language (SPARQL), are used to model, query and infer information about subjects, objects, relations and attributes [9]. The core facts represented by triples extracted from policy rules and formal sources of information (e.g., law enforcement, Department of State and Department of Homeland Security databases) are stored as an ontology. The representation enables a common and standard format for data usage and sharing. Note that this paper uses a homeland security ontology for demonstration purposes.

The primary advantage of an ontology is the ability to use reasoners [4]. Reasoners are key components of semantic web technologies that can infer implicit facts from existing ones and provide explanations about relationships.

A context-aware application takes into account the context, which includes social, physiological, biometric, environmental, hardware, computational, temporal, activity, identity and location factors [3]. Contextual reasoning involves the inference of contextual information using ontological reasoners. The selection of questions based on item response theory parameters (e.g., difficulty) ensures that the selected questions align within a semantic context. Note that the modeling context enables a reasoner to infer facts relevant to the subject being questioned.

2.2 Item Response Theory

Item response theory, sometimes called latent trait theory, is used by psychometricians to test individuals. An item response theory score assigned to an individual is said to measure the individual's latent trait or ability. Mathematically, item response theory provides a characterization of what happens when an individual meets an item such as an exam or an interview. In item response theory, each individual is characterized by a proficiency parameter θ that represents the individual's ability. Each item is characterized by a collection of parameters: discrimination (a), difficulty (b) and guessing factor (c). When an individual (examinee) answers a question, item response theory uses the examinee's proficiency level and the item parameters to predict the probability that the examinee answered the item correctly. The probability of answering a question correctly in a three-parameter model is given by [2]:

$$P = c + \frac{(1-c)}{1 + e^{-a(\theta-b)}} \qquad (1)$$

where e is the Euler number.

In order to determine the discrimination and difficulty parameters of a test item, item response theory uses Bayesian estimation, maximum likelihood estimation (MLE) and other similar methods [7, 8]. To estimate the examinee's ability, item response theory utilizes an iterative maximum likelihood estimation process involving an *a priori* value of the ability, item parameters and

```
1.  <<?xml version="1.0" encoding="UTF-8"?>
2.  <Policy xmlns:xsi="http://www.w3.org/2001/XMLSchema-instance"
        PolicyId="urn:oasis:names:tc:example:SimplePolicy1"
        RuleCombiningAlgId="identifier:rule-combining-algorithm:deny-overrides">
3.   <Description>Homeland Security Example -Secure border entry policy
     </Description>
4.   <Target/>
5.        <Rule RuleId="urn:oasis:names:tc:xacml:2.0:example:SimpleRule1"
     Effect="Permit">
6.           <Description>A subject who passes a US embassy interview for F-1 visa, will
     be allowed to enter the country temporarily to finish his degree
     Ex:DiasKadyrbayev.</Description>
7.   <Target><Subjects>
8.   <Subject>
9.        <SubjectMatch MatchId="urn:oasis:names:tc:xacml:1.0:function:rfc822Name-
     match">
10.          <AttributeValue DataType="urn:oasis:names:tc:xacml:1.0:data-
     type:rfc822Name"> DiasKadyrbayev </AttributeValue>
11.  <SubjectAttributeDesignator
     AttributeId="urn:oasis:names:tc:xacml:1.0:subject:subject-id"
                       DataType="urn:oasis:names:tc:xacml:1.0:datatype:rfc822Name"/
                       >
1.   </SubjectMatch></Subject></Subjects></Target>
     </Rule>
```

Figure 1.   Sample XACML policy rule.

response vector:

$$\hat{\theta}_{s+1} = \hat{\theta}_s + \frac{\sum_{i=1}^{N} -a_i[u_i - P_i(\hat{\theta}_s)]}{\sum_{i=1}^{N} a_i^2 P_i(\hat{\theta}_s) Q_i(\hat{\theta}_s)} \qquad (2)$$

where $\hat{\theta}_s$ is the estimated ability in iteration s; a_i is the discrimination parameter of item i ($i = 1, 2, \cdots, N$); u_i is the response of the examinee (one for correct or zero for incorrect); $P_i(\hat{\theta}_s)$ is the probability of correct response according to Equation (1); and $Q_i(\hat{\theta}_s)$ is the probability of incorrect response.

2.3   Access Control and XACML

Access control policies specify the resources that a subject may access and the conditions under which the access may be granted. This work uses the OASIS XML-based Extensible Access Control Markup Language (XACML) to specify access control policies. In particular, XACML specifies subjects, objects and resources using defined attributes (e.g., verified (ID, password) pair as a subject/object attribute). Figure 1 shows a sample policy rule for the homeland security ontology that allows a person whose subject-id attribute value is "DiasKadyrbayev" to enter the United States.

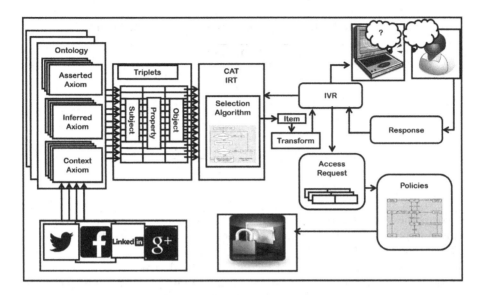

Figure 2. System architecture.

2.4 Interactive Voice Response

Dialog systems provide the means for humans to interact with computer systems. A dialog system uses text, voice and other means to carry out a conversation with a human in order to achieve some objective. Most dialog systems are created with specific objectives in mind and generally involve pre-programmed conversations. An interactive voice response environment incorporates a markup language to specify voice dialogs, a voice recognition engine, a voice browser and auxiliary services that allow a computer to interact with humans using voice and dual tone multi-frequency (DTMF) tones via a key-pad [9]. VoiceXML is a voice markup language used to create audio dialogs that feature synthesized speech, digitized audio, recognition of spoken and DTMF inputs, recording of spoken input, telephony and mixed initiative conversations.

3. System Architecture

Figure 2 shows the overall architecture of the ontology-based interactive voice response system. Axiomatic and derived facts from the ontology are used to create questions asked by the system. Given that a large number of facts can be derived from a context-sensitive ontology, but only a few questions can be asked during an interview, item response theory is used to select the facts that are used to generate questions.

The item response theory module transforms a question into VoiceXML and plays it to the user. The system then waits for the user's response and the system's voice recognition software attempts to recognize the input and check

Table 1. Difficulty assignment based on proof path depth.

Explanations	IRT Difficulty	Level
1	0	Easy
2-3	1	
4-5	1.5	Moderate
6-7	2	
8-9	2.5	
≥ 10	3	Hard

the correctness of the answer. Based on the answer, the item response theory estimation procedure either increases or decreases the *a priori* ability score.

The system uses item response theory to manage and control dialog questions generated from a large pool of ontologically-derived facts in a manner that shortens the length of a dialog while maintaining the maximum accuracy in estimating the user's trustworthiness. When item response theory is not employed, the dialogs tend to be very long or are randomly generated with the possibility of repeated questions.

Another key characteristic of the system is its use of the OWL annotation property to assign item response theory parameters to axioms. Annotations were selected in order to keep the semantics of the original ontology and structure intact. Every asserted axiom in the ontology is annotated with three item response theory parameters, namely discrimination (a), difficulty (b) and guessing (c). Currently, it is assumed that all the asserted axioms have the same default degree of difficulty and a discrimination value of one.

The most important characteristic of the system is that weights are assigned to questions and their answers according to the lengths of the inference or explanation paths. The lengths of the paths are then translated to item response theory difficulty values. Table 1 shows the difficulty value assignment scheme used by the system.

Higher values or weights are assigned according to the number of explanation axioms used to infer a fact. Consequently, such questions are considered to be more difficult than those generated from asserted facts. The item response theory based solution algorithm uses the two-parameter model that relies on the difficulty and discrimination parameters. Figure 3 shows the algorithm used for ability estimation.

After every interactive iteration involving question generation and answering, the item response theory algorithm estimates the ability of the user before selecting and asking the next question. When the ability estimation reaches a predefined threshold, the system concludes the dialog and conveys the decision. Consequently, the decision is based on the item response theory characteristics of the axioms, not on the percentage of correctly-answered questions as in traditional testing.

```
Algorithm 1: IRT Ability Estimation.

Input:  difficultyVector, answerVector, aprioritheta
Output: aposterioritheta

/* calculate theta and standard error */
1:  for (counter < items.length) do
2:      itemDifficulty = parseFloat(difficultyVector[i]);
3:      itemDiscrimination = "1";                  //neutral value
4:      answer=parseFloat(answerVector[i]);
5:      probtheta=calculateProbability(itemDifficulty,
            itemDiscrimination, aprioritheta);   // equation 1
6:      thetaSplus1 = thetaSplus1 + MLE(answer, probtheta);
                                                 // equation 2
7:  endfor;
8:  aposterioritheta = thetaSplus1;
9:  return aposterioritheta;
```

Figure 3. Algorithm for ability estimation using item response theory.

4. Involving Context in Dialog Management

This section describes contextual reasoning strategies for selecting questions based on the current context or a previous context. According to the selection criteria, an item is determined only by the item response theory parameters, which have to be in a range of values close to the interim ability estimation $\hat{\theta}$. This can result in questions that are non-homogeneous and unrelated. For example, one question could be: [*is it true (a isBrotherOf b)?*] while the next question could be: [*is it true (Obama isPresidentOf United States)?*].

Contextual reasoning expands item selection by asking related questions. The concern is not only about the item response theory parameters of a question rendered from an annotated ontology axiom, but also an attempt to continue to ask questions that are related to each other in order to test the user on a branch of knowledge. Compared with the example above, a more relevant series of questions might be [*is it true (a isBrotherOf c)*] followed by [*is it true (b isFriendOf c)*]. Note that the two relations *isBrotherOf* and *isFriendOf* are contextually related by a social relationship context between two people. In order to capture these notions of context, the subject of a previous question is used to generate the next question. Multiple strategies can be used to achieve this objective, such as selecting the next question based solely on subject, solely on property, solely on object or a combination of the three.

A reasoner is used to execute queries in the selection algorithm. A reasoner query using the subject, property or object of a question/axiom is executed to further filter the axioms in the item bank. A contextual reasoning module is incorporated in the architecture to select the axiom elements of the current axiom/question and execute a reasoner query. The addition of this query further filters the triple (subject, property, object) that was previously asserted or inferred by the reasoner. The next axiom/question are determined based on a component of the triple.

The axiom parameters of the current question are examined while the voice rendering loop is executing. Subsequently, a query is passed to the reasoner that returns axioms based on the current context. The next question is generated from the newly executed query result and the item response theory parameters that satisfy the item selection criteria for ability estimation and identification.

In the case of historical contextual reasoning, the current context is expanded by saving the user's session questions and answers in an ontology. A reasoner is executed over the closure of the session with the axioms in the item bank ontology. As a result, questions can be asked in subsequent sessions that are related to the questions posed in previous sessions. Selection strategies for multiple sessions include:

- Asking a question related to a question that a user answered incorrectly in a previous session.

- Asking a question requiring deeper knowledge than a correctly-answered question in a previous session.

- Asking a question about personal relationships related to a previous session (e.g., about co-workers, family members or friends).

This capability provides benefits when evaluating an individual multiple times or a group of related people. For example, related attributes are very likely to be encountered during immigration and security clearance interviews. They also provide the ability to detect abnormal changes in user behavior and personality.

4.1 Context Ontology

Historical context is modeled using an ontology that supports reasoning. Figure 4 shows a context ontology developed with the following classes:

- **Item**: Defines a question generated from an axiom triple (subject, property, object) with respect to difficulty annotation and ID annotation.

- **Session:** Defines an interaction session between the user and the interactive voice response system. The session ID is extracted from the interactive voice response.

- **User:** Defines a user. In our application, the user is the "sameAs" an individual in the item bank ontology.

For each question asked, a set of axioms is added to the context ontology. Some examples are: [User_0001 hasQuestion item_0002]; [Item_0001 wasOfferedIn Session_dd552fcdc5fccef412f96d38818a1c25] and [Session_ dd552fcdc5f-ccef412f96d38818a1c25 timeDateIs Jun 30, 2009 7:03:47 AM]. The existence of

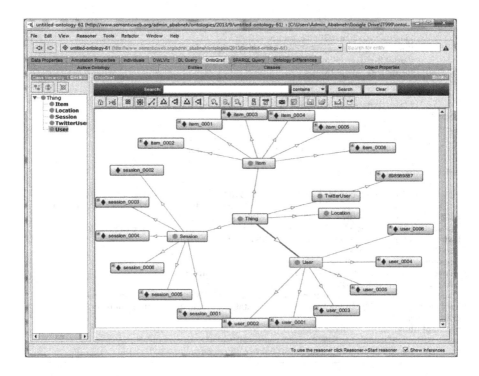

Figure 4. Contextual reasoning ontology.

such axioms makes context-aware reasoning possible. Queries related to questions posed to the current user or to previous users can be executed. This makes it possible to select questions that were previously asked to another user who has a relationship with the current user.

4.2   Contextual Reasoning for Item Selection

The work presented to this point focuses on formal types of policy and knowledge. The axioms must be retained in documents and records. This section discusses how the access control system can be enhanced using knowledge and rules that exist in informal data representations such as social networks (e.g., Facebook, Twitter, LinkedIn and Google+). This is based on the observation that trails, properties, links and photographs contained in social network accounts can be converted to and interfaced with using an ontology to create dialogs used for authentication and authorization. Examples include: Twitter – A isFollowing B; Facebook – B likesPost C; and LinkedIn – C hasContact B and A isGroupMember InformationSecurity.

In the system enhancement, the ontology-based and item-response-theory-supported interactive voice response functionality is augmented with social network information. For example, the system uses Twitter4J APIs [6] associated

```
try{
        long userId=3D97836432, cursor=3D -1;
        IDs ids =3D twitter.getFollowersIDs(userId,cursor);
        // print the user follower IDS=20
        for(long id : ids.getIDs())
                System.out.println(id);
        //tweet or status message
        StatusUpdate statusUpdate =3D new StatusUpdate("Twitter from java =
code");
        //tweet or update status
        Status status =3D twitter.updateStatus(statusUpdate);
        System.out.println("status.toString() =3D " + status.toString());
        }
catch (TwitterException te){

Followers: 2268362549 921276337 84421394 53510732 1162907539 316653147 1311561259
947407448 967877670 383575552 321475980 809284693 454622361 47586577 528672440
81382232 497434232 41674786 199223028 status.toString() =3D
StatusJSONImpl{createdAt=3DThu Jan 23 15:26:59 EST = 2014, id=3D426451015727329281,
text=3D'Twitter from java code', = source=3D'<a href=3D"http://malek.info"
rel=3D"nofollow">Malek =
test</a>', isTruncated=3Dfalse, inReplyToStatusId=3D-1, =inReplyToUserId=3D-1,
isFavorited=3Dfalse, isRetweeted=3Dfalse, = favoriteCount=3D0,
inReplyToScreenName=3D'null', geoLocation=3Dnull, =
place=3Dnull, retweetCount=3D0, isPossiblySensitive=3Dfalse, = isoLanguageCode=3Den,
contributorsIDs=3D[J@433ec72e, = retweetedStatus=3Dnull, userMentionEntities=3D[],
urlEntities=3D[], =
hashtagEntities=3D[], mediaEntities=3D[], currentUserRetweetId=3D-1, =
user=3DUserJSONImpl{id=3D97836432, name=3D'Malek S Athamneh',
=screenName=3D'Malekath', location=3D'Fairfax VA', description=3D'',
```

Figure 5.   Twitter API code and results.

with Twitter. Information extracted from the informal and social knowledge web service is used to populate the context ontology. Figure 5 shows a code snippet and its results, which include the Twitter followers of a specific user and the status of the user. The method `twitter.getFollowersIDs` returns the IDs and the method `twitter.updateStatus` returns the status and location. Axioms such as [User_0001 isFollowing 1162907539], [81382232 isLocatedIn "Fairfax, VA"] and [User_0004 isSameIndividualAs 383575552] are added to the context ontology.

Leveraging the informal data clearly enhances the questions asked by the system. Indeed, questions can be asked about facts collected from formal interviews, official forms, previous sessions as well as social network attributes.

5.   Implementation

This section describes the implementation and the performance characteristics of contextual queries.

5.1   Integrating IVR, Ontology, IRT and Context

The interview begins with a VoiceXML menu hosted on a Voxeo Prophecy web server. The voice browser connects to the web server and converts text-

```
Algorithm 2: Dialog Access Decision Evaluation.

Input:  ontology, contextOntology, user_response,
        difficultyVector, answerVector, aprioritheta
Output: access control decision

/* make access control decision from dialog generated */
/* from ontologies */
1:  domDocument = parse(ontology);
2:  do
3:     subjectArray = getAxiomSubject(domDocument.axiom[i]);
4:     propertyArray = getAxiomProperty(domDocument.axiom[i]);
5:     objectArray = getAxiomObject(domDocument.axiom[i]);
6:     difficultyVector = getAxiomDifficulty(domDocument.axiom[i]);
7:  while (no_more_axioms)
/* use voiceXML and JSP to generate the dialog */
8:  for (counter < items.length) do
9:     <vxml:Prompt> = "auxiliary verb" + propertyArray[i] + " " +
                       objectArray[i] + " " + subjectArray[i];
10:    <vxml:Field> = user_response;
11:    response[i] = Field.voiceRecognition(user_response);
12:    if response[i] = "yes" or "true"
13: answerVector[i] = 1;
14:    else
15:       answerVector[i] = 0;
/* contextual reasoning */
16:    Reasoner.Query([subject][object][property], contextOntology);
17: endfor;
18: theta = IRT_Algorithm(difficultyVector, answerVector,
                          aprioritheta);
19: if theta > thetaThreshold
20:    permit;
21: else
22:    deny;
```

Figure 6. Ontology-IVR algorithm with IRT and context.

to-speech and speech-to-text. Figure 6 shows the algorithm, which integrates interactive voice response, ontology and context. The main steps of the algorithm are:

- **Line 1:** Load and parse the ontology into a Document Object Model (DOM) document.

- **Lines 2–7:** Extract the axiom triple (subject, property, object) and axiom difficulty from axioms and annotations and build separate arrays.

- **Lines 8–17:** Establish a **for** loop to generate a number of questions synthesized from the axiom triple arrays (subject, property, object and difficulty) generated in Lines 2–7. An auxiliary verb such as "is" precedes the triples to indicate a true/false question. VoiceXML and JSP are used to render the format.

- **Lines 10–15:** Obtain the user's response, which is yes/no or true/false. Convert the response to text (0 or 1) and build the response array (vector) used to calculate the ability (theta).

- **Line 16:** Generate questions by contextual reasoning. In addition to the asserted and inferred axioms from the original ontology, a separate context ontology may be used as the target of a reasoner's query in order to ask the next related question. The reasoner's query method uses one of the (subject, property, object) triples as a parameter combined with the context ontology to extract the next related axiom/question.

- **Line 18:** Invoke Algorithm 1 to calculate an estimate of the *a posteriori* θ from the *a priori* θ, which represents the ability or trust.

- **Lines 19–22:** The last *a posteriori* θ is an estimate of the user's ability and is compared with a threshold value set by an administrator. Access is granted if θ is greater than the threshold; otherwise, access is denied.

5.2   Context Performance

Using a context for question generation requires frequent querying of the ontology. To evaluate the performance of question generation, a notional experiment was conducted using synthetic ontology samples that were generated via Java and OWLAPI. SPARQL queries were then executed to return relevant axioms related to specific subjects.

Ontologies were generated for various numbers of students and axioms from a foreign student database. Axioms such as [Student_(randomNumber) isA Student], [Student_(randomNumber) hasVisa F-1] and [Student_(randomNumber) isFromCountry Country_(randomNumber)] were added to produce attributes representative of the Lehigh University Bench Mark (LUBM) ontology [5]. Specifically, an ontology has the following structure:

- There are a number of student individuals of type Student.

- There are 200 countries.

- There are two types of student visas, F-1 and J-1.

- Every student in the ontology has a visa, either F-1 or J-1.

- Every student is a national of one of the 200 countries.

- Every student has a random number of friends (one to twenty) who are also students.

Table 2. Synthetic homeland security ontology statistics.

	HS_100	**HS_1k**	**HS_5k**	**HS_10K**	**HS_50K**
No. Students	0.1K	1K	5K	10K	50K
No. Axioms (approx.)	2.5K	23K	0.1M	0.2M	1.1M

	HS_75K	**HS_100K**	**HS_200K**	**HS_250K**
No. Students	75K	100K	200K	250K
No. Axioms (approx.)	1.7M	2.2M	4.6M	5.7M

- Every student has participated in a random number of sessions with the system (one to twenty).

Table 2 presents the sample statistics, including the numbers of axioms and their sizes.

To test the performance of contextual reasoning queries, three contextual SPARQL queries were created and executed on the data set. Additionally, two baseline queries were developed for comparison.

- Query15 returns all the predicates and objects participating in an axiom with a designated subject.

- Query16 returns all the predicates and subjects participating in an axiom with a designated object.

- Query17 returns the union of the results of Query15 and Query16.

- Query18 returns all the axioms to provide a baseline for comparison with Query15, Query16 and Query17.

- Query18_100 is a version of Query18 that limits the retrieval of results to 100.

Table 3. SPARQL query execution results.

Query	HS_100	HS_1k	HS_5k	HS_10K	HS_50K	HS_75K	HS_100K
Query15	21	21	44	27	30	29	27
Query16	0	0	9	7	16	2	3
Query17	21	21	53	34	46	31	30
Query18	835	3,018	24,535	239,566	1,199,949	NA	NA

Table 3 shows the SPARQL query execution results after each successful execution. Note that Query18_100 is not included in the table because the

Table 4.   SPARQL query execution time (milliseconds).

Query	HS_100	HS_1k	HS_5k	HS_10K	HS_50K	HS_75K	HS_100K
Query15	8	7	13	9	9	10	10
Query16	6	3	8	7	6	7	8
Query17	9	7	10	9	10	9	8
Query18	66	142	1,353	12,133	58,918	NA	NA
Query18_100	20	19	17	18	21	18	23

intent is to show the correctness of the queries. As expected, Query17 shows the union of Query15 and Query16, which is a subset of the total number of axioms returned by Query18.

Table 4 shows the SPARQL query execution time. For a data set containing 10,000 students, Query18 takes approximately twelve seconds to retrieve the results. However, Query15, Query16 and Query17 all require less than 10 milliseconds.

Overall, the three contextual queries perform adequately, returning the expected results in an acceptable period of time. Indeed, the findings suggest that the contextual reasoning queries are executed efficiently and are not expected to cause recognizable delays in question generation that could affect the overall quality of the dialog during an interview.

6.   Conclusions

The implementation of an interview system using ontologies, item response theory and contextual reasoning is certainly feasible. The use of ontologies and reasoning is critical to developing dialogs with items that are differentiated quantitatively. Item response theory provides a means to quantitatively characterize dialog items and to measure user trustworthiness and ability. Contextual reasoning provides the means to select the most appropriate questions quantitatively as well as questions that are semantically-relevant to the domain and subject of focus. The enhancement of contextual reasoning with social media information effectively supplements policy and ontology formal attributes with static and dynamic social attributes.

The paper also demonstrates that social media information is very useful for driving dialogs in interviews. However, the information was used without any analysis. Sentiment analysis is a growing area of research that attempts to predict trends in the inclinations or feelings of groups of people towards life issues. By leveraging social media, it is possible to deduce an individual's sentiments about a variety of issues, especially those related to national security. Our future research will focus on implementing a sentiment analysis module that builds on the social attributes module. The use of social media raises some legal concerns. At this time, we assume that individuals provide consent to use public social media information; however, a comprehensive evaluation of the legal ramifications is required before social media can be used in real interviews of individuals who seek access to controlled areas or sensitive information.

References

[1] M. Ababneh and D. Wijesekera, Dynamically generating policy compliant dialogs for physical access control, *Proceedings of the Conference on Enterprise Information Systems*, pp. 361–370, 2013.

[2] F. Baker, *The Basics of Item Response Theory*, ERIC Clearinghouse on Assessment and Evaluation, University of Maryland, College Park, Maryland, 2001.

[3] B. Beamon and M. Kumar, HyCoRE: Towards a generalized hierarchical hybrid context reasoning engine, *Proceedings of the Eighth IEEE International Conference on Pervasive Computing and Communications Workshops*, pp. 30–36, 2010.

[4] Information Systems Group, HermiT OWL Reasoner, Department of Computer Science, University of Oxford, Oxford, United Kingdom (`hermit-reasoner.com`).

[5] Semantic Web and Agent Technologies Laboratory, SWAT Projects – The Leehigh University Benchmark (LUBM), Department of Computer Science, Lehigh University, Bethlehem, Pennsylvania (`swat.cse.lehigh.edu/projects/lubm`).

[6] Twitter4J, Twitter4J (`twitter4j.org/en/index.html`).

[7] H. Wainer, N. Dorans, R. Flaugher, B. Green and R. Mislevy, *Computerized Adaptive Testing: A Primer*, Routledge, New York, 2014.

[8] D. Weiss and G. Kingsbury, Application of computerized adaptive testing to educational problems, *Journal of Educational Measurement*, vol. 21(4), pp. 361–375, 1984.

[9] World Wide Web Consortium, OWL 2 Web Ontology Language Primer, Massachusetts Institute of Technology, Cambridge, Massachusetts (`www.w3.org/TR/owl2-primer`), 2012.

Chapter 9

A SURVEY OF CRITICAL INFRASTRUCTURE SECURITY

William Hurst, Madjid Merabti, and Paul Fergus

Abstract   Traditionally, securing against environmental threats was the main focus of critical infrastructure protection. However, the emergence of cyber attacks has changed the focus – infrastructures are facing a different danger that has life-threatening consequences and the risk of significant economic losses. Clearly, conventional security techniques are struggling to keep up with the volume of innovative and emerging attacks. Fresh and adaptive infrastructure security solutions are required. This paper discusses critical infrastructures and the digital threats they face, and provides insights into current and future infrastructure security strategies.

Keywords: Critical infrastructures, security, survey

1.   Introduction

The critical infrastructures work together to provide a continuous flow of goods and services, which range from food and water distribution, power supply, military defense and transport, to healthcare and government services, to name but a few [32]. A failure in one infrastructure can directly impact multiple other infrastructures. Beyond the traditional critical infrastructures, non-traditional infrastructures have emerged; these include telephone systems, banking, electric power distribution and automated agriculture. A well-established critical infrastructure network is considered to be the hallmark of an advanced society, and nations are usually judged by the quality of their critical infrastructure networks and the services they provide to citizenry [12]. However, critical infrastructures also represent one of the greatest weaknesses of modern society, due to the fact that a disruption of a critical infrastructure can result in life-threatening and general debilitating consequences to the population, economy and government [40]. As the dependence of society on critical infrastructures

J. Butts and S. Shenoi (Eds.): Critical Infrastructure Protection VIII, IFIP AICT 441, pp. 127–138, 2014.

increases, it is vital that the infrastructures are protected and the potential for disasters is reduced to the maximal extent.

Historically, the main focus was on developing infrastructures that would be resilient to environmental conditions [36] and natural disasters. The shutdown of the Torness nuclear power station in Scotland by a large bloom of jellyfish that blocked the water intake system demonstrates the unpredictability of nature and the importance of planning for damaging natural phenomena.

As technology advanced [7], critical infrastructures increasingly came to rely on digital control systems and networking; this has expanded the focus of critical infrastructure protection to include cyber threats as well as environmental incidents and accidents [3]. Critical infrastructure assets are tempting targets for hackers, criminal organizations, terrorist groups and nation states. Remote attacks on critical infrastructures are a new approach for conducting warfare, with the potential to bring about at least as much damage as traditional physical attacks. Cyber attacks make it possible to incapacitate a country and cause harm to its population. Indeed, because of the interconnectivity and interdependence of critical infrastructures across national borders, there is a high risk that a failure in one infrastructure can propagate to other infrastructures, resulting in cascading failures [21] that could affect practically all aspects of society in multiple countries [26].

This paper presents a survey of computer security techniques currently used to protect critical infrastructures. Also, it discusses why effective protection methods are essential for modern critical infrastructures.

2.   Motivation

The threat levels that currently face critical infrastructures are higher than ever before. Not only do critical infrastructures have to cope with accidents and changing environmental conditions, but the scope, magnitude and sophistication of cyber attacks are placing great strain on defensive mechanisms. Critical infrastructure protection strategies must continually evolve to keep up with new and emerging threats.

2.1   Cyber Threats

Cyber threats are a major concern to corporations and governments [31]. Former U.S. Secretary of Defense Leon Panetta has compared the potential impact of successful cyber attacks to that of the terrorist attacks of September 11, 2001. In the United Kingdom, the large volume of cyber attacks that target government services and multinational corporations has been the subject of much coverage, including discussion and debate in Parliament. While many of the attacks, such as email messages containing Trojan horses [30], are modest, the sheer volume of attacks is cause for concern.

The malicious email threat is difficult to counter because email contents often appear to be genuine [16]. The malicious messages typically contain links to unsafe websites or contain attachments that, once opened, infect the receivers' computer systems and networks. During the last few months of 2011, several malicious email attacks were directed at British Government officials. The email messages, which contained viruses, were doctored to look like they had been sent by government colleagues or White House officials.

Phishing attacks are engineered to steal information that is used for identity theft and financial profit. These attacks have many forms, but one of the most common is to direct a user to a fake website that closely resembles a legitimate website. The counterfeit website is often used to collect user names and passwords as well as banking and credit card information [39].

A common but more complex attack involves distributed denial of service [33], in which computer systems are sent large volumes of traffic that consume their resources and cause them to crash. Distributed denial-of-service attacks are effective because legitimate resource requests and bad requests are often practically indistinguishable, making the attacks difficult to block [1]. Another sophisticated technique is a man-in-the-middle attack [34] that interposes malicious code between system components in order to insert fabricated commands and/or responses. A man-in-the-middle attack can have effects ranging from information theft to system disruption; such an attack can be mitigated by employing an authentication protocol to ensure that communications reach their intended recipients [11].

MI5, the British security service, has announced its intention to invest millions of pounds in cyber defense activities to combat system vulnerabilities and counter cyber threats; other government organizations are also focusing on defensive measures [10]. Meanwhile, several other countries have reported steep increases in attacks. China reported that millions of cyber attacks a day were targeted at Beijing Olympic Games venues in 2008 [24]. While an Olympic Games is not an infrastructure, it is an iconic gathering of people from around the world and would be one of the highest profile targets imaginable.

2.2 Physical Consequences

Critical infrastructures are faced with the unexpected when it comes to cyber threats. Attackers have found ingenious ways to cause infrastructure disruptions. Physical parameters, such as temperatures, pressures, speed and flow rates, are measured and controlled digitally, offering tempting targets. Weaknesses that can result in physical failures must be identified and addressed prior to their exploitation.

During the last decade, several successful high-profile cyber attacks have been covered by the media. The most prominent of these is the Stuxnet worm [19]. Designed to target Siemens industrial software and equipment, Stuxnet reportedly disrupted Iran's uranium hexafluoride centrifuges, significantly delaying the progress of its nuclear weapons program. Stuxnet has clearly demonstrated the sophistication of cyber attacks. If it was possible to successfully target what was, arguably, one of Iran's most protected infrastructures, one can only imagine how easy it would be to target vital infrastructures such as information technology and telecommunications systems, water supply and treatment systems, oil and gas pipelines, and, of course, the electric power grid, which is certainly the most important critical infrastructure to modern society.

3.   Critical Infrastructures

The complexity of critical infrastructures and tight demands for services coupled with operational efficiency and reliability have led to the widespread use of control systems in critical infrastructures. However, control systems require extensive networking resources, which introduce numerous vulnerabilities.

3.1   Infrastructure Complexities

Automation has contributed to design complexities in critical infrastructures. An infrastructure may contain thousands of components distributed across a vast area, all of them connected to a control station. Often the individual components are heterogeneous in nature and have to be integrated in order to control operations [37]. The complexity and scale of the infrastructure mean that there are more potential targets for attack. Additionally, increased automation often leads to reduced resilience and new weaknesses due to design complexities and the dependence on computing systems and networks.

The reliance on wireless networking has introduced design complexities as well as other problems [4]. Wireless networks are difficult to protect because they provide numerous potential entry points. Energy requirements of wireless nodes are also an issue; when their energy is depleted, nodes can no longer perform their designated tasks [28]. One way of attacking a wireless sensor network is to identify and exploit nodes with special roles. A node that has a key role in the functioning of an infrastructure is often overburdened; an attacker can increase the probability causing a disruption by targeting the special node as opposed to a random node. One result is the exposure to a weakness-to-sleep attack, which involves denying nodes in an energy-constrained sensor network the ability to sleep; this attack prevents packets (commands) from reaching their destinations. As Zhang, *et al.* [41] emphasize, since critical infrastructures must provide services 24 hours a day, 365 days a year, disruptions of wireless sensor networks used in these infrastructures are unacceptable.

Business operations and supervisory control operations often require real-time access to the same information and computing resources as critical infrastructure assets. This results in critical infrastructure assets being directly or indirectly connected to other networks, including the Internet [5].

The key lesson from Stuxnet is that even the most sensitive system that is heavily secured and strongly air-gapped can be breached indirectly (e.g., using a USB drive). As a result, critical infrastructure protection is now focused on cyber security and human-initiated cyber attacks [14]. Indeed, the destructive potential of cyber attacks could be just as significant as that of a natural disaster, primarily because cyber attacks could be orchestrated to achieve the maximal effects.

Consider, for example, the Fukushima Daiichi nuclear disaster of March 2011. The 9.0 magnitude earthquake destroyed the electric power infrastructure in the region, causing a large-scale power outage. The subsequent tsunami flooded the rooms that housed the emergency diesel generators, rendering them non-operational. Emergency battery-powered systems were able to provide power to the reactor coolant loops. However, they ran out of power a day later, shutting down the active coolant loops and causing the reactors to heat up, ultimately resulting in the meltdown of three of the six nuclear reactors at the facility. While the Fukushima Daiichi disaster was caused by natural events with an extremely low probability, it is clear that the widespread power outage and the destruction of the back-up diesel generators could be caused by coordinated cyber attacks.

3.2 Control Systems

Critical infrastructures use industrial control systems that enable operators to monitor and control components such as valves, pressure gauges, switches and nodes from remote locations [15]. Industrial control systems may be broadly divided into two categories: supervisory control and data acquisition (SCADA) systems and distributed control systems. SCADA systems are typically used in critical infrastructure assets such as oil and gas pipelines and electric power grids that span large geographical regions [9]. Distributed control systems are used in more localized settings such as chemical plants and manufacturing facilities.

A typical SCADA system consists of a network of sensors that acquire physical process data and actuators that manipulate physical processes. SCADA systems include a master terminal unit, remote terminal units and various communications links. The master terminal unit acquires data from and sends instructions to remote terminal units via the communications links. The remote terminal units interface with hardware components and mechanical devices. Communications in SCADA systems occur over fiber optic, microwave, telephone, pilot cable, radio and/or satellite links. Operators use human machine interfaces and engineering workstations to interact with SCADA devices and ultimately with physical processes. SCADA systems also incorporate databases for storing past information (historians) and business information systems.

The connectivity of SCADA systems and distributed control systems and their increasing use of off-the-shelf components renders them more vulnerable to cyber attacks [9]. Recent cyber attacks include Flame and Stuxnet, which targeted SCADA and distributed control systems. Nicholson, *et al.* [23] identify several types of malicious actors that target industrial control systems:

- **Nation States:** Several countries are investing heavily in cyber warfare technologies. Nation state attacks are characterized by their sophistication and their potential to severely impact control systems and the critical infrastructure assets they operate [17].

- **Insiders:** Insider attacks are among the most serious threats to critical infrastructure assets. Insiders, who may be motivated by revenge or greed, are knowledgeable about infrastructure assets and their weaknesses, and often have high-level access privileges or know how to bypass security controls [17].

- **Organized Crime:** Attacks by criminal entities are usually driven by money. Attacks on critical infrastructure assets may be launched for intimidation, ransom or on behalf of third parties on a for-hire basis.

- **Hobbyists and Script Kiddies:** Attacks by hobbyists are typically motivated by curiosity [17]. Attacks by script kiddies, which are executed because of curiosity, for a thrill or to gain attention, are generally unsophisticated, but can still be damaging.

- **Hacktivists:** Attacks by hacktivists are typically undertaken for political reasons or to gain attention [17]. Hacktivist attacks can be very sophisticated. For example, the shadowy group known as Anonymous has conducted several high-profile attacks, including some that targeted law enforcement websites in the United Kingdom.

4.   Critical Infrastructure Security

This section describes strategies for securing critical infrastructure assets. In particular, it describes the defense-in-depth strategy, along with conventional and future security approaches,

4.1   Defense-in-Depth Strategy

The impact of a critical infrastructure failure has four dimensions: (i) safety; (ii) mission; (iii) business; and (iv) security. Safety refers to the loss of life, serious personal injury or damage to the environment. Mission refers to the inability of an infrastructure to provide vital services; an example is a water supply failure that would not result in an immediate loss of life, but the consequences of a long-term outage could be devastating. Business refers to significant economic losses. Security refers to the loss, damage or destruction of physical, cyber or human assets.

Because of the potentially high impact of a failure, most critical infrastructure assets adopt a defense-in-depth security strategy. Defense in depth involves the implementation of multiple layers of security with different technologies and intrusion detection systems in each layer to ensure that an attack that penetrates one layer will not automatically bypass the next layer. Kumar, *et al.* [18] note that a defense-in-depth security strategy is most effective when the layers operate independently. A typical defense-in-depth implementation may involve three levels of security: low, medium and high. The low level is designed for general employees who have only basic access to infrastructure assets and related information to perform their tasks, while the medium and high levels are designed for individuals such as system administrators, managers and key executives who would require access to infrastructure assets and information systems of increasing sensitivity.

A defense-in-depth implementation positions intrusion detection systems in the different layers to detect hostile activities and raise alerts [41]. The intrusion detection systems typically perform anomaly detection and/or signature-based detection. Anomaly detection involves the detection of abnormal system and/or network behavior (e.g., a sudden, unexpected increase in data flow in a certain part of a system). Signature-based detection involves the use of known attack signatures; on its own, this technique is ineffective at detecting new (i.e., zero-day) attacks [20]. For this reason, critical infrastructure assets typically incorporate multiple intrusion detection systems based on different detection modalities to maximize protection.

One of the problems with using intrusion detection systems in critical infrastructures is that their relatively large footprint makes it difficult to implement them on field devices that have limited computing resources. Additionally, the systems are often unable to identify the most serious attacks and they tend to impact system operation (especially, the tight timing requirements of SCADA systems) [8, 38]. Moreover, intrusion detection systems may generate large numbers of false positive errors, resulting in false alerts. Given the scale of critical infrastructures, massive numbers of alerts could be generated [25], potentially misleading operators and masking real attacks [6].

Unified threat management (UTM) systems, which first appeared in 2004, are now widely used to secure large-scale information technology systems [41]. UTM systems use a combination of firewalls, pattern recognition systems, intrusion detection systems and embedded analysis middleware to implement strong protection within the hardware, software and network layers. The utility of UTM systems for critical infrastructure protection derives from their provision of multiple security features within a unified architecture [41].

The benefits of using UTM systems include lower costs because of the reduced number of security appliances. The systems are also easy to deploy, which makes them ideal for organizations with limited technical capabilities. However, one of the main problems with UTM systems is their integration of multiple security technologies (e.g., control interfaces, message formats, communication protocols and security policies), which can complicate administrative and management activities; the result is that applications tend to work independently of each other.

4.2 Conventional Security Approaches

Several solutions have been proposed to address the security problems facing computer networks used in critical infrastructures. Shiri, *et al.* [29] have proposed the use of multiple (parallel) intrusion detection systems. This design increases efficiency by sharing the detection workload, but it does not enhance security performance in terms of the types of attacks that are detected.

Wen [35] has proposed the use of intrusion detection systems involving a combination of technologies to detect intrusions that originate from internal and external sources. The approach, which uses pattern matching and log file analysis to scan internal network activity and incoming network packets for anomalies, helps combat the insider threat as well as external attacks.

Nai Fovino, *et al.* [22] have developed an innovative approach to detect complex attacks on SCADA systems. Their approach combines signature-based intrusion detection with state analysis. The system can be enhanced by incorporating *ad hoc* rules to detect sophisticated attacks on SCADA systems.

In addition to focusing on network intrusions, it is important to address attacks that have successfully breached network security. This is accomplished using host-based monitoring and anomaly detection. The approach requires the careful analysis of normal operating conditions to establish baselines and thresholds for identifying anomalous activities. The baselines and thresholds should be adjusted continually to reduce false positive errors.

Wang, *et al.* [33] have proposed an augmented attack tree model to combat distributed denial-of-service attacks. Their approach creates attack trees to model attacks and guide the development of attack detection and mitigation strategies. While the approach is innovative, specifying attack trees for the multitude of possible attacks is an arduous task. Moreover, the attack models have to be tuned to the specific infrastructure asset being protected.

Schweitzer, *et al.* [27] discuss how one would know if an attack is actually taking place. They posit that an attack would initially involve probes for collecting information about the targeted infrastructure to be used in conducting the attack. Once the main attack is underway, it is necessary to focus on the intruders' movements within the infrastructure. Schweitzer and colleagues emphasize the need to use multiple, independent communications channels, so that if one channel is compromised, an alternative channel exists to signal an alarm. SCADA systems used in critical infrastructures typically incorporate redundant communications channels to ensure reliable operations; this feature can be leveraged to signal attacks as well as to mitigate their effects.

4.3   Future Security Approaches

As critical infrastructure technology evolves, new threats and vulnerabilities continue to emerge. The introduction of smart meters in electrical power infrastructures demonstrates this trend [2]. Smart meters, which are important features of future smart grids, allow two-way communications between electric utilities and consumers. They enable utilities to use power resources efficiently, provide dynamic pricing and reduce power outages; they offer consumers detailed feedback on energy use and the ability to dynamically adjust their usage patterns to lower electric bills. However, one of the key features of a smart meter is that it has a remote off-switch, which is controlled by the utility. Anderson and Fuloria [2] point out that attackers could potentially manipulate these remote off-switches to create massive power outages.

Clearly, the resilience of critical infrastructures is negatively impacted as new technologies are incorporated for reasons of convenience and cost reduction [2]. Consequently, it is imperative to develop innovative defensive mechanisms that replace or augment existing critical infrastructure protection systems. A promising solution is to design protection systems that operate with a broad view of a critical infrastructure and implement coordinated responses to disruptions using behavioral analysis [13]. This approach constructs and leverages a model of correct behavior based on diverse information about computing systems, networks, industrial control devices and physical processes. Indeed, it offers protection that is at once holistic, proactive and resilient – addressing security issues before they become serious problems and helping critical infrastructures respond gracefully when attacks do succeed.

5.   Conclusions

Critical infrastructures are becoming more and more indispensable as populations grow and demands are placed for new and increased service offerings. Clearly, modern society cannot function if major components of the critical infrastructure are damaged or destroyed. Despite governmental policy and regulation and massive injections of funding and resources, the vast majority of critical infrastructure assets may not be able to cope with sophisticated and evolving cyber threats. Critical infrastructures are large, complex and expensive assets. Since it is not possible to rebuild these assets from scratch to ensure "baked in" security, the only option is to focus on integrating conventional and innovative security mechanisms in comprehensive defense-in-depth approaches founded on risk management and resilience to ensure that successful attacks do not result in catastrophes.

References

[1] A. Al Islam and T. Sabrina, Detection of various denial-of-service and distributed denial-of-service attacks using RNN ensemble, *Proceedings of the Twelfth International Conference on Computers and Information Technology*, pp. 603–608, 2009.

[2] R. Anderson and S. Fuloria, Who controls the off switch? *Proceedings of the First IEEE International Conference on Smart Grid Communications*, pp. 96–101, 2010.

[3] M. Brownfield, Y. Gupta and N. Davis, Wireless sesnsor network denial-of-sleep attack, *Proceedings of the Sixth Annual IEEE SMC Information Assurance Workshop*, pp. 356–364, 2005.

[4] L. Buttyan, D. Gessner, A. Hessler and P. Langendoerfer, Application of wireless sensor networks in critical infrastructure protection: Challenges and design options, *IEEE Wireless Communications*, vol. 17(5), pp. 44–49, 2010.

[5] K. Claffy, S. Bradner and S. Meinrath, The (un)economic Internet? *IEEE Internet Computing*, vol. 11(3), pp. 53–58, 2007.

[6] L. Coppolino, S. D'Antonio, L. Romano and G. Spagnuolo, An intrusion detection system for critical information infrastructures using wireless sensor network technologies, *Proceedings of the Fifth IEEE International Conference on Critical Infrastructure*, 2010.

[7] L. Coyle, M. Hinchey, B. Nuseibeh and J. Fiadeiro, Guest editors' introduction: Evolving critical systems, *IEEE Computer*, vol. 43(5), pp. 28–33, 2010.

[8] F. Deng, A. Luo, Y. Zhang, Z. Chen, X. Peng, X. Jiang and D. Peng, TNC-UTM: A holistic solution to secure enterprise networks, *Proceedings of the Ninth IEEE International Conference for Young Computer Scientists*, pp. 2240–2245, 2008.

[9] C. Esposito, D. Cotroneo, R. Barbosa and N. Silva, Qualification and selection of off-the-shelf components for safety critical systems: A systematic approach, *Proceedings of the Fifth Latin-American Symposium on Dependable Computing Workshops*, pp. 52–57, 2011.

[10] M. Golling and B. Stelte, Requirements for a future EWS – Cyber defense in the Internet of the future, *Proceedings of the Third International Conference on Cyber Conflict*, 2011.

[11] R. Guha, Z. Furqan and S. Muhammad, Discovering man-in-the-middle attacks on authentication protocols, *Proceedings of the IEEE Military Communications Conference*, 2007.

[12] M. Hashim, Malaysia's national cyber security policy: The country's cyber defense initiatives, *Proceedings of the Second Worldwide Cybersecurity Summit*, 2011.

[13] W. Hurst, M. Merabti and P. Fergus, Behavioral observation for critical infrastructure security support, *Proceedings of the Seventh IEEE European Modeling Symposium*, pp. 36–41, 2013.

[14] M. Kaaniche, Resilience assessment of critical infrastructures: From accidental to malicious threats, *Proceedings of the Fifth Latin-American Symposium on Dependable Computing Workshops*, pp. 35–36, 2011.

[15] D. Kang, J. Lee, S. Kim and J. Park, Analysis of cyber threats to SCADA systems, *Proceedings of the IEEE Transmission and Distribution Conference and Exposition: Asia and Pacific*, 2009.

[16] E. Kartaltepe and S. Xi, Towards blocking outgoing malicious impostor emails, *Proceedings of the International Symposium on a World of Wireless, Mobile and Multimedia Networks*, pp. 657–661, 2006.

[17] P. Katsumata, J. Hemenway and W. Gavins, Cybersecurity risk management, *Proceedings of the Military Communications Conference*, pp. 890–895, 2010.

[18] M. Kumar, D. Mukhopadhyay, H. Lele and K. Vaze, Evaluation of operator actions for beyond design basis events for AHWR, *Proceedings of the Second International Conference on Reliability, Safety and Hazards*, pp. 579–582, 2010.

[19] R. Langner, Stuxnet: Dissecting a cyberwarfare weapon, *IEEE Security and Privacy*, vol. 9(3), pp. 49–51, 2011.

[20] P. Li, Z. Wang and X. Tan, Characteristic analysis of virus spreading in ad hoc networks, *Proceedings of the International Conference on Computational Intelligence and Security Workshops*, pp. 538–541, 2007.

[21] A. MacDermott, W. Hurst, Q. Shi and M. Merabti, Simulating critical infrastructure cascading failure, *Proceedings of the Sixteenth IEEE International Conference on Modeling and Simulation*, pp. 323–328, 2014.

[22] I. Nai Fovino, M. Masera, L. Guidi and G. Carpi, An experimental platform for assessing SCADA vulnerabilities and countermeasures in power plants, *Proceedings of the Third International Conference on Human System Interaction*, pp. 679–686, 2010.

[23] N. Nicholson, S. Webber, S. Dyer, T. Patel and H. Janicke, SCADA security in the light of cyber warfare, *Computers and Security*, vol. 31(4), pp. 418–436, 2012.

[24] S. Pritchard, Securing the 2012 Olympics, *Infosecurity*, vol. 6(6), pp. 12–15, 2009.

[25] S. Roschke, F. Cheng and C. Meinel, A flexible and efficient alert correlation platform for distributed IDS, *Proceedings of the Fourth IEEE International Conference on Network and System Security*, pp. 24–31, 2010.

[26] C. Scarlat, C. Simion and E. Scarlat, Managing new technology projects: Some considerations on risk assessment in the case of NPP critical infrastructures, *Proceedings of the Second IEEE International Conference on Emergency Management and Management Sciences*, pp. 911–915, 2011.

[27] E. Schweitzer, D. Whitehead, A. Risley and R. Smith, How would we know? *Proceedings of the Sixty-Fourth Annual Conference for Protective Relay Engineers*, pp. 310–321, 2011.

[28] W. Seah, A. Zhi and H. Tan, Wireless sensor networks powered by ambient energy harvesting (WSN-HEAP) – Survey and challenges, *Proceedings of the First International Conference on Wireless Communication, Vehicular Technology, Information Theory and Aerospace and Electronic Systems Technology*, 2009.

[29] F. Shiri, B. Shanmugam and N. Idris, A parallel technique for improving the performance of signature-based network intrusion detection systems, *Proceedings of the Third International Conference on Communication Software and Networks*, pp. 692–696, 2011.

[30] S. Tang, The detection of Trojan horses based on data mining, *Proceedings of the Sixth International Conference on Fuzzy Systems and Knowledge Discovery*, vol. 1, pp. 311–314, 2009.

[31] J. Walker, B. Williams and G. Skelton, Cyber security for emergency management, *Proceedings of the IEEE International Conference on Technologies for Homeland Security*, pp. 476–480, 2010.

[32] C. Wang, L. Fang and Y. Dai, A simulation environment for SCADA security analysis and assessment, *Proceedings of the International Conference on Measuring Technology and Mechatronics Automation*, vol. 1, pp. 342–347, 2010.

[33] J. Wang, R. Phan, J. Whitley and D. Parish, Augmented attack tree modeling of distributed denial of services and tree based attack detection method, *Proceedings of the Tenth IEEE International Conference on Computer and Information Technology*, pp. 1009–1014, 2010.

[34] Y. Wang, H. Wang, Z. Li and J. Huang, Man-in-the-middle attack on BB84 protocol and its defense, *Proceedings of the Second IEEE International Conference on Computer Science and Information Technology*, pp. 438–439, 2009.

[35] W. Wen, An improved intrusion detection system, *Proceedings of the International Conference on Computer Applications and System Modeling*, vol. 5, pp. 212–215, 2010.

[36] T. Wilson, C. Stewart, V. Sword-Daniels, G. Leonard, D. Johnston, J. Cole, J. Wardman, G. Wilson and S. Barnard, Volcanic ash impacts on critical infrastructure, *Physics and Chemistry of the Earth, Parts A/B/C*, vol. 45-46, pp. 5–23, 2011.

[37] S. Wolthusen, GIS-based command and control infrastructure for critical infrastructure protection, *Proceedings of the First IEEE International Workshop on Critical Infrastructure Protection*, pp. 40–50, 2005.

[38] H. Xue, MultiCore systems architecture design and implementation of UTM, *Proceedings of the International Symposium on Information Science and Engineering*, pp. 441–445, 2008.

[39] W. Yu, S. Nargundkar and N. Tiruthani, A phishing vulnerability analysis of web-based systems, *Proceedings of the IEEE Symposium on Computers and Communications*, pp. 326–331, 2008.

[40] F. Yusufovna, F. Alisherovich, M. Choi, E. Cho, F. Abdurashidovich and T. Kim, Research on critical infrastructures and critical information infrastructures, *Proceedings of the Symposium on Bio-Inspired Learning and Intelligent Systems for Security*, pp. 97–101, 2009.

[41] Y. Zhang, F. Deng, Z. Chen, Y. Xue and C. Lin, UTM-CM: A practical control mechanism solution for UTM systems, *Proceedings of the IEEE International Conference on Communications and Mobile Computing*, pp. 86–90, 2010.

III

INFRASTRUCTURE MODELING AND SIMULATION

Chapter 10

A SYSTEM DYNAMICS FRAMEWORK FOR MODELING CRITICAL INFRASTRUCTURE RESILIENCE

Simona Cavallini, Cristina d'Alessandro, Margherita Volpe,
Stefano Armenia, Camillo Carlini, Elisabeth Brein,
and Pierluigi Assogna

Abstract   In recent years, awareness of the potential consequences associated with a major disruption to the critical infrastructure has grown among public and private entities. Indeed, traditional and emerging threats endanger service continuity and, by extension, the normal functioning of modern society. This paper presents an approach for modeling the effects of critical infrastructure failures as a result of unexpected events. The transportation, energy and telecommunications infrastructures are modeled using a system dynamics approach. The work constitutes a component of the CRISADMIN Project that is focused on developing a tool to evaluate the impacts of critical events. The ultimate objective of the project is to provide decision makers with a sophisticated tool to help them mitigate negative effects in emergency situations. The prototype tool described in this paper leverages case studies of terrorist attacks and floods that have occurred in Europe.

Keywords: Interdependencies, critical events, domino effects, system dynamics

1.   Introduction

Critical infrastructures are the backbone of modern society, enabling the vital functionalities that support economic and social interactions. The European Commission's 2008/114/EC Directive [5] defines critical infrastructure as "an asset, system or part thereof located in Member States which is essential for the maintenance of vital societal functions, health, safety, security, economic or social well-being of people, and the disruption or destruction of which would have a significant impact in a Member State as a result of the failure to maintain those functions." It is important to note that system failures in

J. Butts and S. Shenoi (Eds.): Critical Infrastructure Protection VIII, IFIP AICT 441, pp. 141–154, 2014.

a specific critical infrastructure sector can, due to their strategic role in the socio-economic context, produce domino effects that can potentially impact all aspects of society. Understanding the effects and strategic interconnections are essential when responding to events, setting policies and determining protective investments.

Thurlby and Warren [12] state that, in order to rank preventative measures, the economic costs and potential savings (i.e., reduced casualties and/or economic losses) must be evaluated. Thus, there is a growing need to understand the costs for society as a whole – beyond those of the initially-impacted infrastructures – to fully comprehend the magnitude of an event and make appropriate response decisions.

A number of powerful simulation tools have been developed to help understand how networks may be affected by major incidents, many of which help organizations to improve their response readiness. Nevertheless, the relationship between long-term strategic choices and the ability of infrastructure networks to withstand disruptive events are not well understood. Indeed, decision making concerning investments in critical infrastructure assets, particularly those related to network control systems and the people who manage the systems, have not been thoroughly investigated to determine the long-term implications. While it is clear that spending less on assets, systems and people will degrade a system, it is not obvious how much impact any particular choice has over an extended period of time. The primary issues that need to be addressed are:

- How long-term choices related to strategic issues make a network more resilient.

- How these choices and others can minimize service loss when disruptive events occur.

- How strategic and operational choices can minimize the time taken for a network to recover and, thus, minimize the total cumulative loss of services.

The Critical Infrastructure Simulation of Advanced Models for Interconnected Network Resilience (CRISADMIN) Project studies the effects produced by critical events in an environment in which the interdependencies among several critical infrastructure sectors are modeled using a system dynamics approach and simulated in a synthetic environment. This paper discusses the key features of the methodology. The intention is to provide insights into the activities and expected outputs of the project, providing researchers and professionals with a methodology for crisis management.

2.   CRISADMIN Approach

The CRISADMIN Project is focused on developing a tool for evaluating the impacts of critical events on critical infrastructures. The tool is intended to serve as a decision support system that is able to test and analyze critical infrastructure interdependencies, determine the modalities through which they are affected by predictable and unpredictable events (e.g., terrorist attacks and natural disasters), and investigate the impacts of possible countermeasures and prevention policies.

To achieve these challenging objectives, a three step approach has been formulated:

- **Theoretical Model Definition:** The first step is to define the system characteristics in order to establish the investigative boundaries and key reference points. This objective is achieved through the formulation of a theoretical model that identifies variables and parameters that best represent (or approximate) the infrastructures of interest. Special attention is focused on the identification of social system variables (i.e., "soft" parameters that are particularly difficult to quantify). Through careful analysis of the literature, these variables are represented in a manner compatible with system dynamics.

- **System Dynamics Model Development:** Causal relations between the parameters defined in the theoretical model are identified; this facilitates the construction of a number of causal maps. The causal maps provide the foundation for the simulation model structure that is validated using real case studies.

- **Data Collection:** Quantitative data concerning critical infrastructure functionality is collected from a number of case studies. In addition, data related to the socio-economic framework is gathered according to its availability and reliability with reference to critical events that have occurred in Europe in recent years.

Starting with the definition of a theoretical reference framework, the goal is to design a system dynamics model that constitutes the logical base for developing the decision support system. The effort engages case studies for model development and analysis. The models are integrated within the decision support structure to produce a readily accessible and usable decision making tool.

3. Theoretical Model

The theoretical model defines the main factors that should be considered in an emergency situation. The goal is to enhance the preparedness and response capability of all the involved actors in order to mitigate and recover from the negative effects of a catastrophic event. The main factors are investigated in terms of mutual influences, those that reinforce and those that dampen the effects of an event. Special attention is focused on the involved actors (i.e., victims, spectators and individuals responsible for managing the emergency) [3].

As in all complex environments, the vast majority of factors in emergency situations are highly interconnected. The primary objective of the theoretical model is to identify the main dependencies that impact the evolution of an event. Territorial features, the socio-economic environment, event timing (e.g., time and duration) and actor preparedness are included in the analysis. In the

CRISADMIN Project, the effects of a critical event are studied in the context of three critical infrastructure sectors, namely transportation (private and public), energy (electricity distribution and consumption) and telecommunications (mobile and fixed).

Data domains are grouped according to the parameters included in the model. Specifically, four data domains are considered:

- **Territory:** This domain includes the set of variables and parameters that describe the geographic features of the territory. Territorial characteristics are particularly relevant to natural disasters; however, they may also affect the efficiency of responses in other critical situations (e.g., high territorial diversity exerts a negative influence on the promptness of emergency transportation). In this data domain, the main elements are the territorial factors and geographical nature (e.g., extension and locality) that impact vital services and social aspects.

- **Environment:** This domain refers to the set of variables and parameters related to the presence and activities of human beings in the territory, such as energy-related supply chain capacity, public transportation, population density and socio-economic patterns in the affected area. In the case of human-initiated critical events, environmental parameters are essential to successful crisis response.

- **Apparatus:** This domain includes the set of variables and parameters related to the professionals and operators who manage the effects of catastrophic events and the subsequent recovery. Typically, the apparatus includes multiple agencies and organizations, each of which have a specific role in managing minor emergencies as well as unexpected critical events. In some countries, civil authorities coordinate the activities of all the various apparatus organizations in order to mitigate the effects of a critical event.

- **Events:** This domain refers to the set of variables and parameters that define "normal" conditions. The data describes the evolution of normal situations over time (in contrast, the geographical features in the territory domain are time independent). Data related to the environment and apparatus depend on the normal life-cycles and are tied to the hour of the day (e.g., work hours and commuting hours), day of the week (e.g., workday, weekend, bank holiday and special days) and month of the year (e.g., festivals and vacation periods). These dependencies, which can be more or less substantial for the different variables, are considered when modeling the evolution of a critical event from the very first moments after it occurs. After the first parameter adjustment at t_0, the evolution of an event is generally considered to be independent of the hour, day and month because of the emergency effects.

Figure 1 presents the CRISADMIN theoretical model with the four data domains. Examples of parameters related to the three critical infrastructure

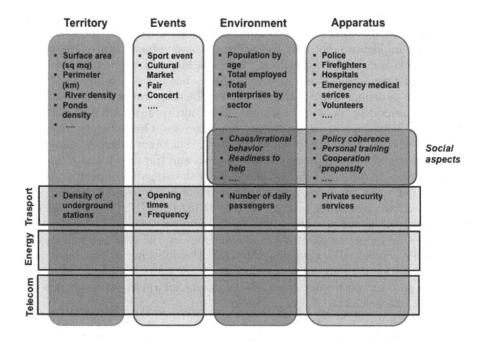

Figure 1. CRISADMIN theoretical model.

sectors are shown to illustrate the items that require investigation when responding to a critical event.

4. Identification of Social System Variables

The data domains capture the stage at which a critical event occurs, where countermeasures should occur and how the damage should be assessed. For this reason, social aspects involved in the preparedness and in the reaction to critical situations are included in the environment and apparatus domains. Special attention should be focused on the actors that participate in the activities being modeled and on the ordinary events that represent normal conditions.

Frequently, discussions about the effectiveness of crisis management focus on the material side (e.g., engineering and structural solutions, effective information technology and transportation networks, safeguarding electric power networks from overload and increasing the number of first responders). These discussions often ignore the thoughts, attitudes, expectations and behavior of individuals and groups who are affected by the crisis or are involved in their management. Indeed, disregarding the social and psychological aspects is problematic because each infrastructure, despite its material nature, is always embedded in the social environment. As Orlikowski and Scott [9] argue, technology is always technology in practice, highlighting the fact that the same technology will be used in very different ways depending on the social context in which it is used; this fact is also true in crises. Therefore, an important premise of the CRISADMIN Project is that, in order to have effective crisis management, it is of vital importance not only to understand how infrastructures and technologies work, but also to understand "how relations and boundaries between humans and technologies are not given or fixed, but enacted in practice" [9]. The realistic modeling of crises clearly requires the inclusion of social variables.

When considering the social variables to be incorporated, it is important differentiate between two categories of human actors. One category includes the people who are actively effected by the crisis. The other category comprises the individuals who attempt to manage the crisis and the subsequent recovery. A critical event induces behavioral changes in both categories of people. Note, however, that these two categories are not necessarily mutually exclusive.

The literature review undertaken by the CRISADMIN Project focused on human behavior in social systems during the response phase. Emphasis was placed on the impact on the individuals affected by the crisis as well as on the individuals involved in managing the crisis. Possible interactions, including inter-organizational coordination in emergency response, leadership in crisis situations and approaches for communication and information dissemination, were taken into account.

The literature review was by no means limited to a specific type of critical event. Indeed, the fundamental assumption was that social system variables in crisis responses are generic in nature and applicable to disparate crises. The CRISADMIN Project specifically considered papers related to crisis management from the theoretical and empirical points of view, papers related to psychological and organizational knowledge based on empirical analysis, and papers related to psychological and organizational knowledge dealing with non-crisis management and based on empirical research. The review identified a total of 34 social variables.

The literature review also yielded several general observations related to the importance of social system variables when modeling critical events:

- For effective crisis management, material needs and social needs should be considered simultaneously.

- Adequate communication is essential immediately after a crisis occurrence.

- Communication flows are core aspects of strategies for systematic crisis management.

- The need for a communication strategy has to be embraced by first responders to improve crisis management.

- Information sharing is significant to successful inter-organizational cooperation.

- A longitudinal perspective should be considered; experience from past critical situations affects current crisis response and reactions.

In addition, cultural and societal settings (e.g., values, attitudes and demographics) that strongly influence the preparation for and the reaction to critical events with regard to victims and first responders in specific environments were taken into account.

5.   System Dynamics Methodology

The CRISADMIN Project employs a computer simulation modeling methodology based on systems dynamics and feedback for studying and managing complex issues and problems encountered during crisis events. The feedback systems, such as social response, are defined as a collection of interacting elements working together for a certain purpose. The key element is to consider the concatenation of causal relations through which any component of a system can influence the behavior of other components that may be proximal or distant in terms of the apparent connections [6].

Originally developed in the 1950s to help corporate managers improve their understanding of industrial processes, system dynamics is currently used to understand the dynamic behavior of complex systems [6]. The application is based on the fact that the structure of any system relies on circular, interlocking and time-delayed relationships among its components.

Sterman [11] stated that the main properties of a system that can be successfully represented using a system dynamics approach are: (i) presence of quantities that vary over time; (ii) variability based on causal dependencies; and (iii) feedback loops containing the main causal influences of a closed system. Additionally, Sterman argued that system dynamics, as a decision modeling approach, is very applicable in contexts where standard analysis is made difficult by the wide range of available data. It is particularly applicable to systems that are highly influenced by soft variables, which are not directly measurable (e.g., trust in first responders, attitudes of the public and panic diffusion).

In recent years, the system dynamics approach has been used to prevent and manage security/defense issues, primarily because it takes into account randomness and interdependencies that characterize behavior in real-world environments. This is made possible by including the soft variables typical of interrelated social systems. The idea behind the system dynamics approach is that if the system structure defines the behavior of the system, then accurately analyzing and determining the interrelationships among the various components of the system produces an accurate understanding of the dynamics of the system [11].

The CRISADMIN Project uses system dynamics to forecast the evolution of the modeled components (i.e., territorial features, timing of the critical event, environmental factors, types of actors involved and social behaviors) from the occurrence of a critical event until the realization of the subsequent impacts. The holistic approach of system dynamics requires that the entire context be considered and that factors perceived as weak or not strictly related be disregarded. This aspect is intended to help avoid defining a model that is difficult to manage and/or interpret.

Table 1.   Example influences among the identified variables.

Influencing Parameter	Influenced Parameter	Notes
Crest (Flood)	(+) Inundation area	Calculated using elevation map
Total Inundation Area	(+) Involved structures	Ascertained by first responders
Energy Production Damage	(−) Electricity disruption	Adjustment of rate on lost power
Electricity Station Damage	(−) Electricity disruption	Adjustment of rate on lost power

The identification of relevant influences within the system dynamics framework makes it possible to understand the connections among critical infrastructures and to model the impacts of critical events, taking into account the dynamics of an infrastructure as a function of the operations of other critical infrastructures that are not affected directly. System dynamics simulations must represent the main mutual influences of the parameters identified in the theoretical model, defining each influence as positive (i.e., reinforcing) or negative (i.e., dampening), and the related value and timing. Table 1 presents example influences among the identified variables.

The overall model uses interactions among influences and additional information to estimate the total direct and indirect impacts arising from a critical event. This approach allows for the comparison of impacts within the socioeconomic context that is represented as a dynamic system. Once they are consolidated, the proposed influences are tested using data gathered from relevant case studies.

6.   Data Collection

In order to apply the CRISADMIN approach, four critical events related to previous terrorist attacks and floods were identified and analyzed. The following criteria drove the selection of the events:

- **Threat Likelihood:** The frequency of terrorist attacks has increased since the events of September 11, 2001, reinforcing the view that a terrorist attack is a real possibility [4]. Floods are also becoming more frequent.

- **Historical Event Frequency:** Special attention is placed on terrorist attacks in Spain and the United Kingdom – countries that have suffered from ethnic terrorism for decades, from the Euskadi Ta Askatasuna (ETA) and the Irish Republican Army (IRA), respectively, and, more recently, have had to deal with attacks by Islamic terrorist groups. Meanwhile, Europe has seen increased flooding incidents; examples are the 2002 Glasgow flood in the United Kingdom, the 2001 Po river floods in Italy and the 2011 Genoa flood in Italy.

■ **Critical Infrastructure Impact:** Terrorist attacks and floods destroy essential assets, and impact critical infrastructures directly or indirectly. These events tend to have major impacts on the transportation, energy and telecommunications sectors.

Four case studies were used to apply and validate the CRISADMIN approach. The case studies include: (i) Madrid bombings of 2004; (ii) London bombings of 2005; (iii) Central and Eastern Europe floods of 2002; and (iv) United Kingdom floods of 2007. The following sections briefly describe the selected case studies and highlight their essential elements and impacts.

6.1 Madrid Bombings (2004)

On the morning of March 11, 2004, explosive devices were detonated aboard four commuter trains in Madrid [10]. The affected trains were traveling on the same line and in the same direction between the Alcala de Henares and Atocha stations. A total of thirteen improvised explosive devices were placed on the trains. Ten of the devices exploded; two of the remaining three devices were detonated by Spanish Police bomb disposal experts at the Atocha and El Pozo stations. The thirteenth bomb was not found until later in the evening, having been stored inadvertently with luggage taken from one of the trains. In the following days, official investigations made by the Spanish Judiciary determined that the attacks were directed by a Muslim terrorist cell, which was inspired by al-Qaeda, although no direct al-Qaeda participation was ever established [8].

The terrorists boarded the four commuter trains, each with a capacity of 6,000 passengers. They hid thirteen bomb bags (backpacks) amongst passenger luggage in several carriages before disembarking. Each backpack contained approximately ten kilograms of dynamite; some of the bags were filled with nails and other shrapnel to cause serious wounds to commuters. The explosive devices, which were activated by mobile phone alarms, were set to explode at various commuter stations to maximize casualties and property damage.

The bombings killed 177 people instantly and wounded approximately 1,858 others. Fourteen of the injured people subsequently died, bringing the final death toll to 191. More than 550 staff members and 100 vehicles from SAMUR Civil Protection were involved in the rescue and management activities. Within 90 minutes, SAMUR mobilized more than 325 people, increasing their staffing from 75 to 400 people, and recalled 70 vehicles. Healthcare-related activities in the emergency areas were performed by SAMUR and other local institutions.

The transportation sector was the only one to be directly affected by the bombings, in particular the four trains and the stations where the explosions occurred. The four trains were on the same track, heading towards Atocha Station (main commuting point in Madrid), El Pozo Station, Santa Eugenia Station and Calle Tellez Station. The energy and telecommunications infrastructures were not directly targeted by the bombing attacks. However, the telecommunications infrastructure experienced massive overloads due to general panic and crisis management needs.

6.2   London Bombings (2005)

On July 7, 2005, three London subway stations (Aldgate, Edgware Road and Russel Square) were attacked by suicide bombers. In addition, a bomb was placed in a double-decker bus that detonated in Travistock Square [7]. The bombings were carried out by four Islamic extremists, who were angered by Britain's involvement in the Iraq War. At about 8:50 A.M., three almost simultaneous explosions detonated in the tunnel between Liverpool Street and Aldgate stations, on the line at Edgware Road and in a Piccadilly Line tunnel between King's Cross and Russell Square.

Almost an hour later, at 9:47 A.M., the bomb placed in the double-decker bus was detonated at Travistock Square. The location of the bomb inside the bus resulted in the front of the vehicle remaining mostly intact. Indeed, most of the passengers in the front of the top deck survived, as did those near the front of the lower deck, including the driver. Individuals at the top and lower rear of the bus suffered more serious injuries. Several passersby were injured by the explosion and some surrounding buildings were damaged by debris. In order to ensure the maintenance of normal security and civil protection services in the city, the choice was made to send only critical staff to the bombing sites – leaving non-essential personnel, equipment and materials at headquarters in the stand-by state. Only the transportation infrastructure was directly affected by the bomb blasts.

6.3   Central and Eastern Europe Floods (2002)

In August 2002, severe flooding affected portions of Austria, the Czech Republic and Germany [13]. Heavy rainfall from storms that crossed central Europe during early August triggered sequential flood waves along two major river systems. The flood waves moved down the Danube through Austria and down the Vltava and Elbe rivers in the Czech Republic and Germany. The flooding event covered a period of approximately fourteen days from August 6 until August 20, 2002. The event included precipitation as well as flash floods along the involved rivers in Central and Eastern Europe.

The August 2002 floods were due to two major factors: unusual meteorological conditions and human activities (e.g., housing construction, land drainage and deforestation). The flood event was triggered by unusual meteorological conditions, which included two periods of intense rainfall during the first half of August 2002. As usual, the water temperatures in the Adriatic and Mediterranean were significantly higher in August than in the spring, causing substantial amounts of atmospheric moisture that fueled the extreme rainfall. The first period of rain on August 6 and 7, 2002 fell in the southwestern Czech Republic and northeastern Austria, immediately north of a weak area of low pressure. Rainfall accumulations were generally less than 125 mm over the two-day period, but intense rainfall of up to 255 mm was observed in some locations.

The rainfall triggered flood waves in the upper portions of the Danube and Vltava catchment areas. One flood wave progressed down the Danube through Austria, Slovakia and Hungary, causing minor damage. A more critical flood wave progressed down the Vltava through Prague and down the Elbe through northern Bohemia and Germany. Upon reaching Germany, the flood waters in the Elbe inundated Dresden, causing damage to residential and commercial property as well as many historical buildings in the city center. The increase in river height in Dresden was more gradual and of greater magnitude than the flood peak in Prague. Although Prague itself was hardly hit by the flash flood, damage occurred in the historical and residential parts of the city center.

The greatest number of fatalities (58) was caused by floods resulting from the first wave on the eastern coast of the Black Sea. Seventeen people died in the Czech Republic, 21 in Dresden and more than 100 fatalities were reported across Europe. Direct and indirect impacts on the transportation and energy infrastructures were registered.

6.4   United Kingdom Floods (2007)

In June and July 2007, the United Kingdom was stricken by a series of severe floods arising from heavy rainfall during an unseasonably wet weather pattern [2]. The severe flooding events were attributed to two major causes: (i) position of the Polar Front Jet Stream; and (ii) high North Atlantic sea surface temperatures.

Heavy rainfall is not unusual in the United Kingdom during the summer months, but the frequency and spatial extent of the rainfall in June and July 2007 were unprecedented. Exceptional rainfall events occurred on June 25 and July 20, which caused widespread floods across England. The floods ranged from small, localized flash floods to widespread events affecting major river basins. First, northeastern England was badly affected by severe rainfall events in June, which caused floods in Sheffield, Doncaster, Rotherham, Louth and Kingston-upon-Hull. Some areas were hit again by further flooding after severe rain in July that affected a much larger area of central England, including Oxford, Gloucester, Tewkesbury, Evesham and Abingdon. The intense rainfall saturated the catchment areas, resulting in rivers flooding their banks in several major river basins. Disruptions to power and water supplies during the July floods were caused by flooding at the Castlemeads power substation near Gloucester and at the Mythe water treatment plant in Tewkesbury.

A total of thirteen people died as a result of the floods and approximately 48,000 homes were damaged. The scale and speed of the floods came as a shock. Although most people were aware of the impending heavy rain that was forecasted, they did not anticipate the magnitude of the rainfall. Indeed, most people involved in the incident had never experienced such flooding and did not know how to react. At the peak of the flooding, around 350,000 homes across Gloucestershire were left without water and 50,000 homes without power.

7.   CRISADMIN Prototype

The CRISADMIN Project seeks to demonstrate, by means of a prototype, that a flexible system dynamics modeling engine can assist first responders and decision makers in managing critical events. During actual events, knowledge of the past, coupled with the current aspects of a given context, form the basis for selecting modeling parameters and defining influences.

The CRISADMIN decision support system takes into account experience gained through participation in projects associated with the design of modeling methods and tools for monitoring and contrasting emergencies [1]. The decision support system incorporates a three-tiered architecture: (i) a back-end that stores variables and parameters associated with the four domains; (ii) a core that houses the system dynamics modeling engine; and (iii) a front-end that maintains the parameters, activates the functions and presents results.

The simulation model will be made available to institutions and organizations across the European Union – public entities (e.g., civil protection and fire brigades) as well as private entities (e.g., infrastructure asset owners and operators). Crisis management is typically performed in interconnected operations control rooms (OCRs) that continuously monitor critical events. The CRISADMIN decision support system is designed for use by analysts in OCRs as they coordinate activities during critical events. The decision support tool will be used to support operational decisions that benefit from the continuous monitoring capabilities provided by OCRs. The tool will provide decision makers with a starting point that is both expandable and customizable. The tool environment will also engage several fixed and non-customizable scenarios and situations that encompass different crisis situations. This feature will enable decision makers to understand the dynamics of interacting critical infrastructure assets. The prototype will also provide decision makers with points of reference as they select appropriate policy alternatives for crisis management.

8.   Conclusions

Decision makers responsible for infrastructure protection and crisis management must understand the consequences of policy and investment options before they enact solutions. This notion is particularly important due to the highly complex alternatives that must be considered when protecting critical infrastructures in the current threat environment. An effective way to examine and pursue trade-offs involving risk reduction and protection investments is to utilize a decision support system that incorporates information about threats and the consequences of disruptions. System dynamics modeling, simulation and analysis can be used to conduct impact assessments and risk analyses based on realistic scenarios.

The system dynamics approach developed under the CRISADMIN Project provides decision makers with a methodology for understanding and evaluating potential risks. The approach can be readily applied in contexts where standard analysis is made difficult by the wide range of available data and/or relationships. The approach is especially suited to systems that are greatly influenced by the "soft" variables associated with human behavior.

The CRISADMIN effort has identified the main parameters associated with the dependencies that impact the evolution of critical events. The result is a simple, yet effective, representation of how an event influences the behavior of a larger interconnected system. As new threats from terrorism and environmental factors emerge, a tool that enables decision makers to anticipate the impacts of critical events would provide them with precious insights for crafting protection strategies and implementing response actions.

Acknowledgements

This research, conducted by personnel from the Department of Computer, Control and Management Engineering of La Sapienza University, FORMIT Foundation, Erasmus University Rotterdam, Theorematica and Euro Works Consulting, was performed under the CRISADMIN Project. The CRISADMIN Project is supported by the Prevention, Preparedness and Consequence Management of Terrorism and Other Security-Related Risks Program launched by the Directorate-General of Home Affairs of the European Commission.

References

[1] P. Assogna, G. Bertocchi, A. Di Carlo, F. Milicchio, A. Paoluzzi, G. Scorzelli, M. Vicentino and R. Zollo, Critical infrastructures as complex systems: A multi-level protection architecture, *Proceedings of the Third International Workshop on Critical Information Infrastructure Security*, pp. 368–375, 2008.

[2] BBC News, The summer floods: What happened (`news.bbc.co.uk/2/hi/uk_news/7446721.stm`), June 25, 2008.

[3] L. Bourque, K. Shoaf and L. Nguyen, Survey research, *International Journal of Mass Emergencies and Disasters*, vol. 15(1), pp. 71–101, 1997.

[4] W. Enders and T. Sandler, *The Political Economy of Terrorism*, Cambridge University Press, Cambridge, United Kingdom, 2012.

[5] European Commission, Identification and Designation of European Critical Infrastructures and the Assessment of the Need to Improve Their Protection, Council Directive 2008/114/EC, Brussels, Belgium, December 8, 2008.

[6] S. Friedman, Learning to make more effective decisions: Changing beliefs as a prelude to action, *The Learning Organization*, vol. 11(2), pp. 110–128, 2004.

[7] London Assembly, 7 July Review Committee, Volume 4: Follow-Up Report, London, United Kingdom (`legacy.london.gov.uk/assembly/reports/7july/follow-up-report.pdf`), 2007.

[8] E. Nash, Madrid bombers "were inspired by Bin Laden address," *The Independent* (`www.independent.co.uk/news/world/europe/madrid-bombers-were-inspired-by-bin-laden-address-423266.html`), November 7, 2006.

[9] W. Orlikowski and S. Scott, Sociomateriality: Challenging the separation of technology, work and organization, *The Academy of Management Annals*, vol. 2(1), pp. 433–474, 2008.

[10] E. Owen, Bomb squad link in Spanish blasts, *The Times Online* (`www.timesonline.co.uk/tol/news/world/article447363.ece`), June 19, 2004.

[11] J. Sterman, *Business Dynamics: Systems Thinking and Modeling for a Complex World*, McGraw-Hill/Irwin, Columbus, Ohio, 2000.

[12] R. Thurlby and K. Warren, Understanding and managing the threat of disruptive events to the critical national infrastructure, *Proceedings of the Asset Management Conference*, pp. 1–10, 2012.

[13] U. Ulbrich, T. Brucher, A. Fink, G. Leckebusch, A. Kruger and J. Pinto, The Central European floods of August 2002: Part 1 – Rainfall periods and flood development, *Weather*, vol. 58(10), pp. 371–377, 2003.

Chapter 11

REINFORCEMENT LEARNING USING MONTE CARLO POLICY ESTIMATION FOR DISASTER MITIGATION

Mohammed Talat Khouj, Sarbjit Sarkaria, Cesar Lopez, and Jose Marti

Abstract   Urban communities rely heavily on the system of interconnected critical infrastructures. The interdependencies in these complex systems give rise to vulnerabilities that must be considered in disaster mitigation planning. Only then will it be possible to address and mitigate major critical infrastructure disruptions in a timely manner.

This paper describes an intelligent decision making system that optimizes the allocation of resources following an infrastructure disruption. The novelty of the approach arises from the application of Monte Carlo estimation for policy evaluation in reinforcement learning to draw on experiential knowledge gained from a massive number of simulations. This method enables a learning agent to explore and exploit the available trajectories, which lead to an optimum goal in a reasonable amount of time. The specific goal of the case study described in this paper is to maximize the number of patients discharged from two hospitals in the aftermath of an infrastructure disruption by intelligently utilizing the available resources. The results demonstrate that a learning agent, through interactions with an environment of simulated catastrophic scenarios, is capable of making informed decisions in a timely manner.

Keywords: Disaster response, Monte Carlo estimation, decision assistance agent

1.   Introduction

All of modern society, but in particular urban communities, rely heavily on the system of interconnected critical infrastructures. These systems are inherently complex in terms of interconnections and interdependencies. Thus, they are vulnerable to major disruptions that could cascade to other dependent systems with possible disastrous consequences. For example, the Indian Blackout of 2012 – the largest power blackout in history – caused massive disruptions

J. Butts and S. Shenoi (Eds.): Critical Infrastructure Protection VIII, IFIP AICT 441, pp. 155–172, 2014.

to medical facilities, transportation systems, water treatment plants and other interconnected infrastructures. It resulted in the loss of power to 600 million people, trapping miners, stranding railway passengers and plunging hospitals into darkness [6]. Such catastrophic incidents reveal the need for efficient planning and, more importantly, the need for careful decisions to be taken during the first few hours following an incident. The decisions are critical to successful mitigation, damage management, death prevention, injury, structural loss, control of financial costs and, ultimately, the overall resolution of the crisis [9].

This paper describes an intelligent decision making system that optimizes the allocation of resources following an infrastructure disruption and suggests how the resources may be utilized during disaster response. An underlying intelligent learning agent interacts continuously with a simulated environment and uses reinforcement learning (RL) to discover a policy that optimizes a long-term reward. The learning system employs Monte Carlo (MC) estimation for policy evaluation in reinforcement learning to gain experiential knowledge over a massive number of simulations using the interdependent critical infrastructure simulator (i2Sim). The approach enables the learning agent to explore and exploit the possible trajectories that lead to an optimum goal in a reasonable period of time.

2.   Related Work

This section describes related work in the areas of disaster mitigation in interdependent critical infrastructures, agent-based modeling for disaster mitigation and disaster mitigation applications using reinforcement learning.

2.1   Disaster Mitigation

Critical infrastructures are characterized by complex interconnections and interdependencies. These systems are vulnerable to major disturbances that can cascade to other dependent systems, potentially leading to national disasters (Figure 1). Interdependencies between infrastructures are bi-directional relationships through which the state of one infrastructure is influenced by or correlated with the states of other infrastructures [15]. Thus, it is essential to address the resource allocation problem in the context of interdependent critical infrastructures for better mitigation planning.

The optimization of resource allocation in interconnected critical infrastructures is a topic that has been addressed extensively. For instance, Min, *et al.* [13] have presented an integrated system to model the physical and financial impacts attributed to critical infrastructure interdependencies. Their framework comprises a system dynamics model, functional model and a non-linear optimization model. The purpose of the system dynamics model is to analyze the interdependencies between individual infrastructure components. The functional model is used to define the data requirements and the information exchanged between the models. The non-linear model enables the determination of optimal values of the control variables. The purpose of the work is to enable officials to respond to potential disruptions in a timely and effective manner.

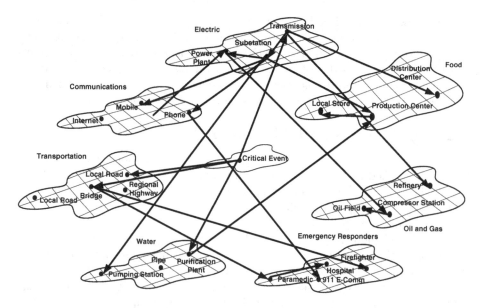

Figure 1. Interconnected critical infrastructures.

O'Reilly, *et al.* [14] have specified a system dynamics model that describes the interactions between interconnected critical infrastructures. They use the model to analyze the impact of a telecommunications infrastructure failure on emergency services. The important conclusion is that lost communications negatively impacts medical services and drastically increases treatment costs.

Similarly, Arboleda, *et al.* [2] have addressed the impact of failures of interdependent infrastructure components on the operation of healthcare facilities. The goal was to determine the unsatisfied demand of interconnected infrastructure systems and the resulting costs using a network flow model. Linear programming was used to assess the level of interdependency between a healthcare facility and the primary infrastructure systems linked to it.

In other work, Arboleda and colleagues [1] examined the internal operating capabilities of healthcare facilities in terms of the interactions between different service areas (emergency room, intensive care unit, operation room and wards). This was performed using a system dynamics simulation model. The goal was to assess the vulnerabilities of a healthcare facility during a disaster. The approach enabled the identification of policies to best mitigate the effects of a disruption.

Arboleda, *et al.* [3] have also integrated a network flow model and system dynamics model. This was done to simulate the impact of infrastructure system disruptions on the provision of healthcare services.

These studies and others make it clear that wise decisions to reallocate and utilize the available resources are vital when dealing with interconnected critical infrastructures. Informed decisions can potentially mitigate death and devastation following natural or human-initiated catastrophes. The decisions must be made on the basis of sound knowledge and experience. In fact, the work described in this paper is motivated by the fact that decisions need to be carefully studied and pre-assessed before they are implemented. Moreover, they must be monitored and modified as the situation evolves. The next section discusses the application of agent-based models to address these issues.

2.2   Agent-Based Modeling

An agent-based model is a system of multiple autonomous decision making entities called agents. The agents are capable of sensing and interacting with each other within a modeled environment based on a set of predefined rules. The rules govern the behavior of the modeled agents and enable them to perform appropriate actions.

Agent-based modeling offers three key advantages in the context of real-world applications [5]. First, it can capture emergent behavior that results from the interaction of individual entities (agents). Second, it facilitates detailed system descriptions by modeling and simulating the behavior of interacting entities. Third, it provides great flexibility to tune the complexity of individual entities to scenarios of interest.

These advantages have encouraged the application of agent-based modeling approaches by the disaster response community, the objective being to enhance disaster mitigation efforts. Atanasiu and Leon [4] have developed a multi-agent system based risk assessment tool for seismic hazards. Their tool, which incorporates an adaptive knowledge base, is designed to help create a risk management plan for better earthquake safety and response. The approach simulates emergency response actions for a set of earthquake scenarios at different urban locations. The results, which are displayed using a geographic information system (GIS), helps improve the quality of decision making. The decisions are typically made post-event for restoration and recovery operations aimed at rehabilitating the damaged infrastructure.

Thapa, *et al.* [18] have proposed an agent-based model for patient information acquisition and real-time decision making during emergencies. The model seeks to promote timely diagnosis and treatment of high-risk patients during emergency situations. The approach engages reinforcement learning in conjunction with an embedded dynamic programming mechanism to evaluate and improve a system value function and its policy.

2.3   Reinforcement Learning

Applications of reinforcement learning in agent-based models have attracted the interest of the critical infrastructure research community. The machine learning technique enables an agent to gain experiential knowledge by interacting with a massive number of disaster scenarios. The trained agent is then able to assist in disaster mitigation.

Wiering and Dorigo [19] have developed an intelligent system that enables decision makers to mitigate the consequences of natural and human-initiated disasters (e.g., forest fires). Such disasters involve many interacting sub-processes that make it difficult for human experts to estimate costs. The system of Wiering and Dorigo uses reinforcement learning to learn the best policy or actions to be chosen in a variety of simulated disaster scenarios.

Su, *et al.* [16] have proposed a path selection algorithm for disaster response management. The algorithm is designed for search and rescue activities in dangerous and dynamic environments. The algorithm engages reinforcement learning to help disaster responders discover the fastest and shortest paths to targeted locations. To accomplish this, a learning agent interacts with a two-dimensional geographic grid model. After a number of trials, the agent learns how to avoid dangerous states and to navigate around inaccessible states.

3. Intelligent Decision Making

This section discusses how a reinforcement learning agent can be used for resource allocation in simulated interdependent critical infrastructures. The scenarios are modeled using i2Sim, a hybrid discrete-time simulator, which can handle vast numbers of interactions with the reinforcement learning agent. The simulated environment is based on an urban community similar to the Downtown Vancouver Model [8]. The model incorporates four electrical power substations (P1, P2, P3 and P4), a water pumping station (W) and infrastructure assets such as venues (V1 and V2) and hospitals (H1 and H2). The continued interactions enable the agent to learn, improve its performance and make optimal decisions.

3.1 i2Sim

i2Sim is a hybrid discrete-time simulator that combines agent-based modeling with input-output production models. The simulator can model and play out scenarios involving interdependent systems. i2Sim is designed as a real-time simulator that can also serve as a decision support tool while a disaster is actually occurring. The simulation capability of i2Sim enables decision makers to evaluate the predicted consequences of suggested actions before they are executed [10].

The dynamic aspects of an i2Sim model are implemented by the movement of tokens between i2Sim production cells (i.e., modeled infrastructures such as power stations) through designated channels (i.e., lifelines such as water pipes). In fact, i2Sim cells and channels correspond to discrete entities in the real world. Figure 2 presents an example i2Sim model.

In i2Sim, each production cell performs a function. A function relates the outputs to a number of possible operating states – physical modes (PM) and resource modes (RM) – of the system. At every operating point along an event timeline, the i2Sim description corresponds to a system of discrete time equations expressed as a transportation matrix (Figure 3). The transportation

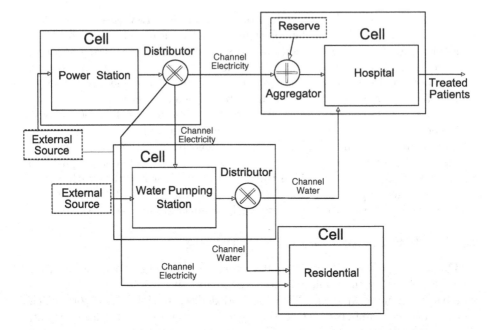

Figure 2.   Example i2Sim model [11].

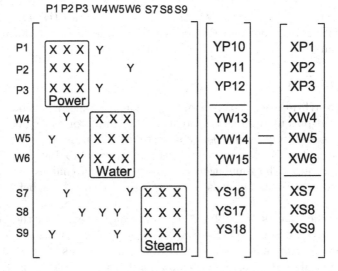

Figure 3.   Transportation matrix showing infrastructure interdependencies [11].

matrix shows the interdependencies between the simulated quantities. In particular, the matrix in Figure 3 relates input quantities (XP1, XP2, ..., XS8, XS9) that arrive at the cells with the quantities that are produced as outputs of other cells (YP10, YP11, ..., YS17, YS18). These outputs can be distributed (via distributors) or aggregated (via aggregators) before being supplied to other cells. For instance, a water pumping station depends on water and electricity that are supplied by other cells (water supply and electrical power station). In row W5 of the transportation matrix, XW5 (water arriving at cell 5) comprises water that outputs from cells YW13, YW14 and YW15 (through X coefficients (internal links)) and power that outputs from cell YP10 (through Y coefficients (interdependent links)). The pumped water is distributed to a number of interconnected critical infrastructures [11].

3.2   Reinforcement Learning

Reinforcement learning [17] is a machine learning technique based on interactions between an agent and its environment. These interactions enable a reinforcement learning agent to maximize a time-delayed goal in the presence of uncertainty. Reinforcement learning occurs through the accumulation of experience, with the goal of finding actions that yield the greatest long-term rewards.

The actions taken in a given situation are determined by a policy realized by an action-value function. In general, reinforcement learning provides three ways of learning the policy: (i) dynamic programming; (ii) Monte Carlo estimation; and (iii) temporal difference. Monte Carlo estimation and temporal difference are the favored methods because they are model free. We have chosen to employ Monte Carlo estimation because it is well suited to learning from episodic problems of the type encountered in the disaster mitigation domain. Experimental results involving similar work [8] reveal that convergence using step-by-step updates as prescribed by temporal difference learning take 2.6 times longer than episode-by-episode based updates as used in Monte Carlo estimation. The goal of the learning agent is to approximate the optimal action-value function leading to the best long-term reward that corresponds to the best trajectory. This recursive-learning algorithm uses incremental episode-by-episode back-ups to solve the well-known Bellman equation [17].

The back-up formula is defined by the following equations for terminal and non-terminal states, respectively:

$$Q(s,a) \quad \leftarrow \quad Q(s,a) + \alpha[R_I + \gamma R_T - Q(s,a)] \text{ (terminal)} \tag{1}$$
$$Q(s,a) \quad \leftarrow \quad Q(s,a) + \alpha[R_I + \gamma max_a Q(s',a') - Q(s,a)] \text{ (non-terminal)} \tag{2}$$

where $Q(s,a)$ is the action-value function of the current state-action pair; $Q(s',a')$ is the action-value function of the next state-action pair; α is the learning rate (i.e., extent to which the newly-required information overrides old information); R_I is the immediate reward; R_T is the terminal reward; and γ is the discount rate (i.e., influence that future rewards have on the learning process).

In Monte Carlo estimation, the back-up equation is used to recursively apply the terminal reward starting at the terminal state and back-stepping all the way

Table 1. Sample lookup table (s: state, a: action).

$(<s>, <a>)$	Q(s,a)
$(<PMXP4, RMYP4, PMXW, RMYW>, <DP4, DW>)$	–
–	–
–	–
–	–

to the start state. The estimate is computed by averaging the samples that are returned.

The action-value function can be implemented as a lookup table. The table associates a long-term predicted reward $Q(s, a)$ value with each state-action pair defined for the modeled system. The table represents the acquired experience of the reinforcement learning agent and is updated during the learning process.

Note that the simulated system presents the state of the modeled environment that is detected by the learning agent. In the example considered here, the state is defined using two critical infrastructures: Power Station 4 and the Water Pumping Station. The physical mode (PM) and the resource mode (RM) of Power Station 4 and the Water Pumping Station are specified as PMXP4 and RMYP4 for power, and PMXW and RMYW for water. The values of X and Y range from one to five. When X has a value of one, the modeled infrastructure has no physical damage; when X is equal to five, the modeled infrastructure has collapsed completely. Similarly, when Y has a value of one, all the required resources to maintain the minimum functionality of the modeled infrastructure are available; when Y is equal to five, the required resources are not available.

Table 1 presents a sample lookup table used by the learning agent. In the table, the state-action pairs are captured using the variables: PMXP4, the Power Station 4 physical mode (state); RMYP4, the Power Station 4 resource mode (state); PMXW, the Water Pumping Station physical mode (state); RMYW, the Water Pumping Station resource mode (state); DP4, the Power Station 4 distributor (action); and DW, the Water Pumping Station distributor (action).

3.3 RL-MC Based Learning

The primary contribution of this paper is the application of reinforcement learning with Monte Carlo estimation (RL-MC) to problems involving interconnected and interdependent critical infrastructures. In the RL-MC approach, the problem is formulated as follows: the operating mode (physical mode and resource mode) of each modeled infrastructure unit represents the state of the targeted system. The distribution ratio of the available resources (associated with every modeled critical infrastructure) represents the actions that the agent can perform at every visited state. Every state-action pair is represented by a utility function that estimates the probability of obtaining the long-term reward

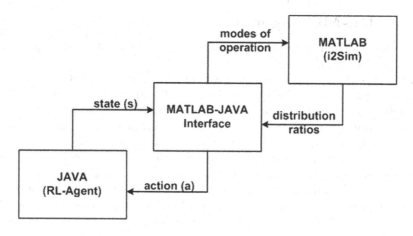

Figure 4. MATLAB-Java dependency diagram.

upon choosing action a in state s. The estimate is computed by averaging the sampled returns over the long term. (In the scenario considered in this paper, the return is the expected number of discharged patients from two hospitals, H1 and H2). Terminal (R_T) and immediate rewards (R_I) are applied in the RL-MC approach.

The learning system (RL-MC) is implemented as a Java program that communicates with the simulator (i2Sim), which is realized in MATLAB (Figure 4). Communications are established via a software interface designed to support data transfer between MATLAB and the Java program. The interface allows the states of the simulated system and actions from the learning agent to be exchanged [7]. From i2Sim, the agent recognizes the state of the simulated environment based on the physical operability (PM) and the resource availability (RM) of the modeled infrastructures. The state is identified by the operating conditions of two critical infrastructures, Power Station 4 and Water Pumping Station (PMXP4, RMYP4, PMXW, RMYW). Accordingly, the agent selects the best distribution ratios (actions) for the distributors associated with Power Station 4 and the Water Pumping Station (DP4 and DW). The chosen action uses the distribution of the monitored resources (power and water) that maximizes the total number of discharged patients from hospitals H1 and H2.

The choice of Monte Carlo estimation over the temporal difference and dynamic programming approaches is also motivated by the need to reduce intra-system communications in the architecture. In a reinforcement learning with temporal difference (RL-TD) approach, communications between the agent and i2Sim (Figure 4) introduce an overhead that is incurred at every time step [8]. In fact, a significant portion of the computational time is due to the MATLAB-Java communications interface alone. In the case of RL-MC, the communications overhead occurs only twice per episode, once at the beginning and once at the end. Consequently, the communication time is reduced by almost a factor of three, which is advantageous when modeling complex systems.

3.4   RL-MC Algorithm

This section provides a technical description of how the RL-MC approach is realized within i2Sim.

In the RL-MC approach, the learning agent interacts with the modeled environment episodically. The agent follows a policy defined by the state-action value function. The agent attempts to learn an optimal policy. This sampling process terminates at a terminal state. At the terminal state, the estimation of the terminal state-action value function $Q(s, a)$ is determined based on the total return that is observed at the end of each episode using Equation (1). This process averages the observed total returns of the visited states in the trajectory. For non-terminal states, the estimation of $Q(s, a)$ occurs by back-stepping Equation (2) to all state-action values in the sampled trajectory for each episode. In the limit, the learning agent successfully discovers the optimum trajectory.

The learning system implements the tabular form of the Q-learning algorithm using RL-MC. The lookup table is used to determine the action that is to be performed at the next state of the modeled environment. At any given state s, the learning agent performs an action a that delivers an adequate amount of resources (power and water) to the interconnected infrastructures. Note that 110 actions ($N_a = 110$) and 225 states ($N_s = 225$) are considered in modeled system. Each action a comprises instructions that specify the ratios of the five outputs of the P4 distributor (DP4) and the two outputs of the water distributor (DW). DP4 distributes power from Power Station 4 to five interconnected critical infrastructures: Hospital 1 (H1), Water Pumping Station (W), Venue 1 (V1), Power Station 2 (P2) and other interconnected infrastructures (Oth.). DW distributes the pumped water to the two modeled hospitals, H1 and H2.

The action vector a expresses the distribution ratios of the two distributors:

$$a = \begin{pmatrix} DP4 \to H1 \\ DP4 \to W \\ DP4 \to V1 \\ DP4 \to P2 \\ DP4 \to Oth. \\ DW \to H1 \\ DW \to H2 \end{pmatrix} \tag{3}$$

Given an initially-untrained lookup table, the RL-MC algorithm seeks to find the optimal action to perform in each state (optimum trajectory). If it is available, real-world experience could be used to initialize the lookup table as a starting estimate of the optimum schedule.

The environment state s is a vector that represents the operating conditions of the two modeled production cells (Power Station 4 and Water Pumping Station). The Power Station 4 and Water Pumping Station states are given by

PMXP4 and RMYP4 for power and PMXW and RMYW for water, respectively. This can be represented at any given time by:

$$
s = \begin{pmatrix}
PM1P4 & RM1P4 & PM1W & RM1W \\
PM1P4 & RM1P4 & PM1W & RM2W \\
\vdots & \vdots & \vdots & \vdots \\
PM1P4 & RM5P4 & PM5W & RM5W \\
PM2P4 & RM2P4 & PM1W & RM1W \\
PM2P4 & RM2P4 & PM1W & RM2W \\
\vdots & \vdots & \vdots & \vdots \\
PM2P4 & RM5P4 & PM5W & RM5W \\
\vdots & \vdots & \vdots & \vdots \\
PM3P4 & RM5P4 & PM5W & RM5W \\
\vdots & \vdots & \vdots & \vdots \\
PM4P4 & RM5P4 & PM5W & RM5W \\
\vdots & \vdots & \vdots & \vdots \\
PM5P4 & RM5P4 & PM5W & RM5W
\end{pmatrix}
\tag{4}
$$

The first row in the equation above corresponds to state s_1 = (PM1P4, RM1P4, PM1W, RM1W), where PM1P4 is the Physical Mode 1 of Power Station 4, RM1P4 is the Resource Mode 1 of Power Station 4, PM1W is the Physical Mode 1 of the Water Pumping Station and RM1W is the Resource Mode 1 of the Water Pumping Station.

The number of states N_s in the model (total number of rows in vector s) is given by:

$$
N_s = Z^K = 15^2 = 225 \text{ states}
\tag{5}
$$

where Z is the number of resource modes available for each controlled production cell; and K is the number of controlled production cells.

The number of available actions N_a is given by:

$$
N_a = DP4 \times DW = 10 \times 11 = 110 \text{ actions}
\tag{6}
$$

where $DP4$ is the distributor associated with Power Substation 4; and DW is the distributor associated with the Water Pumping Station.

The size of the lookup table L_S is given by:

$$
L_S = N_s \times N_a = 225 \times 110 = 24,750 \text{ rows.}
\tag{7}
$$

The states and actions, as described above, suggest a theoretical maximum lookup table size of 24,750 elements.

As the simulation progresses, the history of actions and immediate rewards of each visited state (according to the policy) are accumulated. The immediate reward R_I is applied at every time step by computing the difference in the discharged patients between the current and previous states:

$$R_I = (N_{H1} + N_{H2})_{current} - (N_{H1} + N_{H2})_{previous} \qquad (8)$$

where N_{H1} is the number of discharged patients from Hospital 1; and N_{H2} is the number of discharged patients from Hospital 2. Note that the intermediate reward is a function of the number of patients discharged.

The terminal reward R_T is calculated and applied at the final time step only (terminal state) based on the total number of discharged patients from both hospitals:

$$R_T = N_{H1} + N_{H2}. \qquad (9)$$

Each state-action value $Q(s, a)$ is updated according to Equation (1) for a terminal state or according to Equation (2) for a non-terminal state.

At the end of the episode, according to the RL-MC algorithm, this information and the terminal reward R_T are back-stepped through the sequence of state-action values performed during the episode.

4.   Example Scenario

This section uses an example scenario to demonstrate the application of the learning agent to an urban community model simulated by i2Sim (Figure 5). The goal of the agent is to find the optimum trajectory that leads to the maximum outcome. The expectation is that this approach will converge quickly to the maximum number of discharged patients.

4.1   Environment Description

The simulated urban community model consists of nine interdependent critical infrastructure cells. The modeled cells are connected to each other through channels (e.g., underground cables, water pipes and roads). The resources generated by different cells are aggregated or distributed to other interconnected cells by control elements called aggregators and distributors such as power aggregators and water distributors. A pre-defined scenario defines the capacity and the operating parameters (input variables) of the modeled entities. The information is obtained from public domain data or directly from facility managers.

Four power cells are incorporated in the electricity infrastructure: Power Station 1, Power Station 2, Power Station 3 and Power Station 4. The cells determine the amount of power distributed to the system that comes in from the high-voltage supply system. The stations are geographically separated. Each power substation supplies a specific amount of power to its interconnected critical infrastructures. For example, Power Station 4 supplies 586 MW to its connected infrastructures (Hospital 1 and Water Pumping Station).

Similarly, the Water Pumping Station provides water to the connected hospitals (Hospital 1 and Hospital 2). The Water Pumping Station obtains power

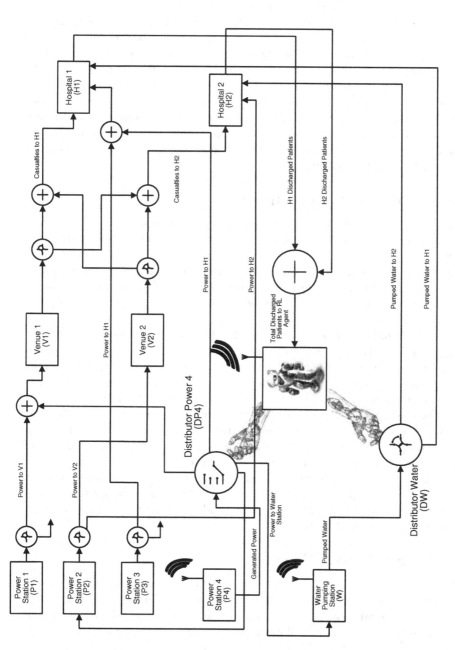

Figure 5. Schematic diagram of i2Sim and RL-MC.

from Power Station 4 and water from an external source. The output of the cell is high pressure pumped water that goes to a water distributor, which distributes the water via water channels (water pipes).

Venue 1 and Venue 2 are facilities that contain large numbers of people. Venue 2 is more than $65,000\,\text{m}^2$ in area and hosts up to 60,000 people. Venue 1 is slightly smaller at about $44,000\,\text{m}^2$ and hosts up to 20,000 people. It is assumed that both venues are hosting events and are fully occupied. Thus, the total population is 80,000.

Two hospitals are modeled, Hospital 1 (main hospital) and Hospital 2 (alternative hospital). The input resources come from the four electrical power stations (electricity) and the water pumping station (water). Based on the availability of these resources, the rate of discharged patients for each hospital is known from historical data.

4.2   Scenario Description

The scenario was configured to reflect the damage caused by an earthquake. The simulated earthquake damaged Power Station 4. The physical structure of the power substation was not affected, but the resource availability RM was reduced due to a failure in one of the electrical feeders, RM2P4. Subsequently, as a result of the reduced electrical power, the water facility was not able to operate at full capacity and the power delivered to the venues and hospitals was also affected.

The earthquake produced casualties due to panic and chaos as people attempted to leave the venues. It was assumed that medical triage at the venues takes an average of 30 minutes per injured person. Upon completion of the assessment, emergency vehicles carried injured people to the emergency units at the hospitals for treatment. The travel time was assumed to be ten minutes.

At the emergency units, all the arriving patients were served on a first-come-first-serve basis. Thirty minutes was assumed to be required to stabilize each trauma patient. The ability of the hospital to function at full capacity was, of course, impacted due to the limited supply of power and water.

The goal of the learning agent was to experience this scenario and to suggest a way to mitigate the impact on the hospitals. This was accomplished by adjusting the distribution ratios of the power and water distributors intelligently, as discussed in the next section.

4.3   Simulation Results

The simulations involved 100 scenarios per test, where each scenario represented a ten-hour period following the disaster event. Upon starting a scenario, the physical operability that represents the damage to the cells and channels was set to model a disaster. Following this, no further changes were made with regard to the extent of the damage. However, the available resources of the associated infrastructures change as the scenario evolves. The lookup table was

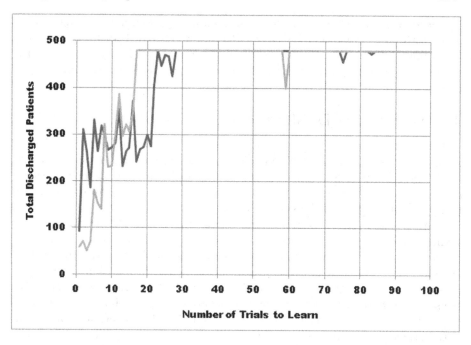

Figure 6. Agent learning behavior under RL-MC.

initialized randomly at the start of the first scenario and learning continued from one scenario to the next.

The model simulated a period of ten hours in five-minute increments. The statistics and system latencies used by the simulator were taken from an internal technical report [7]. The report helped guide the rates used in the simulation. For example, a crowd of 80,000 is expected to have up to 480 injuries.

Figure 6 shows the results for two consecutive sets of trials that were initialized independently (light and dark lines). In both cases, the convergence to an optimum solution occurred and all 480 patients were discharged from both emergency units during the lifetime of the simulation.

During the early phases of learning in both trials, the agent had little or no experience and was unable to maximize the number of discharged patients. However, this was not the case in the later runs, where the agent showed an ability to fully satisfy the demands of the modeled interconnected critical infrastructures by carefully balancing resources across all the infrastructure components.

In contrast, a naive decision maker might select a resource configuration that would only favor the hospitals, but this would be a sub-optimal solution. Instead, the actions taken by the trained agent were those that intelligently utilized the available limited resources (power and water) without exhausting them, which ultimately satisfied the sudden needs of all the interconnected critical infrastructures, including the venues and, most importantly, the hospitals.

The simulation of each scenario required about three minutes using a computer with an Intel Core i5 2.8 GHz CPU and 8 GB RAM. In total, 100 runs took about 600 minutes. This is important in real-world deployments because simulations should be faster than real time in order to assist emergency responders in making informed decisions as a situation unfolds.

4.4   System Deployment

We envisage that the intelligent agent would be deployed as part of a larger software system aimed at providing decision assistance during actual emergencies. The software system would incorporate an i2Sim simulator, a learning agent, a library of pre-configured scenarios and an interface through which a user would interact with the system.

The suggested usage flow would first require the user to identify the disaster taking place in terms of the affected infrastructures. The system would provide a list of scenarios from which the user would pick the best match (instead of defining and entering a new scenario from scratch). In addition to the pre-configured scenario, the system would make available a pre-trained agent for the scenario. Should the scenario match be satisfactory, the human emergency responder can look to the agent for suggested actions in the situation at hand. If the scenario does not match the actual disaster, the user would have to manually adjust the scenario to accurately reflect the real-world situation. The pre-trained agent for the closest-matching scenario could still be used as a starting point.

Using a pre-trained agent is the best option for reducing agent learning time; learning by a trained agent is much faster than when an agent starts with a blank slate. A second approach relies on human knowledge acquisition. Important components of the knowledge and experience of trained emergency responders would have to be identified and captured. The output of this activity would be used to initialize the agent to reduce its learning time.

5.   Conclusions

The modeling and analysis framework presented in this paper is an innovative approach for studying the impact of natural or human-initiated disasters on critical infrastructures and optimally allocating the available resources during disaster response. The framework relies on i2Sim and reinforcement learning using Monte Carlo policy estimation (RL-MC). i2Sim permits the simulation of complex interconnected critical infrastructures while the RL-MC approach supports rapid learning based on experiential knowledge in order to provide intelligent advice on allocating limited resources. The experimental results reveal that decision makers can reduce the impact of disruptions by employing the look-ahead and optimization features provided by the framework. The loosely coupled nature of reinforcement learning also enables it to be applied to a variety of resource optimization scenarios.

Our future research will analyze the computational aspects of the learning system. A speed versus accuracy trade-off exists between approaches that use the conventional lookup table implementation of an action-value function and other approaches that use function approximation techniques.

Acknowledgement

This research was partially supported by the Ministry of Higher Education of the Kingdom of Saudi Arabia.

References

[1] C. Arboleda, D. Abraham and R. Lubitz, Simulation as a tool to assess the vulnerability of the operation of a health care facility, *Journal of Performance of Constructed Facilities*, vol. 21(4), pp. 302–312, 2007.

[2] C. Arboleda, D. Abraham, J. Richard and R. Lubitz, Impact of interdependencies between infrastructure systems in the operation of health care facilities during disaster events, *Proceedings of the Twenty-Third Joint International Conference on Computing and Decision Making in Civil and Building Engineering*, pp. 3020–3029, 2006.

[3] C. Arboleda, D. Abraham, J. Richard and R. Lubitz, Vulnerability assessment of health care facilities during disaster events, *Journal of Infrastructure Systems*, vol. 15(3), pp. 149–161, 2009.

[4] G. Atanasiu and F. Leon, Agent-based risk assessment and mitigation for urban public infrastructure, *Proceedings of the Sixth Congress on Forensic Engineering*, pp. 418–427, 2013.

[5] E. Bonabeau, Agent-based modeling: Methods and techniques for simulating human systems, *Proceedings of the National Academy of Sciences*, vol. 99(3), pp. 7280–7287, 2002.

[6] F. Daniel, India power cut hits millions, among world's worst outages, *Reuters*, July 31, 2012.

[7] M. Khouj and J. Marti, Modeling Critical Infrastructure Interdependencies in Support of the Security Operations for the Vancouver 2010 Olympics, Technical Report, Department of Electrical and Computer Engineering, University of British Columbia, Vancouver, Canada, 2010.

[8] M. Khouj, S. Sarkaria and J. Marti, Decision assistance agent in real-time simulation, *International Journal of Critical Infrastructures*, vol. 10(2), pp. 151–173, 2014.

[9] K. Kowalski-Trakofler, C. Vaught and T. Scharf, Judgment and decision making under stress: An overview for emergency managers, *International Journal of Emergency Management*, vol. 1(3), pp. 278–289, 2003.

[10] J. Marti, J. Hollman, C. Ventura and J. Jatskevich, Dynamic recovery of critical infrastructures: Real-time temporal coordination, *International Journal of Critical Infrastructures*, vol. 4(1/2), pp. 17–31, 2008.

[11] J. Marti, C. Ventura, J. Hollman, K. Srivastava and H. Juarez-Garcia, i2Sim modeling and simulation framework for scenario development, training and real-time decision support of multiple interdependent critical infrastructures during large emergencies, presented at the *NATO RTO Symposium on How is Modeling and Simulation Meeting the Defense Challenges out to 2015*, 2008.

[12] J. Marti, E. Yanful and M. Ulieru, Disaster Response Network Enabled Platform, CANARIE Project Final Report, Department of Electrical and Computer Engineering, University of British Columbia, Vancouver, Canada, 2012.

[13] H. Min, W. Beyeler, T. Brown, Y. Son and A. Jones, Toward modeling and simulation of critical infrastructure interdependencies, *IIE Transactions*, vol. 39(1), pp. 57–71, 2007.

[14] G. O'Reilly, H. Uzunalioglu, S. Conrard and W. Beyeler, Inter-infrastructure simulations across telecom, power and emergency services, *Proceedings of the Fifth International Workshop on the Design of Reliable Communication Networks*, 2005.

[15] S. Rinaldi, Modeling and simulating critical infrastructure and their interdependencies, *Proceedings of the Thirty-Seventh Annual Hawaii International Conference on System Sciences*, 2004.

[16] Z. Su, J. Jiang, C. Liang and G. Zhang, Path selection in disaster response management based on Q-learning, *International Journal of Automation and Computing*, vol. 8(1), pp. 100–106, 2011.

[17] R. Sutton and A. Barto, *Reinforcement Learning: An Introduction*, Bradford/MIT Press, Cambridge, Massachusetts, 1998.

[18] D. Thapa, I. Jung and G. Wang, Agent based decision support system using reinforcement learning under emergency circumstances, *Proceedings of the First International Conference on Natural Computation*, pp. 888–892, 2005.

[19] M. Wiering and M. Dorigo, Learning to control forest fires, *Proceedings of the Twelfth International Symposium on Computer Science for Environmental Protection*, pp. 378–388, 1998.

Chapter 12

ACCURACY OF SERVICE AREA ESTIMATION METHODS USED FOR CRITICAL INFRASTRUCTURE RECOVERY

Okan Pala, David Wilson, Russell Bent, Steve Linger, and James Arnold

Abstract   Electric power, water, natural gas and other utilities are served to consumers via functional sources such as electric power substations, pumps and pipes. Understanding the impact of service outages is vital to decision making in response and recovery efforts. Often, data pertaining to the source-sink relationships between service points and consumers is sensitive or proprietary, and is, therefore, unavailable to external entities. As a result, during emergencies, decision makers often rely on estimates of service areas produced by various methods. This paper, which focuses on electric power, assesses the accuracy of four methods for estimating power substation service areas, namely the standard and weighted versions of Thiessen polygon and cellular automata approaches. Substation locations and their power outputs are used as inputs to the service area calculation methods. Reference data is used to evaluate the accuracy in approximating a power distribution network in a mid-sized U.S. city. Service area estimation methods are surveyed and their performance is evaluated empirically. The results indicate that the performance of the approaches depends on the type of analysis employed. When the desired analysis includes aggregate economic or population predictions, the weighted version of the cellular automata approach has the best performance. However, when the desired analysis involves facility-specific predictions, the weighted Thiessen polygon approach tends to perform the best.

Keywords: Service area estimates, recovery, Thiessen polygons, cellular automata

J. Butts and S. Shenoi (Eds.): Critical Infrastructure Protection VIII, IFIP AICT 441, pp. 173–191, 2014.

1.   Introduction

Electric power, water, natural gas, telecommunications and other utilities are served to consumers using functional sources (facilities) such as power substations, pumps and pipes, switch controls and cell towers. Each of these sources is related to a geographical service area that includes consumers. Data pertaining to the source-sink relationships between service points and consumers is often sensitive or proprietary and is, therefore, unavailable to external entities. During emergencies, decision makers who do not have access to utility information must rely on estimates of service areas derived by various methods. Decision makers have a strong interest in quantifying the accuracy of critical infrastructure service area estimation methods and developing enhanced estimation techniques [14, 22, 25].

This paper assesses the accuracy of four methods that are commonly used to estimate infrastructure impact after a disruptive event. The term "impact" refers to the inability of a utility to provide a service, such as power or gas, due to infrastructure damage. The paper focuses on two types of impacts: (i) aggregate impacts, such as economic activity and the population affected by the outage; and (ii) point data impacts, such as whether specific assets are included in an outage. The methods include Voronoi (Thiessen) polygons, Voronoi (Thiessen) polygons with weights, cellular automata and cellular automata with weights. The methods are compared using a reference model of a power distribution network for a mid-sized U.S. city.

2.   Background

Power, gas, water and other infrastructures serve customers in geographical regions called service areas. Although infrastructure operators have detailed information about the source-sink relationships between their assets, this information is neither organized to facilitate large-scale analyses nor is it documented by public regulatory agencies. In addition, the data is often highly sensitive or proprietary.

Determining service areas in the absence of data has long been a problem, but estimating the service areas accurately is very important in disaster recovery situations [7, 14, 22, 25]. Typically, the geographic boundary of a service point is required to estimate the source-sink relationships between serving entities (sources) and served entities (sinks). Increasing the accuracy of the estimates could lead to more efficient recovery. Moreover, understanding the comparative merits of different estimation approaches is necessary to enable decision makers to select the right mitigation and remediation strategies in disaster situations. This paper focuses on Voronoi diagram (Thiessen polygon) and cellular automata estimation approaches.

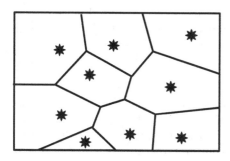 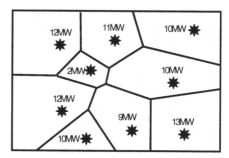

Figure 1. (a) Thiessen polygons; (b) Thiessen polygons with weights.

2.1   Voronoi Diagrams (Thiessen Polygons)

Voronoi diagrams are named after the Russian mathematician Georgy Voronoi, who defined them in 1908. Voronoi diagrams are also called Thiessen polygons after Alfred Thiessen, who in 1911, used the approach to estimate the average rainfall of a region from a set of values recorded at individual stations. Three aspects of Voronoi diagrams (Thiessen polygons) have been investigated over the years: (i) modeling natural phenomena; (ii) investigating geometrical, combinatorial and stochastic properties; and (iii) developing computer-based representations [2].

Thiessen polygons have been used in a variety of ways to present and analyze data. The success of the method comes from its ability to uniformly and systematically partition a geographical region. Given points in a Euclidean plane, a Thiessen diagram divides the plane according to a nearest-neighbor rule, where each point is associated with the region of the plane closest to it [2]. To create the boundaries, straight lines are drawn between all the points; from the mid-point of each line, a perpendicular line is drawn at equal Euclidean distances to each joining point. The Thiessen polygons take shape when the perpendicular lines are trimmed at their intersections with other lines (Figure 1(a)). Interested readers are referred to [23] for additional details about Thiessen polygons and to [1, 16, 22, 24] for details about using the approach to generate critical infrastructure service boundaries.

One drawback of the Thiessen polygon approach is that it assumes that each point is homogenous (as shown in Figure 1(a)). This is generally not the case because each source point provides varying degrees of service. For example, electric power substations have different load outputs and natural gas transportation systems have different pressures and output capacities.

Using weights based on source points can enhance Voronoi-based methods such as the Thiessen polygon approach. A weighted approach creates Thiessen polygons by computing the weighted Euclidean distances [13, 15]. The approach assigns smaller service areas to critical infrastructure elements with lower out-

puts. This approach is potentially more realistic than an approach that uses
Thiessen polygons with equal weights. For example, as shown in Figure 1(b), a
2 MW electric power substation serves a smaller area than neighboring power
substations with larger power outputs.

2.2   Cellular Automata

Cellular automata are discrete computational systems that comprise finite
or denumerable sets of homogeneous, simple cells as part of spatially and tem-
porally discrete grid structures [4]. They are often used to create mathematical
models of complex natural systems that contain large numbers of simple and
identical components with local interactions [38].

A cellular automata is formally defined as a system composed of adjacent
cells or sites (usually organized as a regular lattice) that evolves in discrete
time steps. Each cell represents an internal state from a finite set of states.
The states in the automata are updated in parallel according to a local rule
that considers the neighborhood of each cell [9].

The cellular automata approach originated with digital computing in the
late 1940s [34–36]. However, it was first used in geographical science in the
1970s [3, 26]. The interest in geographical information technologies in the 1990s
led to numerous geographical applications [12, 17, 28, 30–32]. In retrospect,
the adoption of cellular automata by the geographical science community was
natural because both fields intrinsically rely on proximity, adjacency, distance,
spatial configuration, spatial composition and diffusion. Cellular automata also
share mathematical and algorithmic structures with remote sensing, relational
databases and object-oriented programming [29].

Although cellular automata have been applied to a variety of fields, cellular
automata techniques were not used for service area calculations until the last
decade [14, 18]. Like Thiessen polygon approaches, cellular automata algorithms can be run with equal weights or weights based on the actual substation
loads. Tools that use cellular automata approaches to estimate service and
outage areas include the Interdependency Environment for Infrastructure Simulation Systems (IEISS) [6], TranSims [6, 14, 28] and Water Infrastructure
Simulation Environment [19, 33].

3.   Assessment Methodology

Four algorithms are used to estimate service areas for electric power: (i)
Thiessen polygons; (ii) Thiessen polygons with weights based on the electric
power substation loads; (iii) cellular automata; and (iv) cellular automata with
weights based on the electric power substation loads.

An electric power network in a mid-sized U.S. city comprising roughly 150
substations is used in the evaluation. The reference dataset includes the transmission network, substations, power demand and substation service areas. The
reference substation service areas, which are polygonal in shape, were drawn
up by an electric power system expert. Economic and population information

derived from the 2010 LandScan dataset [5] is incorporated, along with the daytime/nighttime population information from [8, 20].

The ESRI suite of GIS tools was used to implement the Thiessen polygon approach. The weighted Thiessen polygons were created using the publicly-available ArcGIS extension [13]. IEISS [6] was used to create the cellular automata and weighted cellular automata polygons; this algorithm grows cells in a raster format starting from each source point (i.e., electric power substation) until it runs out of space or electric power resources.

3.1   Aggregated Impacts

Aggregated impacts are used in situations where coarse information about service areas is required. Examples include total population, total economic activity and total area. In these situations, an error in the spatial extent of a service area is acceptable as long as the extent of the area produces the correct values. To perform the comparisons, the daytime population of each polygon associated with a substation is computed using each of the four methods. The results obtained for each method are compared with the actual population associated with the substation in the reference model. In the comparisons, the method with the lowest error is considered to exhibit better performance.

The process is repeated for the nighttime population, economic activity indicators and total area. The economic activity indicators include direct, indirect and induced economic impacts, as well as the economic impact on business and employment. Similarly, the approach that yields the lowest error with respect to the reference dataset is considered to have the best performance. Direct economic impact is based on the types of businesses in a service area. Indirect economic impact is based on the suppliers of commodities in a service area. Induced economic impact is based on the reduction in factor income in a service area. The economic impact on business and employment considers the overall effect on known businesses and employment [21].

3.2   Point Data Impacts

The spatial accuracy of a service area is important for certain types of analyses, such as if an infrastructure outage impacts other infrastructure assets. For example, an asset that depends on electric power from a substation may be unable to function if the substation is out of service. The analysis computes the spatial agreement between the reference service areas and the calculated service areas. Spatial accuracy is evaluated using a point accuracy test. The metric uses 10,000 (10K) points randomly located within a study area.

Figures 2 through 5 show the service areas created by the four methods overlaid on the random points. Point analysis assesses the accuracy of matching critical facilities with their corresponding service source points through service areas. This type of analysis is widely used in land cover classification accuracy assessments [10, 11]. For each randomly-placed point, the service area to which the point belongs in the reference model is determined; the same deter-

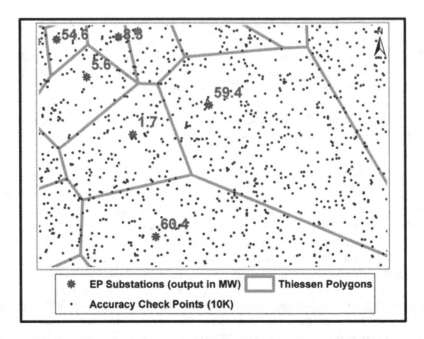

Figure 2. Point layer (10K) overlaid with Thiessen polygon layer.

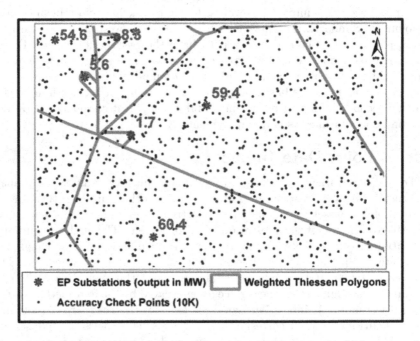

Figure 3. Point layer (10K) overlaid with weighted Thiessen polygon layer.

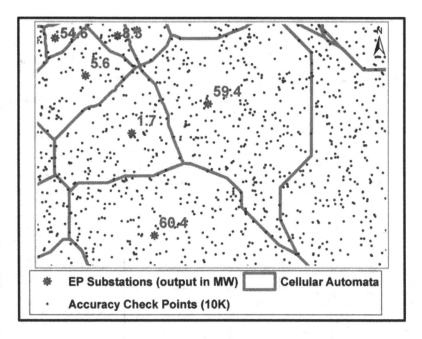

Figure 4. Point layer (10K) overlaid with cellular automata polygon layer.

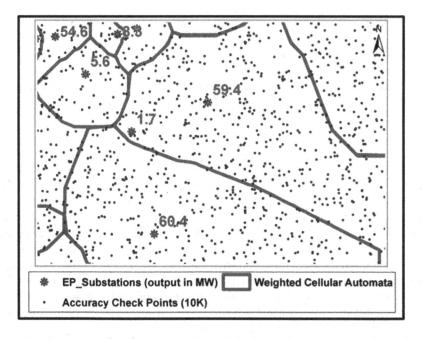

Figure 5. Point layer (10K) overlaid with weighted cellular automata polygon layer.

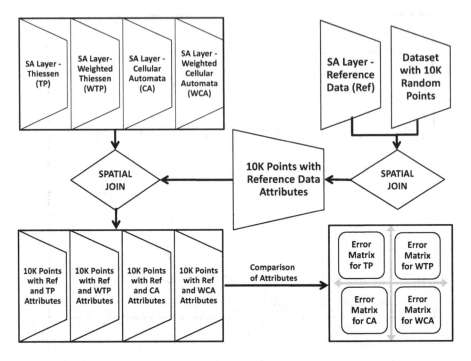

Figure 6. Point accuracy assessment data preparation flowchart.

mination is performed for the Thiessen polygon, weighted Thiessen polygon, cellular automata and weighted cellular automata approaches (Figure 6). This information is used to create error matrices for evaluating the approaches.

The following equation is used to extract the overall accuracy measure from an error matrix [11]:

$$Overall\ Accuracy = \frac{\sum_{i=1}^{k} n_{ii}}{k}$$

where k is the number of substations, n is the number of sample points and n_{ii} is a cell along the matrix diagonal corresponding to row i and column i.

Figure 7 shows an error matrix. The rows are the values for a particular method (e.g., weighted cellular automata) and the columns are the reference values. Four matrices are created (one for each method) to assess the accuracy of each calculated dataset compared with the reference dataset. For each sample point, the reference and calculated polygons in which the point falls (i and j, respectively) are determined. If both polygons represent the service area for the same substation, then the ID fields match (i.e., $i = j$), which causes the n_{ij} cell in the matrix to be incremented by one.

Proximity confidence analyses are also performed to evaluate if the proximity to the source point in a polygon affects the accuracy of an estimate. In the analyses, the distance between the source point and the substation (defined as a

		Reference (Ground Truth) Service Area Data							
		Substation 1	Substation 2	Substation 3	Substation 4	....	..... Substation i	Row Total
Service area data for each method	Substation 1	n_{11}	n_{21}	n_{31}	n_{41}			
	Substation 2	n_{12}	n_{22}	n_{32}	n_{42}			
	Substation 3	n_{13}	n_{23}	n_{33}	n_{43}			
	Substation 4	n_{14}	n_{24}	n_{34}	n_{44}			
	....							
	....							
	Substation k						n_{kk}	
								Overall Accuracy: $(\sum_{i=1}^{k} n_{ii})/n$

Figure 7. Error matrix.

serving point in the reference dataset) is measured for each polygon. To classify the points uniformly based on their proximity to the serving source point, the distances are normalized based on the size of the service area polygon that overlays the point for each method. This approach enables a decision maker to quantify the quality of the results based on where a point is located within a service area. Facilities located closer to the service source (i.e., electric power substation) have higher confidence values than those that are further away from the service source. This reduction in confidence can, in fact, be quantified.

As an example, consider two hospitals as point data. The first hospital is located 500 yards away from Substation A and the second hospital is two miles away from Substation B. If the service area sizes are the same for both substations, it is reasonable to compare the hospital to substation distances and to calculate the confidence that the hospitals are correctly associated with the substations. However, if the service area of Substation A is much smaller than that of Substation B, then the distances must be normalized.

Normalization and point classification are based on the distance to the source. Let $P(s)$ be the service area polygon for service point s, A be the area of polygon P and r be the radius of a circle with the same area A as the service area polygon $P(s)$. Furthermore, let i be a randomly-placed point in the agreement zone (i.e., region where the reference data polygon and the polygon produced by the service area estimation method overlap), d be the distance between i and service point s, which is normalized and classified as follows:

(i) Point i is classified in Proximity Class #1 (closest 25%) if $d < r/4$.

(ii) Point i is classified in Proximity Class #2 (25–50%) if $r/4 < d < r/2$.

(iii) Point i is classified in Proximity Class #3 (50–75%) if $r/2 < d < 3r/4$.

(iv) Point i is classified in Proximity Class #4 (farthest 25%) if $d < 3r/4$.

All the points are classified using the normalized distances and the classifications are used to measure the effect of proximity on the accuracy of point data and to quantify the confidence in a method when reference data is unavailable.

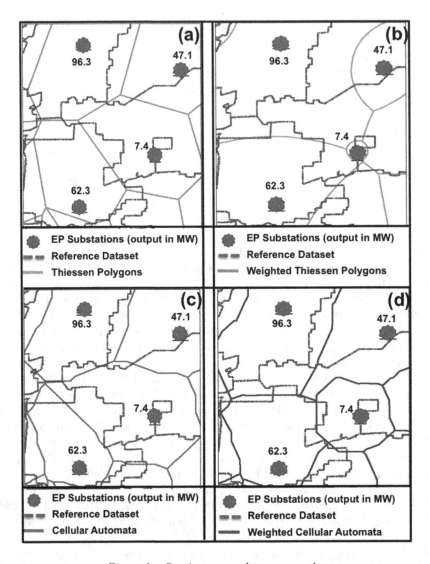

Figure 8. Service area polygon examples.

We also investigate the ability of the methods to accurately estimate the service-sink relationships when neighboring polygons are also considered. This is performed by creating a lookup table for each method. The lookup table lists all the existing service area polygons for all the methods along with the neighboring polygons. The table is used to recalculate the point accuracy values. For each point that is misplaced in the reference dataset, it is determined if the point is correctly associated with a neighboring polygon. Taking into account the neighboring service area polygons makes it possible to test the accuracy of determining source-sink relationships for critical point locations.

Table 1. Mean differences in populations.

Estimation Approach	Daytime Population	Nighttime Population
Thiessen Polygons	2,640	3,754
Weighted Thiessen Polygons	2,554	3,505
Cellular Automata	3,189	4,847
Weighted Cellular Automata	1,754	541

4. Experimental Results

This section presents the results of the performance analysis of the four approaches, namely the standard and weighted versions of the Thiessen polygon and cellular automata approaches. For the weighted methods, peak energy consumption (in MW) is used for the weights.

Figure 8 shows the results obtained for the four approaches. Each sub-figure displays one service area creation method along with the reference dataset. Figure 8(a) compares the Thiessen polygon approach results with the reference set while Figure 8(b) compares the weighted Thiessen polygon approach results with the reference set. Figures 8(c) and 8(d) show the corresponding results for the cellular automata and weighted cellular automata approaches, respectively.

The first set of results pertains to aggregate statistical accuracy. In particular, the area, population and various economic indicators are compared with the results of the reference service areas.

Table 1 shows the mean differences in the daytime and nighttime populations between the calculated and reference service areas. A smaller value is a better result because the population value produced by the method is closer to the population value produced for the reference service area. For the daytime and nighttime populations, the weighted cellular automata approach yields the best results (smallest differences) compared with the reference data. On the other hand, the cellular automata approach yields results with the highest differences.

Table 2. Sum of differences in populations.

Estimation Approach	Daytime Population	Nighttime Population
Thiessen Polygons	319K	367K
Weighted Thiessen Polygons	286K	326K
Cellular Automata	376K	417K
Weighted Cellular Automata	79K	24K

Similar results were obtained for the sum of differences in populations (Table 2). The weighted cellular automata approach yields the best results. The

Table 3. Mean differences in economic impact (direct, indirect and induced).

Estimation Approach	Direct (dollars)	Indirect (dollars)	Induced (dollars)
Thiessen Polygons	1.07M	1.54M	2.12M
Weighted Thiessen Polygons	533K	707K	952K
Cellular Automata	330K	448K	611K
Weighted Cellular Automata	11K	8K	16K

Table 4. Mean differences in economic impact (employment and business).

Estimation Approach	Employment (dollars)	Business (dollars)
Thiessen Polygons	6,200	560
Weighted Thiessen Polygons	2,700	80
Cellular Automata	1,900	200
Weighted Cellular Automata	150	10

weighted Thiessen polygon approach yields better results than the standard Thiessen polygon and cellular automata approaches.

Tables 3 and 4 show the means of the differences in the economic impact for various metrics (direct, indirect, induced, employment and business). In all cases, the difference is the lowest for the weighted cellular automata approach, second lowest for the cellular automata approach and third lowest for the weighted Thiessen polygon approach. The only exception is the economic impact on business (Table 4), for which the weighted Thiessen polygon approach and cellular automata approach swap places. The largest mean difference value is produced by the Thiessen polygon approach. Although the mean difference for the weighted Thiessen polygon approach is larger than that for the cellular automata approach (except for the economic impact on business), the differences are not as notable as the differences for the other categories.

Table 5. Sum of differences in economic impact (direct, indirect and induced).

Estimation Approach	Direct (dollars)	Indirect (dollars)	Induced (dollars)
Thiessen Polygons	59M	85M	116M
Weighted Thiessen Polygons	25M	33M	44M
Cellular Automata	16M	22M	31M
Weighted Cellular Automata	500K	360K	714K

Tables 5 and 6 show the results corresponding to the sums of the differences; the results have the same trends as in the case of the mean differences.

Table 6.   Sum of differences in economic impact (employment and business).

Estimation Approach	Employment (dollars)	Business (dollars)
Thiessen Polygons	340K	31K
Weighted Thiessen Polygons	127K	4K
Cellular Automata	96K	11K
Weighted Cellular Automata	6.4K	0.5K

Table 7.   Average service area polygon size.

Estimation Approach	Mean (acres)	RMS (acres)
Reference Data	1,033	2,241
Thiessen Polygons	1,054	2,145
Weighted Thiessen Polygons	1,106	2,536
Cellular Automata	898	1,822
Weighted Cellular Automata	921	2,299

The final aggregate statistic is the total surface area of the polygons. The results of the total surface area comparisons indicate that the average reference polygon area is 1,033 acres. As shown in Table 7, the weighted cellular automata and Thiessen polygon approaches yield polygons that are the closest in size (on average) to the reference polygon sizes. The cellular automata approach yields the least accurate approximation for this metric.

Table 8.   Overall accuracy through point analysis.

Estimation Approach	Acccuracy (%)
Thiessen Polygons	54.1
Weighted Thiessen Polygons	68.9
Cellular Automata	52.3
Weighted Cellular Automata	59.5

For the point accuracy analysis, 10,000 points were selected randomly across the study area and an error matrix was created for each method. The matrices were used to calculate the overlay agreement accuracy. Table 8 shows that the weighted Thiessen polygon approach yields the best overall results (68.9%), followed by the weighted cellular automata approach (59.5%), while the cellular automata approach has the lowest accuracy (52.3%).

As shown in Table 9, the results are nuanced. The weighted cellular automata approach has the highest point accuracy (91%) when points in the closest 25% area of each polygon are considered, followed by the weighted

Table 9. Proximity confidence analysis accuracy (%).

Estimation Approach	25% Area	25%-50% Area	50%-75% Area	75%-100% Area
Thiessen Polygons	81	65	40	31
Weighted Thiessen Polygons	86	75	58	50
Cellular Automata	85	68	38	27
Weighted Cellular Automata	91	76	54	41

Thiessen polygon approach (86%), the cellular automata approach (85%) and the Thiessen polygon approach (81%). Farther away from the source point, a drop in the accuracy of the unweighted approaches (Thiessen polygon and cellular automata) is observed. The accuracies of the weighted approaches decrease considerably, but they are still higher than the accuracies of the unweighted approaches.

Table 10. Point accuracy analysis based on polygon neighborhood relaxation.

Estimation Approach	Acccuracy (%)
Thiessen Polygons	96.5
Weighted Thiessen Polygons	97.4
Cellular Automata	95.2
Weighted Cellular Automata	97.9

It is important to note that the accuracies of all the approaches improve dramatically when neighboring polygons are included. Instead of assigning a point to a single polygon, a point is assigned to a single polygon and a neighboring polygon. This relaxes the analysis to indicate that a point is associated with a source facility from a set of source facilities. The corresponding results are shown in Table 10, where the points are correctly assigned to a set of source facilities more than 95% of the time for all four approaches.

5.   Discussion

Critical infrastructures, such as electric power, natural gas, water and telecommunications, provide vital services to society. In the event of an outage, these services must be restored as soon as possible to bring the situation back to normal and reduce the negative impacts of the outage. Several factors make it difficult for decision makers to assess the impacts of an outage. Critical infrastructure networks are inherently complex and the relationships between network elements as well as those between other networks are not well understood. Outage propagation is complicated to trace, especially in the case of an electric power disruption. In addition, information on source-sink relationships is not readily available. Therefore, prioritizing restoration and repair for network elements can be an extremely challenging task.

Moreover, critical infrastructure networks are interconnected and it is often the case that networks depend on other networks to function. For example, an electric network provides power to water pumps, which are part of a water network. Likewise, telecommunications towers and hubs also require electricity to function. Therefore, an electric power network outage can cascade within the network as well as to other networks. The accurate determination of service areas is vital to modeling cross-infrastructure effects. Applying four well-known estimation methods, namely standard and weighted Thiessen polygon and cellular automata approaches, to service area determination for electric power networks yields interesting insights. In general, the weighted cellular automata approach is the best performer while the Thiessen polygon approach has the worst performance. However, for points closest to the boundaries of service areas, the weighted Thiessen polygon approach has the best accuracy.

Visual inspection of the weighted cellular automata polygons compared with the reference dataset polygons provides some insights into the point accuracy results. Two situations lead to the lower accuracy of weighted cellular automata polygons in the point accuracy analysis. The first involves weighted cellular automata polygons at the outer edge of the study area and is an artifact of how the cellular automata algorithm is designed. Cellular automata algorithms favor growth in unconstrained regions and, thus, polygons at the edges tend to grow outward rather than inward, leading to unrealistic results. This behavior can be controlled by introducing boundaries that limit cellular automata growth. The second situation occurs for a few cases in the dataset where the ratio of power output for a specific substation to the total service area in the reference dataset is too large (e.g., when some of the power is provided to an industrial complex). Including substations with large outputs and small area coverage in the reference dataset also contributes to errors.

Finally, cellular automata algorithms incorporate several parameters that must be tuned. This study has used "out of the box" parameters for cellular automata to allow for the least-biased comparisons with Thiessen polygon approaches. However, while parameter tuning can dramatically improve the performance of cellular automata approaches, the tuning is highly specific to the application domain.

6. Conclusions

Sophisticated modeling and simulation tools are vital to enable decision makers to predict, plan for and respond to complex critical infrastructure service outages [27, 37]. However, modeling and simulation tools cannot function effectively without adequate, good-quality data. Unfortunately, data pertaining to critical infrastructure assets is highly sensitive and is, therefore, difficult to obtain; detailed data about infrastructure dependencies is even more difficult to obtain.

In the absence of data of adequate quantity and quality, the only feasible solution is to rely on estimation methods to predict the impacts of critical infrastructure service outages on populations, regional economies and other critical infrastructure components. The empirical evaluation of service area estimation techniques described in this paper reveals that the weighted cellular automata and weighted Thiessen polygon approaches produce better estimates than their standard (unweighted) counterparts. Also, the results demonstrate that the weighted cellular automata approach has the best aggregate statistical accuracy while the weighted Thiessen polygon approach has the best point accuracy. However, parameter tuning dramatically improves the performance of the cellular automata approach.

Future research will proceed along three directions. First, other critical infrastructures will be investigated to gain an understanding of the aspects that are unique to critical infrastructures and those that are common between critical infrastructures. Second, other comparison metrics will be developed; for example, substation loads (in MW) could be compared with the expected consumptions by populations and businesses in service areas to assess the accuracy of the computed polygons. Third, formal probability-based methods will be investigated to cope with the error and uncertainty that underlie service area algorithms.

References

[1] K. Akabane, K. Nara, Y. Mishima and K. Tsuji, Optimal geographic allocation of power quality control centers by Voronoi diagram, *Proceedings of the Power Systems Computation Conference*, 2002.

[2] F. Aurenhammer, Voronoi diagrams: A survey of a fundamental geometric data structure, *ACM Computing Surveys*, vol. 23(3), pp. 345–405, 1991.

[3] A. Barto, Cellular Automata as Models of Natural Systems, Ph.D. Dissertation, Department of Computer and Communication Sciences, University of Michigan, Ann Arbor, Michigan, 1975.

[4] F. Berto and J. Tagliabue, Cellular automata, in *The Stanford Encyclopedia of Philosophy*, E. Zalta (Ed.), Stanford, California (plato.stanford.edu/archives/sum2012/entries/cellular-automata), 2012.

[5] E. Bright, P. Coleman and A. Rose, LandScan 2011 Global Population Database, Oak Ridge National Laboratory, Oak Ridge, Tennessee, 2012.

[6] B. Bush, A. Bush, R. Fisher, S. Folga, P. Giguere, J. Holland, J. Hurford, J. Kavicky, A. McCown, M. McLamore, E. Pontante, L. Rothrock, M. Salazar, S. Shamsuddin, C. Unal, D. Visarraga and K. Werley, Interdependent Energy Infrastructure Simulation System – IEISS Version 2.1 Technical Reference Manual, Technical Report LANL-D4-05-0027, Los Alamos National Laboratory, Los Alamos, New Mexico, 2005.

[7] S. Castongia, A Demand-Based Resource Allocation Method for Electrical Substation Service Area Delineation, M.A. Thesis, Department of Geography and Earth Sciences, University of North Carolina at Charlotte, Charlotte, North Carolina, 2006.

[8] J. Ching, M. Brown, T. McPherson, S. Burian, F. Chen, R. Cionco, A. Hanna, T. Hultgren, D. Sailor, H. Taha and D. Williams, National Urban Database and Access Portal Tool, *Bulletin of the American Meteorological Society*, vol. 90(8), pp. 1157–1168, 2009.

[9] B. Chopard, Cellular automata modeling of physical systems, in *Computational Complexity: Theory, Techniques and Applications*, R. Meyers (Ed.), Springer, New York, pp. 407–433, 2012.

[10] R. Congalton, A review of assessing the accuracy of classifications of remotely sensed data, *Remote Sensing of Environment*, vol. 37(1), pp. 35–46, 1991.

[11] R. Congalton and K. Green, *Assessing the Accuracy of Remotely Sensed Data: Principles and Practices*, CRC Press, Boca Raton, Florida, 2009.

[12] M. Creutz, Self-organized criticality and cellular automata, in *Computational Complexity: Theory, Techniques and Applications*, R. Meyers (Ed.), Springer, New York, pp. 2780–2791, 2012.

[13] P. Dong, Generating and updating multiplicatively weighted Voronoi diagrams for point, line and polygon features in GIS, *Computers and Geosciences*, vol. 34(4), pp. 411–421, 2008.

[14] J. Fenwick and L. Dowell, Electrical substation service-area estimation using cellular automata: An initial report, *Proceedings of the ACM Symposium on Applied Computing*, pp. 560–565, 1999.

[15] M. Gahegan and I. Lee, Data structures and algorithms to support interactive spatial analysis using dynamic Voronoi diagrams, *Computers, Environment and Urban Systems*, vol. 24(6), pp. 509–537, 2000.

[16] M. Held and R. Williamson, Creating electrical distribution boundaries using computational geometry, *IEEE Transactions on Power Systems*, vol. 19(3), pp. 1342–1347, 2004.

[17] H. Kuo and Y. Hsu, Distribution system load estimation and service restoration using a fuzzy set approach, *IEEE Transactions on Power Delivery*, vol. 8(4), pp. 1950–1957, 1993.

[18] S. Linger and M. Wolinsky, Estimating electrical service areas using GIS and cellular automata, presented at the *Environmental Systems Research Institute International Conference*, 2001.

[19] T. McPherson and S. Burian, The Water Infrastructure Simulation Environment (WISE) Project, *Proceedings of the Seventh Annual Symposoum on Water Distribution Systems Analysis*, 2005.

[20] T. McPherson, J. Rush, H. Khalsa, A. Ivey and M. Brown, A day-night population exchange model for better exposure and consequence management assessments, *Proceedings of the Sixth Symposium on Urban Development*, 2006.

[21] National Infrastructure Simulation and Analysis Center, FastEcon Tool Summary Report: Fiscal Year 2008, Technical Report LA-UR-09-00558, Los Alamos National Laboratory, Los Alamos, New Mexico, 2008.

[22] K. Newton and D. Schirmer, On the methodology of defining substation spheres of influence within an electric vehicle project framework, presented at the *Environmental Systems Research Institute User Conference*, 1997.

[23] A. Okabe, B. Boots, K. Sugihara and S. Chiu, *Spatial Tessellations: Concepts and Applications of Voronoi Diagrams*, John Wiley, Chichester, United Kingdom, 2000.

[24] A. Okabe, T. Satoh, T. Furuta, A. Suzuki and K. Okano, Generalized network Voronoi diagrams: Concepts, computational methods and applications, *International Journal of Geographical Information Science*, vol. 22(9), pp. 965–994, 2008.

[25] L. Sulewski, A Geographic Modeling Framework for Assessing Critical Infrastructure Vulnerability: Energy Infrastructure Case Study, Ph.D. Dissertation, Department of Geography, University of South Carolina, Columbia, South Carolina, 2013.

[26] W. Tobler, Cellular geography, in *Philosophy in Geography*, S. Gale and G. Olsson (Eds.), Springer, Dordrecht, The Netherlands, pp. 379–386, 1979.

[27] W. Tolone, D. Wilson, A. Raja, W. Xiang, H. Hao, S. Phelps and E. Johnson, Critical infrastructure integration modeling and simulation, *Proceedings of the Second Symposium on Intelligence and Security Informatics*, pp. 214–225, 2004.

[28] G. Toole, S. Linger and M. Burks, Automated utility service area assessment under emergency conditions, *Proceedings of International Conference of the Society for Computer Simulation*, 2001.

[29] P. Torrens, Cellular automata, in *International Encyclopedia of Human Geography*, R. Kitchen and N. Thrift (Eds.), Elsevier, London, United Kingdom, pp. 1–4, 2009.

[30] P. Torrens and I. Benenson, Geographic automata systems, *International Journal of Geographical Information Science*, vol. 19(4), pp. 385–412, 2005.

[31] P. Torrens and A. Nara, Modeling gentrification dynamics: A hybrid approach, *Computers, Environment and Urban Systems*, vol. 31(3), pp. 337–361, 2007.

[32] P. Torrens and D. O'Sullivan, Cellular automata and urban simulation: Where do we go from here? *Environment and Planning B: Planning and Design*, vol. 28(2), pp. 163–168, 2001.

[33] D. Visarraga, B. Bush, S. Linger and T. McPherson, Development of a Java based water distribution simulation capability for infrastructure interdependency analyses, *Proceedings of the World Water and Environmental Resources Congress*, 2005.

[34] J. von Neumann, *The Computer and the Brain*, Yale University Press, New Haven, Connecticut, 1958.

[35] J. von Neumann, *Papers of John von Neumann on Computers and Computing Theory*, MIT Press, Cambridge, Massachusetts, 1986.

[36] J. von Neumann and O. Morgenstern, *Theory of Games and Economic Behavior*, Princeton University Press, Princeton, New Jersey, 1953.

[37] D. Wilson, O. Pala, W. Tolone and W. Xiang, Recommendation-based geovisualization support for reconstitution in critical infrastructure protection, *SPIE Proceedings on Visual Analytics for Homeland Defense and Security*, vol. 7346, 2009.

[38] S. Wolfram, *Cellular Automata and Complexity: Collected Papers*, Westview Press, Boulder, Colorado, 1994.

IV

RISK AND IMPACT ASSESSMENT

Chapter 13

A DECISION SUPPORT TOOL FOR A UNIFIED HOMELAND SECURITY STRATEGY

Richard White, Aaron Burkhart, Edward Chow, and Logan Maynard

Abstract   This paper describes an asset vulnerability model decision support tool (AVM-DST) that is designed to guide strategic investments in critical infrastructure protection. AVM-DST is predicated on previous research on an alternative risk methodology for assessing the current infrastructure protection status, evaluating future protective improvement measures and justifying national investments. AVM-DST is a web-based application that works within the U.S. Department of Homeland Security Risk Management Framework and enables decision makers to view infrastructure assets risk profiles that highlight various features of interest, select protective improvement measures within a given budget based on defined investment strategies or other criteria, and evaluate protective purchases against varying probabilities of attack over a given period of time. In addition to reviewing the concepts and formulations underlying the application, this paper describes the AVM-DST capabilities, functions, features, architecture and performance.

Keywords: Risk management, asset vulnerability model, decision support tool

1.   Introduction

The events of September 11, 2001 and their aftermath exposed the vulnerability of the critical infrastructure to asymmetric domestic attacks. The 2002 Homeland Security Act made critical infrastructure protection a core mission of the Department of Homeland Security (DHS). From the outset, DHS's goal has been to develop a program that would "establish standards and benchmarks for infrastructure protection and provide the means to measure performance" [17]. Quantifiable metrics are not only essential to developing coherent strategy, but they are also the law under the 1993 Government Performance and Results Act. Nevertheless, despite successive attempts over the ensuing years [2–5], a 2010

J. Butts and S. Shenoi (Eds.): Critical Infrastructure Protection VIII, IFIP AICT 441, pp. 195–211, 2014.
© IFIP International Federation for Information Processing 2014

review of DHS's approach to risk analysis conducted by the National Research Council [16] "did not find any DHS risk analysis capabilities and methods that are as yet adequate for supporting DHS decision making." Arguably, the absence of viable metrics and standards have beset attempts to identify the critical infrastructure [15], assess and analyze risks [10] and allocate resources [14] – all of them basic steps in the Risk Management Framework that underpins the current National Infrastructure Protection Plan [7]. While much research has been conducted on infrastructure [11] and terrorism [13] risk modeling, a cursory analysis of 21 models [9] determined that not one of them satisfied fundamental challenges cited in the National Research Council report [22]. That no effective metrics have been found is indicated by the lack of supporting risk analysis in the 2014 DHS budget request to Congress [6]. Without a viable metric, DHS is unable to assess the current protective status, evaluate future protective improvement measures and justify national investments.

This paper describes a decision support tool based on an asset vulnerability model (AVM) that is designed to lend strategic direction to critical infrastructure protection efforts [21]. AVM-DST is a web-based application that allows decision makers to view infrastructure asset risk profiles that highlight various features of interest, select protective improvement measures within a given budget based on investment strategies or other criteria, and evaluate protective purchases against varying probabilities of attack over a given period of time.

2.   AVM Overview

In 2013, an asset vulnerability model (AVM) was developed to overcome the challenges cited in the National Research Council report [16] and provide DHS with a quantitative means to guide strategic investments in critical infrastructure protection [21]. AVM is a risk analysis methodology that works within the DHS Risk Management Framework to provide a baseline analysis, cost-benefit analysis and decision support tools that provide guidance in selecting critical infrastructure protective improvement measures. AVM is predicated on a measure designated as Θ, which represents the attacker's probability of failure. The selection of Θ was informed by the game theoretic research of Sandler and Lapan [18] that evaluates defensive strategies based on an attacker's choice of target. The Θ formulation is constructed from five parameters corresponding to the five phases of emergency management – prevent, protect, mitigate, respond and recover [12]:

$$\Theta = P(dis) \cdot P(def) \cdot P(den) \cdot P(dim) \cdot Pct(dam) \qquad (1)$$

where $P(dis)$ is the probability that an attack can be detected or disrupted, $P(def)$ is the probability that an attack can be defeated, $P(den)$ is the probability that a worst case disaster can be averted, $P(dim)$ is the probability that 100% of the survivors can be saved and $Pct(dam)$ is the decrease in economic output times the percentage increase in mortality rate.

$P(dis)$ corresponds to the "prevent" phase of emergency management and is calculated from known intelligence data by dividing the number of thwarted attacks by the number of planned attacks (only planned attacks that were discovered; presumably they were thwarted before execution) and executed attacks culled from available sources such as the Global Terrorism Database (www.start.umd.edu/gtd). $P(def)$ corresponds to the "protect" phase of emergency management and is derived from the protective measure index (PMI) assessed by Argonne National Laboratory [10] from data collected in DHS security surveys and vulnerability assessments. $P(den)$ corresponds to the "mitigate" phase of emergency management and may be derived from the resilience index (RI), also calculated by Argonne National Laboratory [9], that assesses failure modes and redundancies. $P(dim)$ corresponds to the "response" phase of emergency management and may be expressed as the percentage of survivors that first responders can rescue and treat within 72 hours of a catastrophe as determined by DHS data collected from the Threat and Hazard Identification and Risk Assessment (THIRA) Program [21]. The $Pct(dam)$ parameter represents both the "recovery" phase of emergency management and the magnitude component of the risk formulation. The parameter is computed as the product of the change in the Gross Domestic Product (GDP) and national homicide rates expected from the loss of a particular asset. According to data from the Bureau of Economic Analysis and the National Center for Health Statistics, the 9/11 attacks registered a 47% decrease in the GDP, down from 6.43% in 2000 to 3.38% in 2001, and a 20% increase in national homicides, up from 5.9 to 7.1 deaths per 100,000 from 2000 to 2001.

The chief criticism leveled by the National Research Council was the inability to produce reliable threat estimates (i.e., "probability of attack") for human-initiated (i.e., "threat-driven") events because of a dearth of data to support robust statistical analysis [16]. AVM overcomes this challenge by adopting an "asset-driven" risk assessment methodology and replacing "threat estimation" with "threat localization." Threat localization realizes that even with a robust set of data, as in the case of natural phenomena, it is still impossible to predict exactly where and when the next natural disaster will occur. The best forecasters can do is localize the problem to justify protective investments. Thus, while earthquakes are national phenomena, their prevalence along the West Coast justifies the more stringent seismic standards imposed in California compared with those imposed in Connecticut. Localization can be similarly achieved for the critical infrastructure without the benefit of a robust data set.

Homeland Security Presidential Directive #7 directs the protection of assets "whose exploitation or destruction by terrorists could cause catastrophic health effects or mass casualties comparable to the use of a weapon of mass destruction ... [or] have a debilitating effect on security and economic well-being" [19]. Of the sixteen infrastructure sectors currently categorized by the federal government [20], only the nine sectors listed in Table 1 may be targeted to precipitate mass or debilitating effects.

Table 1.   Targeted critical infrastructure sectors.

ID	Infrastructure Sector
1	Chemical Plants
2	Dams
3	Energy
4	Financial Services
5	Food and Agriculture
6	Information Networks
7	Nuclear Reactors, Materials and Waste
8	Transportation Systems
9	Water and Wastewater Systems

According to the National Research Council, a good risk analysis (i) conveys current risk levels; (ii) supports cost-benefit analysis; (iii) demonstrates risk reduction effects across multiple assets at different levels of management; and (iv) measures and tracks investments and improvement in overall system resilience over time [16]. Working within the DHS Risk Management Framework, AVM can convey current risk levels through a baseline analysis of the critical infrastructure sectors identified in Table 1 using the Θ risk formulation in Equation (1). AVM can further facilitate cost-benefit analyses of proposed protective improvement measures using the following formulation:

$$\Delta\Theta = P(\Delta dis) \cdot P(\Delta def) \cdot P(\Delta den) \cdot P(\Delta dim) \cdot Pct(dam)$$
$$D(\Delta\Theta) = D(\Delta dis) + D(\Delta def) + D(\Delta den) + D(\Delta dim)$$

Each proposed measure has an associated $\Delta\Theta$ protective gain and $D(\Delta\Theta)$ implementation cost. Multiple protective improvement measures may be proposed for a given asset, for assets within a region or for assets across the nation. AVM cost-benefit analysis calculates a $\Delta\Theta$ and $D(\Delta\Theta)$ for every combination of proposed improvement measures and identifies the combination that provides the greatest protective gain for the least cost. In this manner, AVM can narrow down a list of candidates to those that offer the best value.

AVM works with and supports the DHS Risk Management Framework. Starting in Step 2 (Identify Infrastructure) of the framework, AVM restricts the problem set to the nine critical infrastructure sectors identified in Table 1, overcoming past problems with developing a definitive National Asset Database, assessed by a DHS Inspector General as containing "many unusual or out-of-place assets whose criticality is not readily apparent, and too few assets in essential areas" [15]. An AVM baseline analysis unifies data collection efforts by the DHS Enhanced Critical Infrastructure Protection (ECIP) Program [10] working inside the perimeter and by the Threat and Hazard Identification and Risk Assessment System working outside the perimeter [8] in Step 3 (Assess and Analyze Risks) of the Risk Management Framework. AVM cost-benefit analy-

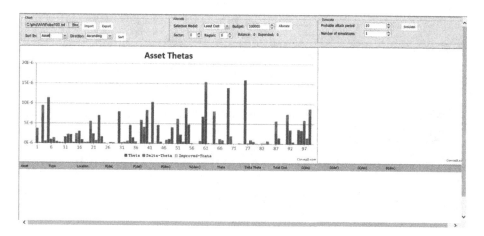

Figure 1. AVM-DST display of 100 simulated assets.

sis, perhaps conducted by the National Infrastructure Simulation and Analysis Center (NISAC), can identify the optimum combination of proposed protective improvements competing for Homeland Security Grant Program (HSGP) funding in Step 4 (Implement Risk Management Activities) of the Risk Management Framework. At every step and at all levels of the Risk Management Framework, AVM-DST can facilitate strategic analysis and decision making as described in this paper.

3. AVM-DST Capabilities and Functions

AVM-DST is a web-based application that allows decision makers to view infrastructure asset risk profiles that highlight various features of interest, select protective improvement measures within a given budget based on defined investment strategies or other criteria, and evaluate protective purchases against varying probabilities of attack over a given period of time.

3.1 Viewing a Risk Profile

Figure 1 shows a critical infrastructure risk profile by asset ID number. Real data is not available because it is protected from disclosure under the 2002 Homeland Security Act, even overriding requests made under the Freedom of Information Act. In the AVM-DST display, the current Θ protective values of assets are represented by blue bars. The current Θ protective values are derived from the AVM baseline analysis. The taller the bar, the better the asset is protected. The notional ID number of an asset is listed on the x-axis. Red bars indicate $\Delta\Theta$, which is the additional protection to be gained by purchasing measures recommended by AVM cost-benefit analysis.

AVM-DST enables decision makers to examine the current critical infrastructure risk profile from a number of different perspectives. For example,

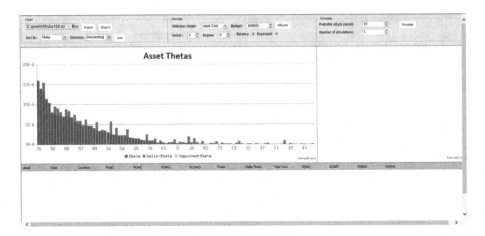

Figure 2.   Critical infrastructure risk profile by Θ value.

Figure 2 shows the same assets sorted by Θ, identifying the most protected to the least protected assets. Similarly, the data may be sorted by asset type to display the relative protection of assets in the same sector, or by asset location to depict the relative protection of assets in a given geographic region. Other views may also be generated as desired.

3.2   Selecting Protective Improvements

AVM-DST assists decision makers with selecting protective improvements for purchase. Each protective improvement, indicated by a red bar in Figure 2, has an associated cost value. AVM-DST assists decision makers in selecting protective improvements within the available budgetary constraints. AVM-DST does this by allowing decision makers to select improvements individually or collectively. Individually, the decision maker can select protective improvements by simply clicking on the associated red bars. Collectively, the decision maker can have AVM-DST automatically select protective improvements based on one of seven investment strategies: (i) least cost; (ii) least protected; (iii) region protection; (iv) sector protection; (v) highest $\Delta\Theta$; (vi) highest consequence; or (vii) random protection.

The least cost investment strategy purchases all protective improvement measures based on the lowest cost. Given a fixed budget, this strategy attempts to purchase as many protection measures as possible, regardless of their individual protective gain. The advantage of this strategy is that it affords the purchase of the largest number of protective measures, which may make it politically attractive to "share the wealth" among more congressional districts.

The least protected investment strategy purchases protective improvement measures for the assets that have the least protection as determined by their Θ values. This strategy has the intuitive advantage of allocating resources where they are most needed or at least towards assets that are the most vulnerable.

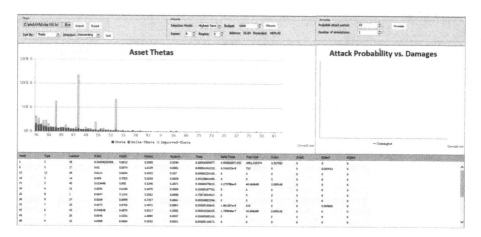

Figure 3. Protective improvement purchase using the highest consequence strategy.

The region protection investment strategy purchases protective improvement measures for regions of the country that are deemed to be more susceptible to attacks than others. This strategy is similar to that used by the Urban Area Security Initiative (UASI) Grant Program administered by DHS.

The sector protection investment strategy allocates funds to a specific sector that is deemed to be more susceptible to attack or whose incapacitation or destruction is considered to have significant damage effects.

The highest $\Delta\Theta$ investment strategy allocates funds to protective improvement measures that provide the highest $\Delta\Theta$ protection gain regardless of cost. This may be considered to be a cost optimization scheme by purchasing protective measures that provide the highest return on investment.

The highest consequence investment strategy allocates funds to assets with the highest magnitude component in terms of national economic and mortality consequences as determined by the product of their $P(dim)$ and $Pct(dam)$ values. Like the least protected investment strategy, this strategy has the intuitive advantage of allocating resources where they are most needed in terms of the damaging effects.

The random protection investment strategy purchases protective improvements without regard to any properties of the measure or asset. This strategy was created to gain insight into the effects of non-systematic purchases, roughly mimicking current practice.

To engage a strategy, the decision maker must select the desired strategy, enter the amount of budgeted funds and click "Allocate." AVM-DST automatically selects the available protective improvements within the given budget amount and uses green bars to indicate their purchase. Additional information regarding each selected improvement is displayed in the detail grid panel as shown in Figure 3. Decision makers may further customize their choices by clicking on asset records in the detail grid panel and deleting them from the selection.

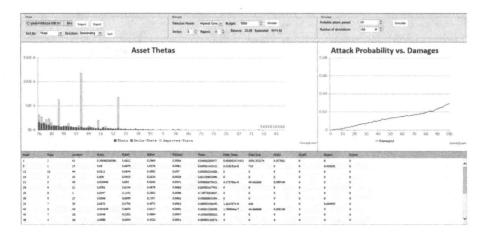

Figure 4. AVM-DST attack simulation and damage estimate.

3.3   Evaluating Protective Improvements

AVM-DST assists decision makers in evaluating their proposed protective improvement purchases through an attack simulator. The attack simulator is engaged by specifying the probable period of attack and number of simulations before clicking the "Simulate" button. The attack simulator graphs the total amount of damage suffered over the probable attack period across a range of attack probabilities as shown in Figure 4. Clauset and Woodard [1] have estimated that there was an 11% to 35% chance of a 9/11-scale terrorist attack in the 40-year period between 1968 and 2007. Moreover, they estimated a 19% to 46% chance of another such attack over the next ten years.

AVM-DST uses the revised Θ values from protective improvement purchases to compute the damage based on the probability of a successful attack. The simulation begins by calculating an annual attack expectancy. The attack expectancy is calculated by dividing the current probability of attack by the probable attack period. So, for example, an estimated 30% probability of attack over ten years has a 3% annual attack expectancy. AVM-DST generates a uniform random number between zero and one that represents the probability of attack during a given year. A probability of attack that is less than the annual attack expectancy indicates that an attack was initiated. Whether or not the attack is successful depends on the target. AVM-DST selects the target with the lowest Θ value in accordance with the position of Sandler and Lapan [18] that attackers will choose targets for which they are the least likely to fail. AVM-DST then generates a uniform random number between zero and one that represents the attacker's probability of success. Next, it calculates a probability of failure as the product of $P(dis)$, $P(def)$ and $P(den)$ for the selected target. These components correspond to the prevent and protect phases of emergency management. If the probability of success is greater than the probability of failure, then the attack is deemed a success and the asset

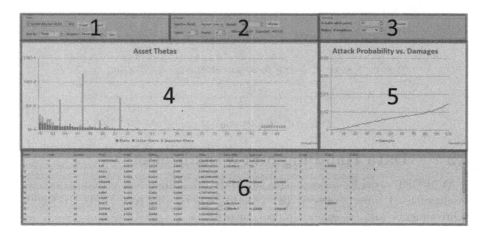

Figure 5. Application user interface.

is removed from further simulation. AVM-DST calculates the damage from a successful attack as the product of $P(dim)$ and $Pct(dam)$ corresponding to the response and recovery phases of emergency management. The collective damage assessments for each attack probability are averaged over the number of specified simulations. More simulations provide finer results, but they also take longer to execute.

4. AVM-DST User Features and Options

The range of AVM-DST robust capabilities and functions are easily accessible from a compact interface that supports a variety of user features and options.

4.1 Compact User Interface

The AVM-DST user interface is differentiated into six display panels presented on a single screen as shown in Figure 5. Each panel facilitates a different application function. The three panels at the top are the control panels, which facilitate user input and control over AVM-DST capabilities. The two panels in the middle are the chart panels: Panel 4 is the main chart that shows assets by their current and improved Θ protective values and Panel 5 is the secondary chart that shows the damage results from attack simulations across a range of probabilities. Both chart panels are fully interactive and support zooming and panning. Panel 6 at the bottom is the asset detail grid panel, which displays detailed record information for each asset selected for protective improvement purchases. This panel is interactive in that records may be added, sorted and deleted from display.

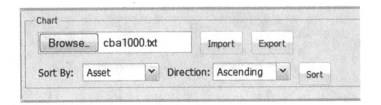

Figure 6. Chart control panel.

4.2 Data Handling and Visualization

AVM-DST provides an extensive set of data handling and visualization capabilities to (i) import assets; (ii) visualize assets; (iii) sort assets; (iv) edit improvements; and (v) export improvements.

- **Import Assets:** AVM-DST imports critical infrastructure asset data from AVM cost-benefit analysis in the comma-separated value (CSV) format. The output file from AVM cost-benefit analysis contains a single record for each asset that identifies its attributes and nominated protective improvements. The following actions must be performed to import an asset file:
    - Click the "Browse" button on the chart control panel (Figure 6).
    - Select the desired asset file to upload.
    - Click "Open" to import the file.

- **Visualize Assets:** Imported assets are automatically displayed in the main chart panel. Each asset is depicted as a bar that represents its current Θ value. The greater the value, the more the asset is protected. The Θ value is updated and displayed as a green bar when protective improvements are selected. The main display also places an "X" below assets that are destroyed in an attack simulation. The damage results from an attack simulation is displayed in the secondary chart panel. The chart shows the calculated damage for different attack probabilities. The following actions must be performed to zoom and pan in each display:
    - Zoom into the chart by clicking and dragging from one point on the chart to another to expand the corresponding subsection of the chart.
    - Pan the chart after it has been zoomed by clicking "Pan" and then click and drag the chart to scroll the chart horizontally. To go back to the zoom mode, click "Zoom."
    - Click "Reset" to restore the chart to maximal zoom.

- **Sort Assets:** AVM-DST also allows users to examine critical infrastructure assets from different perspectives by sorting assets in the main chart panel. The following actions must be performed to sort assets:

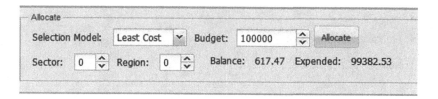

Figure 7. Allocate control panel.

— Click the "Sort By" box and select the field to use in sorting.

— Click the "Direction" for sorting and select either ascending or descending.

— Click "Sort" to update the chart.

- **Edit Improvements:** The record details for assets selected to receive protective improvements are displayed in the asset detail grid panel. AVM-DST allows users to sort this data by clicking the column header associated with the field that is to be sorted. AVM-DST also allows users to remove selected asset improvements by right clicking on the desired record and choosing "Delete."

- **Export Improvements:** Selected improvements may be exported in a CSV file to support implementation efforts. The following actions must be performed to export selected improvements:

  — Click "Export" on the chart control panel (Figure 6).

  — Depending on the browser being used, open the file immediately by selecting the program with which to open it or save the file to the browser-specific download directory.

4.3   Selection of Protective Improvements

As described above, AVM-DST assists decision makers in selecting the desired protective improvements either individually or collectively. To select an improvement individually, a user has only to click on the desired asset indicated by a blue or red bar. The Θ value for the selected asset is updated and is replaced by a green bar. Additionally, the record details associated with the selected asset are displayed in an Excel-like format below the main chart panel. The following actions must be performed to select improvements collectively using one of the predefined investment strategies:

- Click the "Selection Model" dropdown box (Figure 7).

- For the region protection and sector protection models, specify the desired region and sector numbers.

- Enter a dollar amount in the "Budget" field.

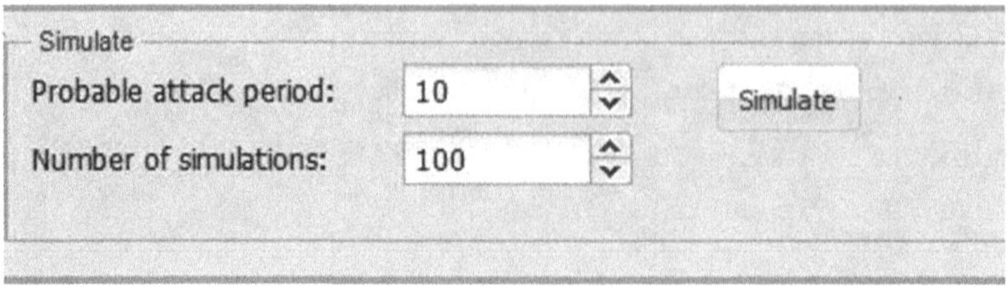

Figure 8. Simulate control panel.

- Click "Allocate."

AVM-DST automatically selects assets based on the user's specifications. The total amount expended and the remaining balance are displayed in the allocate control panel.

4.4 Decision Analysis and Evaluation

As described above, AVM-DST provides a means for a decision maker to assess the effectiveness of an investment strategy by running attack simulations. Each simulation determines if assets are attacked and calculates the total damage due to the attacks over a given period of time. Presumably, the best strategy results in the least amount of damages. The attack simulation results are displayed in the secondary chart panel. The following actions must be performed to run an attack simulation:

- Enter a number of years in the "Probable Attack Period" field in the simulate control panel (Figure 8).

- Enter the number of times to run simulations in the "Number of Simulations" field.

- Click "Simulate."

AVM-DST executes the specified number of simulations and displays the results in the secondary chart, showing the total damage corresponding to each attack probability. The assets that have been destroyed are marked with an "X" on the main chart.

5. AVM-DST Implementation

AVM-DST was constructed in phases using an incremental development process. Phase 1 developed the visualization and data handling capabilities. Phase 2 added the decision support and decision analysis features. AVM-DST is written in JavaScript and utilizes the Ext JS application framework along with the CanvasJS charting plugin. This enables AVM-DST to run with any browser.

5.1   Architecture

AVM-DST is a stand-alone, client-side, browser-oriented web application built using JavaScript and HTML5. It does not currently contain any server side components. It was built using the model-view-controller paradigm, which is recommended, albeit not required, for Ext JS applications. In this paradigm, the model is the representation of the data to be used. The model describes the objects and their fields and specifies object relationships and hierarchies. It also includes the functions used to manipulate the data. Ext JS uses data stores to load, handle and manipulate collections of model instances. A view serves as the visual interface between the user and the application. This includes windows panels and widgets that facilitate input from the user and display output. The controller handles the business logic of the application. It reacts to events and updates the models and views accordingly.

5.2   Development

AVM-DST v1.0 was a proof-of-concept prototype. It included the basic functionality for importing, displaying and sorting asset data. AVM-DST v1.0 used Ext JS built-in charts that did not support zooming and panning. Also, performance issues restricted the number of assets to no more than a few hundred.

AVM-DST v2.0 used CanvasJS to dramatically increase performance and add zooming and panning. This one change enabled AVM-DST to be used to manipulate thousands of assets. It also allowed record details of selected assets to be displayed below the main chart are exported in the CSV format.

AVM-DST v3.0 marked the Phase 2 development by incorporating decision support and analysis tools. It included the control panels, but only the chart and allocate panels were functional. AVM-DST v3.0 did not implement the attack simulation functionality.

AVM-DST v4.0 added the attack simulation functionality. It also added the secondary chart panel to display the results.

AVM-DST v5.0, the current version, fixed the bugs identified in the previous version and optimized the attack simulation algorithm to run faster and accommodate more simulations over longer probable attack periods.

5.3   Performance

AVM-DST was tested on a machine running Windows 7 64-bit with a 3.2 GHz Intel Core i7-4770k CPU and an NVIDIA GeForce GTX 770 GPU. The browser used during testing was Firefox 26.0 and the input test file contained 1,000 records. The least cost investment strategy required the most time to run for this data set, so it was used predominantly during performance testing. Simulation times were recorded using a ten-year probable attack period with ten simulations and 1,000 simulations. The time to run simulations is not always directly proportional to the number of simulations because of a constant

Table 2.   Performance of AVM-DST functions.

AVM-DST Function	Time
Import File	65 ms
Render Main Chart	60 ms
Render Secondary Chart	6 ms
Run Allocation Algorithm	174 ms
Render Grid	840 ms
Run 10 Simulations	96 ms
Run 1,000 Simulations	2,287 ms
Sort Data	67 ms

pre-processing time for tasks (e.g., sorting) that are only done once regardless of the number of simulations. Table 2 shows the run times of various functions.

6.   Lessons Learned

Performance is always a concern when handling thousands of data records, especially when using web technology. AVM-DST is a stand-alone client-side web application. Because it does not require server-side interaction after it is initially loaded, it does not experience network delays or server-side processing delays that are commonly associated with web applications. AVM-DST was tested using a data file containing 1,000 records and is expected to be able to handle much larger data files.

Initially, the application utilized the built-in Ext JS charts that rely on SVG technology. Because of this, AVM-DST experienced performance problems when handling charts. The browser crashed when the application was tested on the 1,000-record file. Efforts were made to mitigate the problem by implementing paging functionality that loads portions of the data at a time. However, this was not ideal. For this reason, CanvasJS was incorporated because it can quickly and seamlessly handle thousands of data points in the charts.

The asset selection decision support tool must sort the data based on the selection model and then iteratively evaluate each asset for selection. This process is fairly quick so the real performance bottleneck arises when populating the grid with the selected assets.

The performance of the decision analysis tool does not depend on the size of the input file because it only considers the asset that is most likely to be attacked at each iteration. Instead, it is dependent on the probable period of attack and the number of simulations to be performed. Before optimization, this algorithm removes the destroyed assets from the data set during each iteration and then restores and re-sorts them during the next simulation. To prevent the browser from becoming unresponsive, the number of simulations was limited to ten and the probability of attack was incremented in five percent intervals. After optimization, the algorithm sorted only once, then maintained a counter that referenced the next asset being considered and incremented the counter when it was destroyed. On the next simulation, the counter was then reset to zero. In this manner, a substantial amount of file overhead was eliminated by performing only a single sort and not removing the destroyed asset records. These changes resulted in significant performance improvement. They also afforded greater simulation resolution, allowing the probability of attack to be incremented only one percent at each iteration, but still executing 1,000 simulations in less than three seconds.

7.   Conclusions

AVM-DST leverages the AVM risk methodology to enable decision makers to view infrastructure asset risk profiles that highlight various features of interest, select protective improvement measures within a given budget based on seven defined investment strategies and other criteria, and evaluate protective purchases against varying probabilities of attack over a given period of time. Built as a stand-alone, client-side, browser-oriented web application using JavaScript and HTML5, AVM-DST offers a robust range of capabilities and functions that are easily accessible from a compact interface supporting a variety of user features and options. Performance tests show that AVM-DST is capable of handling large data sets with no noticeable delays; it promptly displays simulation results for thousands of assets. Indeed, the AVM-DST research demonstrates that it is possible to guide strategic critical infrastructure protection efforts by assessing the current protection status, evaluating future protective improvement measures and justifying national investments.

Future work related to the AVM-DST web application includes developing additional analytics for the analysis and evaluation component, improved simulation of attack scenarios based on intelligence, support for enhanced trade-offs and extensions for including additional investment strategies. Metrics will be added to the simulations to provide insights into the effectiveness of investment strategies. Additionally, display and visualization enhancements will be implemented, especially optimizing the rendering of the grid panel when the investment allocation tool populates it with the selected assets.

References

[1] A. Clauset and R. Woodard, Estimating the historical and future probabilities of large terrorist events, *Annals of Applied Statistics*, vol. 7(4), pp. 1838–1865, 2013.

[2] Department of Homeland Security, Draft National Infrastructure Protection Plan, Base Plan, Draft NIPP v1.0, Washington, DC, 2005.

[3] Department of Homeland Security, Interim National Preparedness Goal, Homeland Security Presidential Directive 8: National Preparedness, Washington, DC, 2005.

[4] Department of Homeland Security, National Infrastructure Protection Plan, Washington, DC, 2006.

[5] Department of Homeland Security, National Infrastructure Protection Plan, Washington, DC, 2009.

[6] Department of Homeland Security, Budget-in-Brief, Fiscal Year 2014, Washington, DC, 2013.

[7] Department of Homeland Security, NIPP 2013: Partnering for Critical Infrastructure Security and Resilience, Washington, DC, 2013.

[8] Federal Emergency Management Agency, Grant Programs Directorate Information Bulletin, Washington, DC, 2012.

[9] G. Giannopoulos, R. Filippini and M. Schimmer, Risk Assessment Methodologies for Critical Infrastructure Protection, Part I: A State of the Art, JRC Technical Note EUR 25286 EN-2012, Institute for the Protection and Security of the Citizen, European Commission Joint Research Centre, Ispra, Italy, 2012.

[10] Government Accountability Office, Critical Infrastructure Protection: DHS Could Better Manage Security Surveys and Vulnerability Assessments, GAO-12-378, Washington, DC, 2012.

[11] T. Lewis, R. Darken, T. Mackin and D. Dudenhoeffer, Model-based risk analysis for critical infrastructures, in *Critical Infrastructure Security*, F. Flammini (Ed.), WIT Press, Southampton, United Kingdom, pp. 3–19, 2012.

[12] M. Lindell, R. Perry, C. Prater and W. Nicholson, *Fundamentals of Emergency Management*, Federal Emergency Management Agency, Washington, DC, 2006.

[13] G. Loo, The evolution of terrorism risk modeling, *Journal of Reinsurance*, vol. 10(3), pp. 1–16, 2003.

[14] T. Masse, S. O'Neil and J. Rollins, The Department of Homeland Security's Risk Assessment Methodology: Evolution, Issues and Options for Congress, CRS Report for Congress, Order Code RL33858, Congressional Research Service, Washington, DC, 2007.

[15] J. Moteff, Critical Infrastructure: The National Asset Database, CRS Report for Congress, Order Code RL33648, Congressional Research Service, Washington, DC, 2007.

[16] National Research Council of the National Academies, *Review of the Department of Homeland Security's Approach to Risk Analysis*, National Academies Press, Washington, DC, 2010.

[17] Office of Homeland Security, National Strategy for Homeland Security, Washington, DC, 2002.

[18] T. Sandler and H. Lapan, The calculus of dissent: An analysis of terrorists' choice of targets, *Synthese*, vol. 72(2), pp. 245–261, 1988.

[19] The White House, Homeland Security Presidential Directive 7: Critical Infrastructure Identification, Prioritization and Protection, Washington, DC, 2003.

[20] The White House, Presidential Policy Directive – Critical Infrastructure Security and Resilience, Presidential Policy Directive/PPD-21, Washington, DC, 2013.

[21] R. White, Towards a Computational Unified Homeland Security Strategy: An Asset Vulnerability Model, Department of Computer Science, University of Colorado at Colorado Springs, Colorado Springs, Colorado, 2013.

[22] R. White, Towards a unified homeland security strategy: An asset vulnerability model, *Homeland Security Affairs*, vol. 10, art. 1, pp. 1-16, 2014.

Chapter 14

ASSESSING THE IMPACT OF CYBER ATTACKS ON WIRELESS SENSOR NODES THAT MONITOR INTERDEPENDENT PHYSICAL SYSTEMS

Valerio Formicola, Antonio Di Pietro, Abdullah Alsubaie, Salvatore D'Antonio, and Jose Marti

Abstract   This paper describes a next-generation security information and event management (SIEM) platform that performs real-time impact assessment of cyber attacks that target monitoring and control systems in interdependent critical infrastructures. To assess the effects of cyber attacks on the services provided by critical infrastructures, the platform combines security analysis with simulations produced by the Infrastructure Interdependencies Simulator (i2Sim). The approach is based on the mixed holistic reductionist (MHR) methodology that models the relationships between functional components of critical infrastructures and the provided services. The effectiveness of the approach is demonstrated using a scenario involving a dam that feeds a hydroelectric power plant. The scenario considers an attack on a legacy SCADA system and wireless sensor network that reduces electricity production and degrades the services provided by the interdependent systems. The results demonstrate that the attack is detected in a timely manner, risk assessment is performed effectively and service level variations can be predicted. The paper also shows how the impact of attacks on services can be estimated when limits are imposed on information sharing.

Keywords: Cyber attacks, wireless sensor networks, attack impact

1.   Introduction

Cyber attacks against supervisory control and data acquisition (SCADA) systems [22] have shown that security violations can compromise the proper functioning of critical infrastructures. The Stuxnet worm [13] exploited vulnerabilities in the information and communications technology layer (primarily

J. Butts and S. Shenoi (Eds.): Critical Infrastructure Protection VIII, IFIP AICT 441, pp. 213–229, 2014.

deficient security policies and bugs in special purpose systems), ultimately affecting the operation of programmable logic controllers and the uranium hexafluoride centrifuges they controlled. Cyber attacks typically induce faults in sensors and actuators, and alter supervisory mechanisms and notification systems. Once activated, the faults become errors and result in improper operations. These can cause failures in critical infrastructures and eventually affect services, facilities, people and the environment.

Sophisticated wireless sensor networks [5] are increasingly used to monitor critical infrastructure assets, including dams and pipelines [4, 18]. In fact, sensor networks are rapidly being integrated in SCADA environments. Wireless sensor networks are often deployed in hydroelectric power plants and dams to monitor feed water supply, power generation, structural stability, environmental conditions and pollution levels. A single dam can have a thousand sensors, with additional sensors deployed in areas surrounding the water reservoir. Wireless sensor networks expose SCADA systems to new threats introduced by the information and communications technology layer. Unlike traditional sensor systems, wireless sensor networks are also vulnerable to signal eavesdropping and physical tampering, along with new ways of compromising data confidentiality, integrity and availability. The effects of cyber attacks against a dam include: (i) anomalous variations in seepage channel flows; (ii) uncontrolled gate opening; (iii) excessive turbine and infrastructure vibrations; (iv) structural instability; and (v) reservoir level variations.

Despite the adoption of security policies and the implementation of countermeasures, SCADA systems and wireless sensor networks continue to be vulnerable [2, 17]. SCADA systems are generally unable to cope with cyber attacks primarily because they were not designed with security in mind. Protection from cyber attacks has to be provided by additional security mechanisms that must be integrated with existing SCADA systems in a seamless manner. Logical security is commonly provided by security information and event management (SIEM) systems, which are specifically designed to manage and operate information and communications technology applications.

This paper presents a next-generation SIEM platform that performs realtime impact assessment of cyber attacks against monitoring and control systems in interdependent critical infrastructures. Run-time service level analysis is performed in the SIEM workflow. This is enabled by three novel contributions: (i) enhanced security event collectors (probes) that perform advanced semantic analysis of non-IP domains (e.g., wireless sensor networks) in the SIEM framework; (ii) impact assessment based on interdependency simulation; and (iii) transformation of SIEM risk assessment metrics to critical infrastructure operational levels (i.e., levels of services provided by the attacked systems). The approach also helps predict service level variations when limits are imposed on information sharing among different critical infrastructures.

Romano, *et al.* [23] have proposed the use of an enhanced SIEM system to monitor the security level of a traditional dam that incorporates legacy control systems and wireless sensor networks; the system was designed to collect data from physical devices (sensors) and correlate physical events with events generated at the logical layer. This paper further enhances the SIEM system to assess the impact of cyber attacks against a dam that exhibits interdependencies with other critical infrastructures. The goal is to improve risk analyses performed by SIEM systems with qualitative and quantitative analysis of service level variations. This ultimately reduces the time required for decision making and improves decision outcomes in the presence of impending failures. The impact assessment module of the SIEM system relies on i2Sim [16], an infrastructure interdependency simulator that models resource flows between critical infrastructures and assesses how the output of one critical infrastructure is affected by the availability of resources provided by other critical infrastructures.

2.   Related Work

This section discusses related work on next-generation SIEM systems for service level monitoring and models for evaluating critical infrastructure interdependencies.

Collections of events occurring in network systems enable the SIEM framework to assess the security level of network domains. A common way to store this information is to save it in logs generated by security probes and logical sensors. Since logs have heterogeneous formats (semantics and syntax), it is necessary to convert log data into a common representation. The overall process encompasses data gathering, parsing, field normalization and format conversion. Mostly, this process is executed by SIEM agents that collect data from several sources. In order to use SIEM systems to protect critical infrastructures, obtain a holistic view of security and enable impact analysis of cyber attacks on service levels, it is necessary to incorporate enhanced data collectors [6]. Specifically, enhanced data processing has to be introduced at the edge of the SIEM architecture to perform multi-level data aggregation and to manage data processing in the organizational domain [6].

Two widely-used data collectors, OSSIM-Agents [1] for the Open Source Security Information Management (OSSIM) SIEM platform and Prelude-LML for the Prelude OSS SIEM system [19], collect data using transport protocols (e.g., Syslog, Snare, FTP and SNMP) and produce OSSIM and IDMEF [8] messages, respectively. Both types of collectors execute format translation tasks, but do not perform content analysis and advanced data manipulation such as aggregation, filtering, correlation, anonymization and content-based encryption. Coppolino, *et al.* [7] have demonstrated that the OSSIM SIEM system can be used to protect critical infrastructures in a non-intrusive manner (i.e., without modifying SIEM framework components). They also show how to process physical layer data on the OSSIM server. Specifically, the server is configured to analyze environmental and physical measurements to detect physical anomalies in the SCADA workflow of a dam infrastructure. The introduction of SIEM technology in a dam protection system enables a massive number of messages to be sent from data sources (measurement collection points) located in the field towards the core of the OSSIM architecture (OSSIM server).

In the area of interdependency models, researchers have adopted a variety of techniques (e.g., agent-based systems, input-output inoperability, system reliability theory, nonlinear dynamics and graph theory) to model different types of interdependency phenomena [9, 21]. Satumitra, et al. [24] have demonstrated that it is possible to distinguish between physical, social, logical, geographical and cyber interdependencies. Ghorbani, et al. [14] have presented a classification and comparison of agent-based interdependency modeling and simulation tools. The work described in this paper is based on i2Sim [16], a simulation environment that models critical infrastructure interdependencies based on resource requirements and distribution. Using specific components called production cells, i2Sim is able to model the high-level behavior of a critical infrastructure by specifying the level of input resources that the critical infrastructure needs in order to provide a certain quantity of output. i2Sim also makes it possible to model the reduction of output quantity due to a reduction of input resources or an internal failure (e.g., due to a physical or cyber event).

Although SIEM systems can be enhanced to provide a multilayer view of system events and cope with sophisticated cyber attacks against service infrastructures, they do not use infrastructure interdependency models to evaluate real-time cascading effects [11]. The approach described in this paper incorporates an infrastructure interdependency model in a SIEM system in order to evaluate how cyber attacks against wireless sensor nodes impact interdependent systems. The proposed methodology is effective in current information sharing contexts where only limited amounts of information can be exchanged between interdependent infrastructures. Theoharidou, et al. [25] discuss related work on risk and impact assessment, but they neither consider security-related risks and technologies nor information sharing constraints.

3.   Cyber Attack Impact Assessment

The proposed SIEM platform analyzes data from diverse sources and assesses the impact of cyber attacks on the services provided by interdependent critical infrastructures. The SIEM platform implements a novel level of intelligence (with respect to state-of-the-art commercial solutions), enabling a holistic view of security. The solution also supports the introduction of sophisticated detection mechanisms to discover attacks in non-IP networks (e.g., wireless sensor networks) and in the business layer. This feature is key to enhancing SIEM system intelligence and assessing the impact of attacks on critical infrastructure services.

Figure 1 shows the architecture of the enhanced SIEM platform. The platform incorporates the following main components:

- **SIEM Collector:** This component collects data from the monitored infrastructures to provide a multilayer view of system events and cross-correlate data in the proximity of the collection points. The modules responsible for data aggregation are called security probes. The security probes observe data related to specific services and detect anomalous

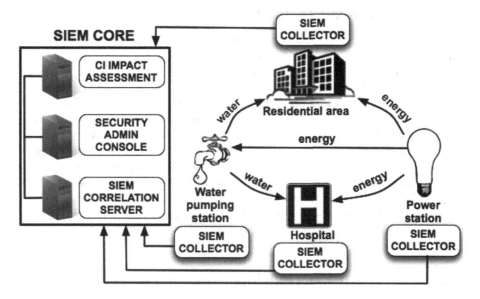

Figure 1. Enhanced SIEM platform architecture.

behavior. Information expressed in the resulting alarms is valuable for security risk assessment as well as service level impact assessment.

- **SIEM Correlation Server:** This component correlates events from security probes located in the proximity of critical infrastructure field systems. The SIEM server generates high-level alarms when cyber attacks against the monitored critical infrastructures are detected. The alarms contain a risk metric and information about the targeted assets. This information is used to assess the impact of attacks on critical infrastructure services. In this work, the SIEM correlation server is the OSSIM server.

- **Critical Infrastructure Impact Assessment:** This component assesses the impact on the services provided by interdependent critical infrastructures, some of which may be victims of cyber attacks. First, a mapping is performed between the alarms triggered by the SIEM correlation server and the operability levels provided by i2Sim. Next, an i2Sim simulation is executed to assess how the services provided by other critical infrastructures are affected by the new operability levels given the existing interdependencies. The alarms are weighted based on the relevance of the targeted assets to other critical infrastructures. The weighted alarms are sent to human experts or to decision support systems (DSSs) to identify the appropriate countermeasures.

3.1   Enhanced Collection

The SIEM collector is called the generic event translation (GET) framework [23]. It comprises modules that gather, parse, filter, anonymize, normalize, translate, aggregate and correlate low-level events (micro-events) across different layers. This workflow generates semantically-rich messages (macro-events) and dramatically reduces the volume of data generated by the sensors and directed to the SIEM server. Moreover, the GET framework confines the processing of private data within the domain boundaries of the collection points (e.g., company and organization networks). The GET framework operates as a data parser (i.e., it preprocesses data and translates content representation) and also correlates and analyzes data. A useful tool for producing pattern detectors is the State Machine Compiler [20], which facilitates the deployment of complex state machines represented as state charts. Each security probe receives messages from a subset of parsers and uses the information to provide input to the state machines.

3.2   Central Correlation

The SIEM correlation server is responsible for analyzing all the events collected by the GET framework. As shown in Figure 1, the SIEM correlation server receives data from event sources installed in the critical infrastructures (e.g., intrusion detection systems, firewalls, and servers running different operating systems) and from security probes in the GET framework.

The correlation engine is typically configured using detection patterns stored in rule databases. In order to assess the security level of the overall system, the SIEM correlation server operates in a centralized manner. By correlating events and security information, the SIEM server reduces the volume of alerts that reach the higher security event analysis layers (e.g., security administrators and, in our case, the critical infrastructure impact assessment module). Indeed, the SIEM server essentially reduces the number of false positives. For instance, consider the deployment of Linux servers and network intrusion detection systems that generate alerts due to malicious packets that target Windows Servers; the alerts are correlated with the current software characteristics (i.e., Linux operating systems) and no alarms are generated. Also, by correlating events from distributed security sources, the SIEM server can reveal malicious activities that are perpetrated in a distributed manner.

Correlation servers differ from each other in the correlation logic (logical tree, complex event processor, etc.). Their main task is to assess the risk posed by the events that occur. Outputs are reported as concise and meaningful alarms containing indicators of the risk levels reached by the events composing an attack sequence. Indicators are expressed as numerical values or qualitative indices. For instance, OSSIM SIEM uses numerical risk values in the range zero (lower risk) to ten (higher risk). Prelude OSS generates alarms with an assessment ("severity" in the IDMEF standard) expressed as *info, low, medium high* along with a flag that states if the attack was successful. In this work, risk (and severity) are important to calculate the impacts of the cyber attacks that are detected.

The impact assessment process can be described as follows:

■ Each event e is normalized by the GET framework in order to have a standard structure and appear as an information vector of the monitored activity $e(x_1, ..., x_N)$ where N is the number of fields that comprise the normalized event format.

■ The SIEM server stores all the information that can help improve the accuracy of detection by the organization that hosts the SIEM system. This information includes the real vulnerabilities that affect a targeted host (e.g., known bugs) and the relevance of the target as a company asset. This information is referred to as "context information" or simply "the context" and is expressed as a vector of the additional data $a(s_1, ..., s_m)$. It is worth noting that this information is known only to the organization in charge of the targeted asset, (e.g., a company that manages the infrastructure) because it includes very sensitive information such as hardware characteristics, IP addresses, software versions and business relevance. This information cannot be shared with other infrastructures.

■ The correlation process operates on sequences of events $(e(k))$ and additional data vectors (a). At the end of the process, alarms may be triggered if the security thresholds are exceeded. The SIEM server applies a risk assessment function R to calculate the risk associated with a sequence of events e in conjunction with the a information, i.e., $R(e, a)$.

For example, consider the implementation of risk assessment as provided by OSSIM SIEM. The OSSIM rules are called directives. When a directive is fired, the following function is applied:

$$Risk = (Priority \times Reliability \times Asset)/25 \qquad (1)$$

In OSSIM, the Priority range is zero to five, the Reliability range is zero to ten and the Asset range is zero to five. Thus, Risk ranges from zero to ten. Priority and Asset are assigned through an offline analysis of host vulnerabilities, the typology of the attack and the relevance of the targeted asset to the organization; these constitute the context vector in the model above. Reliability is computed by observing the e sequence and by summing the Reliability of each event. In OSSIM, Reliability is taken to be the probability that an attack is real, given current events observed in the system. Note that lower Risk values (e.g., zero) are not dangerous because they mean that one of the assessment parameters has very low security relevance.

3.3 Critical Infrastructure Impact Assessment

The core function of the critical infrastructure impact assessment module is provided by i2Sim, which is an event-driven, time-domain simulator that is

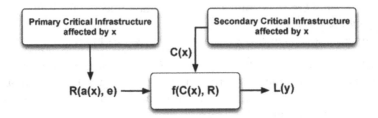

Figure 2.   Metric transformation function.

used to model infrastructure interdependencies. i2Sim uses a cell-channel approach, which provides a multi-system representation at multiple hierarchical levels (e.g., local, municipal and provincial/state) and can be used in real time to assess the effects of resource allocation decisions during disasters. In addition, i2Sim provides a dynamic simulation environment that integrates different systems in a common simulation platform [3]. i2Sim determines the output of a critical infrastructure using two measures: resource mode (RM) and physical mode (PM). RM is determined by the availability of input resources from other critical infrastructures whereas PM is determined by the internal conditions of the critical infrastructure itself (e.g., level of physical damage to a building). Therefore, the output of a critical infrastructure modeled in i2Sim is a function of the availability of input resources and its physical integrity.

3.4   Metric Transformation

In order to relate alarms resulting from SIEM analysis to physical modes of each i2Sim cell, the risk assessment value (R) is combined with the service criticality metric (C). Criticality considers the relationships between the attacked nodes (e.g., sensors and actuators) and services (e.g., electric power and water supply). The mixed holistic reductionist (MHR) approach [9, 10] is used to define service criticality. The approach considers interdependency phenomena using three-layers: (i) a holistic layer that considers the evaluation of an event within a critical infrastructure; (ii) a service layer that specifies the services delivered to end users; and (iii) a reductionist layer that models the functional interdependences among different critical infrastructures. The reductionist layer evaluates the impact on a critical infrastructure. i2Sim translates this impact to the impacts on physical resource flows between infrastructures.

Figure 2 shows the transformation function. The transformation function f is factorized and the parameters are used to adapt the OSSIM risk values to i2Sim (x is the sensor and y is the secondary critical infrastructure). There is a subtle, but substantial, difference between the concepts of context and criticality. Context embraces the relevance of an asset (e.g., sensor) to the primary infrastructure, namely the relevance of an asset to the business of the infrastructure providing a service. Criticality refers to the relevance of an

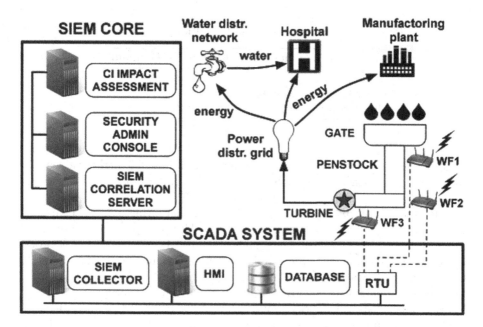

Figure 3. Sample scenario.

asset to the infrastructure that uses a service. Thus, criticality is not a unique parameter, but is strictly dependent on the infrastructure that consumes the service; it is computed by the provider based on information shared with the consumer. Indeed, criticality focuses on the need as indicated by the consumer infrastructure, which is not aware of the systems in the provider infrastructure. Given the information supplied by the consumer, the provider calculates a criticality value for each asset that is involved.

4. Example Scenario

The example scenario uses an attack on wireless sensor network nodes to demonstrate how the enhanced SIEM system can help evaluate the impact of an attack on infrastructure services. Figure 3 shows the scenario involving a dam that feeds a hydroelectric power station, which feeds a power distribution substation through a transmission network (not modeled for simplicity). Arrows in the figure indicate functional dependencies between critical infrastructures.

The dam provides water to the hydroelectric power station through a gate that is remotely controlled to release basin water and activate the power plant turbine. The dam and hydroelectric power station are controlled by a SCADA system that utilizes a wireless sensor network. Water fed to the hydroelectric power station is conveyed through pipes called penstocks. It is important to guarantee that the water flow values in the penstocks are within the operational

Table 1. Electricity demands of the critical infrastructures.

Critical Infrastructure	Electricity Demand
Hospital	13.47 MW
Water Distribution Station	52.5 MW
Manufacturing Plant	9.47 MW

range. Lower values can result in low power generation while higher values can lead to excessive turbine rotational speed and turbine vibration, which can result in physical damage to the infrastructure [15].

A hospital, water distribution station and manufacturing plant receive electricity from the power distribution substation. All the dependencies are modeled using i2Sim. A cyber attack is launched against the wireless sensor network that monitors the dam; the objective is to measure the impact on the operability level of the hospital, which requires electricity and water. Table 1 shows the electrical demands of the critical infrastructures in the scenario.

The wireless sensor network enables the SCADA system to monitor physical parameters. Four types of sensors are used: (i) three water flow sensors placed in the penstocks (WF1, WF2, WF3); (ii) two water level sensors that monitor erosion and piping phenomena under the dam wall (WL1 and WL2); (iii) a tilt sensor placed on the dam gate to measure the gate opening level (inclination); and (iv) a vibration sensor placed on the turbine. The sensors, which correspond to nodes in the wireless sensor network, send their measurements at regular intervals to the wireless sensor network base station (BS). The base station acts as wireless remote terminal unit (RTU) that forwards measurements to the remote SCADA server. Opening commands are issued by the remote SCADA facility to the gate actuator. The information and communications technology components deployed include a network-based intrusion detection system (N-IDS) installed in the remote SCADA server facility, a host-based intrusion detection system (H-IDS) positioned in the dam facility and a SIEM platform with a correlation engine located in a remote office. Figure 4 shows the results of applying the MHR approach, which models the services and equipment that are relevant to the critical infrastructure impact assessment module of the SIEM platform.

4.1   i2Sim Model

The i2Sim model provides a high-level abstraction of the physical components. In the i2Sim ontology, physical infrastructure entities are modeled as cells connected through channels that transport resources (e.g., electricity and water). The implemented model includes five cells that are used to represent the dependent infrastructures: hydroelectric power station, power distribution substation, water distribution station, manufacturing plant and hospital. The hydroelectric power station cell represents both the dam and the turbine. Alarms

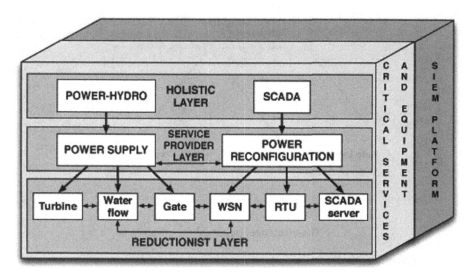

Figure 4. MHR model of the example scenario.

generated by the SIEM correlator are mapped to physical modes of the considered critical infrastructures. Changes to the physical modes of i2Sim result in changes to the RMs of the affected cells that measure their operability levels.

4.2 Attack Execution and Identification

The scenario considers an attack targeting the wireless sensor network nodes that involves several steps. At the end of the attack, the physical measurements collected by the wireless sensor network nodes are altered to induce incorrect situational awareness about the SCADA system. The SIEM framework detects this complex attack by correlating security events generated by the security tools installed in the dam facility, specifically the intrusion detection systems and GET security probes.

The assumption is that the attacker is a dam employee who can physically access wireless sensor network zones and connect to the network that hosts the SCADA server. The attacker has limited administrator rights and is not responsible for the cyber security of deployed systems (e.g., not responsible for security configuration policies and does not know the credentials needed to change the configuration or the cryptographic keys used for wireless sensor network communications).

The attack is performed in two phases. In the first phase, the attacker steals the wireless sensor network cryptographic key (e.g., via a side-channel attack as described in [12]). In the second phase, the attacker targets the SCADA server since he can access a host that monitors the dam (e.g., a human-machine interface (HMI) or engineering station). The attacker exploits a SCADA server

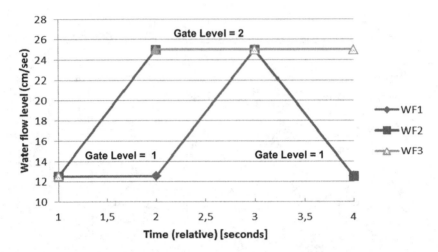

Figure 5.   Water flow measurements forged by a malicious sensor.

vulnerability via malware that is installed by inserting a USB device into a SCADA network machine (as in the case of the Stuxnet worm [13]).

After the SCADA server is compromised, the attacker connects to the wireless sensor network RTU host. Having gained access to the wireless sensor network master node, the attacker reprograms the wireless sensor network nodes (e.g., via over-the-air programming). The new program is configured with the cryptographic key obtained during the previous phase. The new malicious code executes the routing protocol by altering the data forwarded from the water flow sensors to the master RTU. Water flow measurement data is altered in order to exceed the control threshold by adding a constant offset to the measured values. In this way, the gate is forced to limit water release and ultimately cause low turbine rotation. The final effect of the attack is a reduction in the electricity supplied to the power grid.

In order to detect the attack, we consider events generated by the security probes that oversee the wireless sensors. These security probes detect physical inconsistencies in the sensor data and generate alarms that are processed by the SIEM server: seepage channel sensors should report similar values of water levels; water flow sensors should measure values in the same range; and the gate opening sensor should report a value that is consistent with the water flow in the penstocks. The security probes aggregate the sensor data and verify their consistency.

Figure 5 shows the trends in the wireless sensor network data collected by the security probes (measurements). The SCADA server regulates the gate opening level (level 1 is low and level 2 is medium) based on the average water flow level provided by the three sensors. When the gate opening is at level 2, the water flow level is 12.5 cm/sec. The attack compromises the sensors so that they indicate a water flow level of 25.0 cm/sec. This causes the SCADA system to set the gate opening to level 1 to reduce the water flow below the

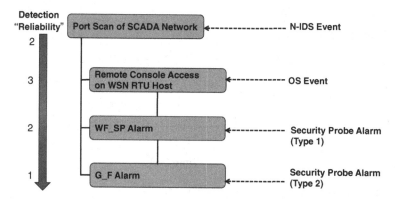

Figure 6. OSSIM rule.

control threshold. The result of the attack is that the gate opening moves to level 1 although measurements indicate that the gate opening is at level 2 (last measurements in the sequence in Figure 5).

The anomaly is revealed by two security probes: the first (WF_SP) reveals an inconsistency in the water flows and the second (G_F) reveals a gate opening level inconsistency for all three sensors. Note that another security probe that monitors the water level in the seepage does not show any inconsistency for WL1 and WL2. The alarms from the security probes are correlated by the SIEM platform according to the rule shown in Figure 6. The rule takes into account the two events from the H-IDS and N-IDS due to the worm activities and access to the wireless sensor network RTU host. The final alarm generated by the SIEM server contains evidence that the wireless sensors exhibit anomalies. In particular, the security probes indicate that WFx in the Penstock1 zone exhibits anomalous conditions. Such parameters, despite being irrelevant to the rule, are crucial to understand the impact of the attack (i.e., reduction in the power supplied by the hydroelectric power station). The parameters are used by i2Sim to evaluate the impact of the attack. In the rule, the Priority is highest (5), Reliability is 8 (sum of single event reliabilities) and Asset has the highest value (5). Thus, the Risk is $(5 \times 8 \times 5)/25 = 8$. This value must be associated with the service criticality of the wireless sensors with respect to the power production service in the critical infrastructure impact assessment module.

4.3 Critical Infrastructure Impact Assessment

Using the MHR approach, services and equipment that exhibit high event criticality can be identified. The graph in Figure 7 shows the estimated rate of treated patients depending on the hospital operability level following the cyber attack on the water flow sensors. As far the scenario is concerned, the flow sensors placed at different points in the penstocks (WF1, WF2 and WF3) exhibit high service criticality because, if attacked, they may alter the water

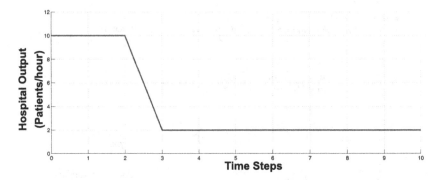

Figure 7.   i2Sim results.

flow measurements and lead to low or over energy production, thus impacting the dependent critical infrastructures.

In this scenario, the Risk (R) of the attack is 8 while the event criticality (C) is in the range 0 to 0.5 (0 is not critical and 0.5 is highly critical). Given that the energy production is affected by the wireless sensor network measurements by a factor of 0.5, the resulting impact is PM = $R \times C = 8 \times 0.5 = 4$. The physical mode (PM) value is the physical mode in i2Sim where a value of one corresponds to fully operational and a value of five corresponds to not operational. Specifically, PM = 4 indicates that the cyber attack moves the physical mode functionality down to its lowest energy production level. The 0.5 factor was chosen because the wireless sensor network affects the total productivity of the power plant. Figure 7 shows a scenario where a cyber attack against the water flow sensors is detected. Due to the existing interdependency phenomena, the cyber attack degrades the operability level of the hospital.

5.   Conclusions

The next-generation SIEM platform described in this paper is designed to support the real-time impact assessment of cyber attacks that affect interdependent critical infrastructures. The platform can detect cyber attacks against wireless sensor network nodes and can conduct real-time assessments of the impact of the attacks on the services provided by the wireless sensor nodes as well as the potential cascading effects involving other critical infrastructures. As demonstrated in the scenario, the i2Sim tool can be used to model the physical layer and services of an interdependent system (i.e., a dam and hydroelectric power plant) in order to analyze the impact of service degradation. The scenario helps understand how the interdependent system reacts to an attack that impacts water flow from the dam. The resulting functioning levels of the hydroelectric power plant and the effects on other critical infrastructures can be provided as inputs to an operator dashboard to help make decisions about appropriate mitigation strategies. Our future research will continue this line of inquiry, in particular, validating the approach and the SIEM platform using a realistic testbed that incorporates a dam equipped with sensors and actuators.

Acknowledgement

This research was supported by the Seventh Framework Programme of the European Commission (FP7/2007-2013) under Grant Agreement No. 313034 (Situation Aware Security Operations Center (SAWSOC) Project). The research was also supported by the TENACE PRIN Project (No. 20103P34XC) funded by the Italian Ministry of Education, University and Research.

References

[1] AlienVault, OSSIM Sensor (`www.alienvault.com/wiki/doku.php?id= documentation:agent`).

[2] C. Alcaraz and J. Lopez, A security analysis for wireless sensor mesh networks in highly critical systems, *IEEE Transactions on Systems, Man and Cybernetics, Part C: Applications and Reviews*, vol. 40(4), pp. 419–428, 2010.

[3] A. Alsubaie, A. Di Pietro, J. Marti, P. Kini, T. Lin, S. Palmieri and A. Tofani, A platform for disaster response planning with interdependency simulation functionality, in *Critical Infrastructure Protection VII*, J. Butts and S. Shenoi (Eds.), Heidelberg, Germany, pp. 183–197, 2013.

[4] X. Bai, X. Meng, Z. Du, M. Gong and Z. Hu, Design of wireless sensor network in SCADA system for wind power plant, *Proceedings of the IEEE International Conference on Automation and Logistics*, pp. 3023–3027, 2008.

[5] P. Baronti, P. Pillai, V. Chook, S. Chessa, A. Gotta and Y. Hu, Wireless sensor networks: A survey on the state of the art and the 802.15.4 and ZigBee standards, *Computer Communications*, vol. 30(7), pp. 1655–1695, 2007.

[6] L. Coppolino, S. D'Antonio, V. Formicola and L. Romano, Enhancing SIEM technology to protect critical infrastructures, *Proceedings of the Seventh International Workshop on Critical Information Infrastructure Security*, pp. 10–21, 2010.

[7] L. Coppolino, S. D'Antonio, V. Formicola and L. Romano, Integration of a system for critical infrastructure protection with the OSSIM SIEM platform: A dam case study, *Proceedings of the Thirtieth International Conference on Computer Safety, Reliability and Security*, pp. 199–212, 2011.

[8] H. Debar, D. Curry and B. Feinstein, The Intrusion Detection Message Exchange Format (IDMEF), RFC 4765, 2007.

[9] S. De Porcellinis, S. Panzieri and R. Setola, Modeling critical infrastructure via a mixed holistic reductionistic approach, *International Journal of Critical Infrastructures*, vol. 5(1/2), pp. 86–99, 2009.

[10] A. Di Pietro, C. Foglietta, S. Palmieri and S. Panzieri, Assessing the impact of cyber attacks on interdependent physical systems, in *Critical Infrastructure Protection VII*, J. Butts and S. Shenoi (Eds.), Heidelberg, Germany, pp. 215–227, 2013.

[11] A. Di Pietro and S. Panzieri, Taxonomy of SCADA systems security testbeds, to appear in *International Journal of Critical Infrastructures*.

[12] Z. Dyka and P. Langendorfer, Improving the security of wireless sensor networks by protecting the sensor nodes against side channel attacks, in *Wireless Networks and Security*, S. Khan and A. Pathan (Eds.), Springer-Verlag, Berlin Heidelberg, Germany, pp. 303–328, 2013.

[13] N. Falliere, L. O'Murchu and E. Chien, W32.Stuxnet Dossier, Version 1.4, Symantec, Mountain View, California, 2011.

[14] A. Ghorbani and E. Bagheri, The state of the art in critical infrastructure protection: A framework for convergence, *International Journal of Critical Infrastructures*, vol. 4(3), pp. 215–244, 2008.

[15] J. Hasler, Investigating Russia's biggest dam explosion: What went wrong, *Popular Mechanics* (`www.popularmechanics.com/technology/en gineering/gonzo/4344681`), February 2, 2010.

[16] J. Marti, Multisystem simulation: Analysis of critical infrastructures for disaster response, in *Networks of Networks: The Last Frontier of Complexity*, G. D'Agostino and A. Scala (Eds.), Springer International Publishing, Cham, Switzerland, pp. 255–277, 2014.

[17] D. Martins and H. Guyennet, Wireless sensor network attacks and security mechanisms: A short survey, *Proceedings of the Thirteenth International Conference on Network-Based Systems*, pp. 313–320, 2010.

[18] K. Poulsen, Slammer worm crashed Ohio nuke plant network, *Security Focus* (`www.securityfocus.com/news/6767`), August 19, 2003.

[19] Prelude-IDS, Prelude LML (`www.prelude-ids.org/wiki/prelude/Pre ludeLml`), 2013.

[20] C. Rapp, Home of SMC: The State Machine Compiler (`smc.sourceforge. net`), 2013.

[21] S. Rinaldi, J. Peerenboom and T. Kelly, Identifying, understanding and analyzing critical infrastructure interdependencies, *IEEE Control Systems*, vol. 21(6), pp. 11–25, 2001.

[22] R. Roman, C. Alcaraz and J. Lopez, The role of wireless sensor networks in the area of critical information infrastructure protection, *Information Security Technical Report*, vol. 12(1), pp. 24–31, 2007.

[23] L. Romano, S. D'Antonio, V. Formicola and L. Coppolino, Protecting the WSN zones of a critical infrastructure via enhanced SIEM technology, *Proceedings of the Thirty-First International Conference on Computer Safety, Reliability and Security*, pp. 222–234, 2012.

[24] G. Satumitra and L. Duenas-Osorio, Synthesis of modeling and simulation methods in critical infrastructure interdependencies research, in *Sustainable and Resilient Critical Infrastructure Systems*, K. Gopalakrishnan and S. Peeta (Eds.), Springer-Verlag, Berlin Heidelberg, Germany, pp. 1–51, 2010.

[25] M. Theoharidou, P. Kotzanikolaou and D. Gritzalis, A multi-layer criticality assessment methodology based on interdependencies, *Computers and Security*, vol. 29(6), pp. 643–658, 2010.

Chapter 15

ASSESSING POTENTIAL CASUALTIES IN CRITICAL EVENTS

Simona Cavallini, Fabio Bisogni, Marco Bardoscia, and Roberto Bellotti

Abstract   This paper describes an approach for assessing potential casualties due to events that adversely impact critical infrastructure sectors. The approach employs the consequence calculation model (CMM) to integrate quantitative data and qualitative information in evaluating the socio-economic impacts of sector failures. This is important because a critical event that affects social and economic activities may also cause injuries and fatalities. Upon engaging a structured method for gathering information about potential casualties, the consequence calculation model may be applied to failure trees constructed using various approaches. The analysis of failure trees enables decision makers to implement effective strategies for reducing casualties due to critical events.

Keywords: Cascading effects, consequence calculation, casualties, failure trees

1.   Introduction

The European Commission Directive 2008/114/EC of 2008 [5] defines a critical infrastructure as "an asset, system or part thereof located in [m]ember [s]tates which is essential for the maintenance of vital societal functions, health, safety, security, economic or social well-being of people, and the disruption or destruction of which would have a significant impact in a [m]ember [s]tate as a result of the failure to maintain those functions." The directive clarifies a European critical infrastructure as one that is located in a European Union (EU) member state whose destruction or malfunction would have a significant impact in at least two EU member states. The significance of the impact should be assessed in terms of cross-cutting criteria, including the effects of cross-sector dependencies involving other infrastructures.

According to Article 3 of Directive 2008/114/EC [5], the identification process of each member state should be based on the following cross-cutting criteria:

J. Butts and S. Shenoi (Eds.): Critical Infrastructure Protection VIII, IFIP AICT 441, pp. 231–242, 2014.

- **Casualties Criterion:** Assessed in terms of the potential numbers of fatalities and injuries.

- **Economic Effects Criterion:** Assessed in terms of the significance of economic loss and/or degradation of products and services, including potential environmental effects.

- **Public Effects Criterion:** Assessed in terms of the impact on public confidence, physical suffering and disruption of daily life, including the loss of essential services.

To define and identify critical infrastructures at the national level, each EU member state has adopted a perspective that can be related to one of the following approaches [2]: (i) service-oriented approach, in which the key elements are vital services and/or essential societal functions; (ii) asset-oriented approach, in which the key elements are impact and/or risk assessment; and (iii) operator-oriented approach, in which the key elements are public/private organizations that manage/own infrastructures because of their decision-making role.

A sector-based approach may be considered close to an operator-oriented approach when, in a given area, the number of operators is limited (i.e., natural oligopoly or monopoly) and/or the opportunity to replace their services is difficult in the short term. In this perspective, a critical infrastructure corresponds to key elements of a productive sector at the national level, where the sectors must be identified using official statistical classifications such as NACE in the EU context.

The malfunction or destruction of an infrastructure, especially due to an unexpected event, affects social and economic activities. The relevance of critical infrastructure failures is, in general, not only due to their direct role in socio-economic activities, but also because of their interconnections. Tight interconnections among critical infrastructures and the cascading effects that can occur in the case of failures of one or more infrastructures have been extensively investigated at the theoretical [1, 4] and empirical levels [12]. In both cases, strong connections have been identified in certain sectors that can cause cascading effects in specific cases.

With regard to preventive actions and crisis management, civil protection authorities and first responders would benefit from a preliminary assessment of potential damage caused by accidental or intentional failures of socio-economic sectors. According to an intervention perspective related to the emergency roles of civil protection personnel and first responders, the focus is on evaluating the impacts, especially casualties, in the time frame starting from the end of the direct effect of the event of interest.

This paper describes the consequence calculation model (CCM), which integrates quantitative data and qualitative information in order to evaluate the socio-economic impacts of sector failures. The model has been developed by the FORMIT team and applied in the DOMINO Project [10]. The concrete application of the model provides indications of priorities of intervention in

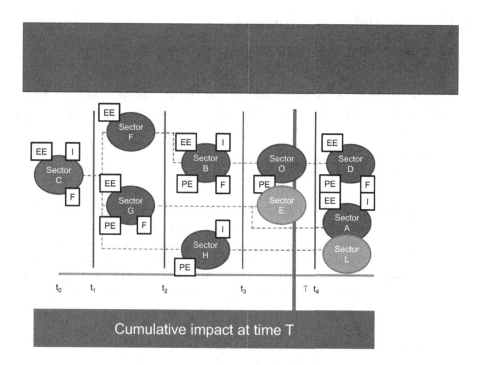

Figure 1. Failure tree reporting effects by sector.

different sectors in order to contain the potential consequences to the extent possible.

2. Consequence Calculation Model

The primary goal of the consequence calculation model is to evaluate the effects of failures of socio-economic sectors, including critical infrastructures. The main inputs to the model are time series of the operativity levels of the sectors of interest. The main outputs are time series of the potential impacts in terms of casualties (injured and fatalities), economic effects and public effects due to failures of the affected sectors. The effect of each sector failure at a certain time instant is summarized by an indicator per impact.

In order to assess the impacts (i.e., casualties, economic effects and public effects) of an unexpected event that affects a country (as in the DOMINO Project), the output of the consequence calculation model can be represented using a failure tree for each of the potential impacts (casualties, economic effects and public effects) that captures the dependencies existing among the impacted sectors. In a failure tree, the sectors affected by a critical event and the sectors affected by disruptions of other sectors are represented by considering the time dimension. Figure 1 shows a failure tree that reports the economic effects (EE), public effects (PE), injuries (I) and fatalities (F) by sector.

2.1   Model Assumptions

The proposed model for computing the consequences of a disruption of each sector relies on the following assumptions:

- **Independence of Sector Impacts from Disruption Causes (A1):** The estimated impacts, in terms of economic effects, public effects and casualties, due to the disruption of the ith sector are not affected by disruptions of other sectors that occur before or after the disruption of the ith sector. The cause of the failure of the "first" sector does not affect the operativity levels of the other sectors.

- **Time Homogeneity (A2):** The estimated impacts are not affected by their absolute time positions in a failure tree. In other words, the sequences of affected sectors shown in failure trees are used as time-invariant information by the consequence calculation model. The total consequences at time t of the entire failure tree is defined as the sum of the individual impacts generated by the disrupted sectors (see Figure 1 for the effects by sector).

- **Lower/Upper Bounded Operativity Levels (A3):** The operativity level x_i of each sector ranges from zero to one. A value of zero corresponds to the total disruption of the sector, while a value of one corresponds to full (normal) operativity of the sector. The consequence calculation model is constructed to work with discrete operativity levels (i.e., $x_i \in \{0, 1\}$) as well as continuous operativity levels (i.e., $x_i \in [0, 1]$).

Note that, according to Assumption A1, the impacts of the affected sectors are independent, while the disruption of one sector is strictly related to the disruption of one or more other sectors.

2.2   Model Hypotheses

The computation of the three indicators of the model relies on the three preceding assumptions and three hypotheses.

The first hypothesis (H1) is that, when a sector fails, its recovery is no longer possible. As a consequence, the effects of a sector disruption and of the consequent failure tree may proceed indefinitely.

The second hypothesis (H2) is that the disruption of a specific sector can occur only once. For example, if the disruption of Sector A could be caused by both Sector B and Sector C, and if, in the failure tree, the disruption of Sector C occurs before the disruption of Sector B, then Sector A fails because of Sector C, but not because of Sector B.

The third hypothesis (H3) is that an outage occurring to a sector cannot be partial, but only complete at least for the first time period. This implies that the operativity levels are discrete.

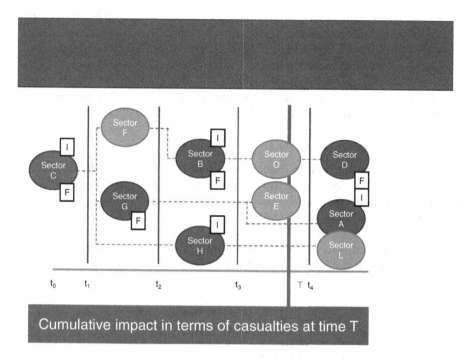

Figure 2. Failure tree reporting eventual effects in terms of casualties by sector.

3. Calculating Potential Impacts

The aforementioned European Commission directive [6] defines casualties (C) in terms of injured persons (I) and fatalities (F). In addition, the non-binding guidelines for the application of the directive specify that:

- A casualty is either an injured person or a fatality.

- An injured person is defined as a person who requires more than 24 hours of hospitalization.

- There is no limit on the maximum time following an event that causes the disruption or destruction of an infrastructure during which fatalities should occur.

The potential impacts in terms of casualties are computed in the consequence calculation model according to the metrics suggested by the European Commission directive [6]. According to the assumptions listed above, the estimated impacts in terms of casualties (C) (injured persons and fatalities) due to the disruption of one sector are not affected by disruptions of other sectors (occurring before or after) (Assumption A1) and by the absolute time position in the potential failure tree (Assumption A2) (Figure 2).

In the case of a critical event, the indicators of the total impacts in terms of injured persons $I(t)$ and fatalities $F(t)$ at time t for the entire failure tree are computed as the sum of the injured persons and the sum of the fatalities occurring in all the affected sectors. Without any loss of generality, the model for assessing the impact in terms of injured persons and fatalities can be described, in general, as casualties and applied to the two cases. Given n sectors, only m_c of the sectors ($m_c \leq n$) suffer effects in terms of casualties. In the proposed model, the casualties caused by the disruption of the jth sector at time t are linked to the operativity levels according to the equation:

$$C_j(t) = \alpha_j \Theta[\theta_j - x_j(t)] \tag{1}$$

where $C_j(t)$ is the number of casualties induced at time t by the disruption of the jth sector; α_j is a positive real parameter that represents the average number of casualties induced by the complete disruption of the jth sector per unit of time (α_j takes different values for injured persons and fatalities); θ_j is a real parameter that can be interpreted as an operativity threshold of the jth sector ranging from zero to one; $x_j(t)$ is the operativity level of the jth sector at time t ranging from zero to one; and Θ is the step function:

$$\Theta[\theta_j - x_j(t)] = \begin{cases} 1, & \text{if } x_j(t) < \theta_j \\ 0, & \text{otherwise} \end{cases}$$

Equation (1), which gives the casualties caused by a disruption of the jth sector at time t, includes a threshold mechanism: the operativity level of the jth sector at time t must fall below the threshold θ_j to contribute to the casualties by an amount α_j at time t. The total casualties at time t, denoted by $y_j(t)$, is the sum over all the sectors that potentially suffer effects in terms of casualties (Assumption A1):

$$y(t) = \sum_j \alpha_j \Theta[\theta_j - x_j(t)]. \tag{2}$$

Equation (2) implies that the outage of the jth sector has an instantaneous effect (at the same instant of time) on the casualties. This is relaxed by introducing a delay time $\bar{t}_j$ for the jth sector and modifying the equation accordingly:

$$y(t + \bar{t}_j) = \sum_j \alpha_j \Theta[\theta_j - x_j(t)]. \tag{3}$$

Thus, the operativity level of the jth sector at time t influences the casualties at time $t + \bar{t}_j$. To this point, the additional hypotheses have not come into play. In the case that the operativity levels do not take values in the real interval $[0, 1]$, but only take discrete values of 0 or 1 (Hypothesis H3), the parameter θ_j has no meaning. In fact, it is perfectly reasonable for a completely functional sector not to have any effect on the casualties, while a completely non-functional sector must have some effect on the casualties. In this case, Equation (3) reduces to:

$$y(t + \bar{t}_j) = \sum_j \alpha_j [1 - x_j(t)]. \tag{4}$$

If the interest is only in the cumulative casualties $Y(T)$, then the integral of the casualties up to the final instant of time T must be computed:

$$Y(T) = \int_0^T y(t)dt. \tag{5}$$

Time delays do not play any role. Indeed, it can be shown that the integrals over time of the terms in Equation (5) are left unchanged by a time translation. Analogously, it is possible to define the cumulative casualties up to time t as:

$$Y(t) = \int_0^t y(t)dt. \tag{6}$$

However, in this case, the time delays can play an important role.

4. Information Collection

Several academic and empirical works have attempted to assess casualties due to critical events. For example, Cavalieri, *et al.* [3] evaluate the number of casualties (injuries and fatalities) based on the number of displaced people in the case of an earthquake or damage to infrastructure systems. Hirsch [7] assesses casualties due to critical events based on health care system response.

Casualty assessment in the consequence calculation model employs a general approach. Four pieces of information are needed to validate the model with discrete operativity level values (Hypothesis H3): (i) sectors that potentially cause casualties (m_c); (ii) average number of casualties induced by the complete disruption of the jth sector per unit of time (α_j); (iii) delay time of the jth sector ($\bar{t}_j$); and (iv) number of casualties induced at time t by the complete disruption of the jth sector (for validation purposes) ($C_j(t)$).

Casualty information needed by the consequence calculation model for an Italian case study was collected from four data sources (DS1–DS4):

- **DS1:** A pilot survey involving nearly 200 sector experts that collected information pertaining to the identification of sector components and the assessment of potential impacts due to sector failures.

- **DS2:** A questionnaire submitted to one expert from each sector that potentially suffers casualties. The information helped refine the assessment of the potential casualties occurring as a result of sector failures.

- **DS3:** Public databases maintained by the Italian National Institute for Statistics (ISTAT) [8].

- **DS4:** Desk research.

4.1   Limitations of Information Collection

Information collected by the pilot survey (DS1) was compared with that in the reference database (DS3) and analysis was conducted using real-world data. The pilot survey (DS1) was used to identify the m_c sectors to be investigated, while the desk research (DS4) enabled the analysis of casualty information (i.e., α_j and $C_j(t)$) pertaining to real-world critical events.

With regard to the assumptions and hypotheses, it is important to emphasize that the estimated effects have to be considered as the maximum potential impact affecting the area of interest. Detailed information provided by experts (DS2) was the primary source for estimating the maximum potential number of injured persons and the maximum potential number of fatalities caused by the complete failure (100% loss of service) of a sector.

Estimating the model parameters involves several considerations. The reason is that a portion of the casualties in a disaster occur as a consequence of outages of critical infrastructures in specific sectors and another portion occur as immediate and direct consequences of the disaster itself (e.g. injuries caused by the collapse of a building during an earthquake).

Another obstacle is the unstructured manner in which information is collected, especially in the case of critical events. In the vast majority of cases, only heterogeneous data is available. For example, official data about the L'Aquila earthquake on April 6, 2009 only provides the total number of deaths (298) and injured (1,500) [11] without any details about their causes.

After selecting the subset of sectors in which an outage might produce casualties, efforts were focused on retrieving information about these sectors from widely-accessible sources (non-specialized press articles, websites, etc). Deep scanning of several types of information sources for unexpected critical events (e.g., peer reviewed articles, newspapers and gray literature) (DS4) did not provide useful indications about the distributions of injured persons and fatalities over time.

Official statistics, such as those disseminated by the Italian National Institute of Statistics [9], provide information on the numbers of injured persons and fatalities by cause, but the majority of them (about 85%) are related to health problems. The remaining 15% include four main causes – accidents, suicides, homicides and undetermined events – a classification that is not appropriate for investigating the consequences of critical events.

4.2   Limitations due to Data Requirements

Information related to the total number of casualties for a critical event is difficult to adapt with respect to the assumption of independence of sector impacts and disruption causes (Assumption A1) and time homogeneity (Assumption A2). The challenge is related to the fact that the idiosyncratic nature of an event (e.g., earthquake or terrorist bombing) causes an unpredictable number of casualties that cannot be reduced in the time frame of the event. Because of the intervention perspective of civil protection personnel and first responders, the main interest is in evaluating the number of casualties caused in the time frame starting right after the end of the direct effects of an event. This perspective is considered in the concrete application of the consequence calculation model, which seeks to provide indications of intervention priorities in different sectors in order to contain the potential consequences. For example, in the case of the L'Aquila earthquake, analysis of the data using the consequence calculation model should discriminate between casualties (injured persons and fatalities) directly caused by the event and the casualties caused by consequent failures of infrastructures in the affected area.

Another challenge arises because, in the consequence calculation model, each sector is supposed to have a deterministic impact in case of a total failure regardless of the timing of the failure (Assumption A2). For example, in the case of the L'Aquila earthquake, data on casualties caused by consequent failures of infrastructures in the affected area were not collected with respect to detailed time frames (e.g., casualties due to the electricity sector outage after one hour, one day or one week).

5.   Direct Collection Approach

The lack of useful structural data from official statistics and information on casualties forced the use of a direct data collection approach for some sectors. In addition, a direct data collection approach was necessary because of the assumption that the numbers of injured persons and fatalities follow the same distributions over time, but with sector-specific parameters.

Direct data collection involved the following steps:

- **Step 1:** Identification of the subset of sectors with potential casualties. For example, these are sectors for which experts questioned in the pilot survey (DS1) answered "Yes" to the question: "According to your opinion/experience, do you believe that a complete service outage of the sector may directly cause fatalities/injuries?" and provided an answer to: "If yes, please quantify the number of casualties as a function of the service outage time (e.g., nothing until two hours, from one to five until 18 hours, and from six to ten until two days)."

- **Step 2:** Second round of interviews with the experts for the selected sectors. The experts were given an *ad hoc* questionnaire (Questionnaire for impact evaluation in terms of casualties in the event of sector failures) (DS2).

- **Step 3:** Final identification of the sectors to be considered.

Step 1 yields the sectors that cause casualties. In theory, a total disruption of any sector would cause casualties in the long term. The sectors that cause casualties are those that have higher probabilities of generating injuries and fatalities in the short term. The selection of sectors was made on the basis of information provided by experts in the pilot survey and a "reasonability

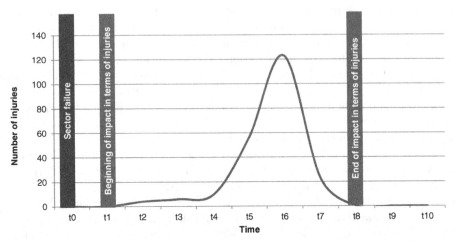

Figure 3. Occurrence of injured persons after a total failure of Sector A.

assessment" made by the research team. A preliminary cut was made of the sectors that might be directly responsible for the occurrence of casualties.

The key element of Step 2 was the interviews of sector experts (DS2). General considerations regarding the propensity of a sector to generate casualties in the short term due to a complete and prolonged outage came with detailed information on the impacts along the time dimension. In particular, the Italian sector experts were asked to provide indications to help construct casualty curves of injured persons and fatalities (Figure 3). The casualty curves can help overcome the limitations of Hypothesis H1 by adding a time after which no more impacts occur. Note that the non-recovery of a sector implies the indefinite generation of new casualties.

The key information provided by the experts for their sectors of reference included:

- The instant of time when the effects start and the instant of time when the effects end with respect to the instant of time when the failure occurs.

- The average percentage of casualties in the total population of interest per time unit.

The two parameters α_j and $t + \bar{t}_j$ in the consequence calculation model were estimated using input from experts. The interviews with experts constituted the final criterion to determine the subset of sectors that potentially suffer effects in terms of casualties. A reduced list of sectors for which the casualty effects can be computed was specified based on the availability of data and the possibility of estimating the parameters needed to generate and propagate the casualties that occur during complete sector failures.

6.   Conclusions

Consolidated approaches are required to assess the consequences of critical events, especially the casualties that potentially occur when critical infrastructures are disrupted, damaged or destroyed. The consequence calculation model is readily applied to any structured classification of socio-economic activities with a predefined geographical scope. The model relies on the definition of sectors of economic activity as identified in official statistical classifications (e.g., NACE for the European context), but it can also be implemented by classifying socio-economic activities in any coherent manner. Moreover, the consequence calculation model can be applied to assess the effects of critical events regardless of the approach used to represent interdependencies (e.g., input-output relationships and direct recognition).

The application of the consequence calculation model in the Italian context proved to be a challenging task. Due to the paucity of publicly-available data, it was necessary to solicit information from sector experts to apply the model and validate the results. Nevertheless, the model and its failure trees are invaluable to operators and strategic decision makers.

Future research will focus on alleviating the limitations induced by the assumptions and hypotheses, thereby providing civil protection personnel and first responders with an effective planning instrument for analyzing potential casualties. Extending the scope to additional countries is another important research topic – it will help tune the model and enhance strategies for reducing event consequences, especially casualties, that directly affect populations.

Acknowledgement

This research was initiated under Project DOMINO, which was supported by the Prevention, Preparedness and Consequence Management of Terrorism and Other Security Related Risks Programme launched by the Directorate-General Home Affairs of the European Commission. Project DOMINO research was conducted by the Ugo Bordoni Foundation (Italy), FORMIT Foundation (Italy) and Theorematica (Italy) with the support of the Presidency of the Council of Ministries (Italy), Home Office (United Kingdom), SGDN (France) and Ministry of Emergency Situations (Bulgaria).

References

[1] F. Bisogni and S. Cavallini, Assessing the economic loss and social impact of information system breakdowns, in *Critical Infrastructure Protection IV*, T. Moore and S. Shenoi (Eds.), Springer, Heidelberg, Germany, pp. 185–198, 2010.

[2] F. Bisogni, S. Cavallini, L. Franchina and G. Saja, The European perspective of telecommunications as a critical infrastructure, in *Critical Infrastructure Protection VI*, J. Butts and S. Shenoi (Eds.), Springer, Heidelberg, Germany, pp. 3–15, 2012.

[3] F. Cavalieri, P. Franchin, P. Gehl and B. Khazai, Quantitative assessment and social losses based on physical damage and infrastructural systems, *Earthquake Engineering and Structural Dynamics*, vol. 41(11), pp. 1569–1589, 2012.

[4] S. Cavallini, S. Di Trocchio, F. Bisogni, M. Tancioni and P. Trucco, Study for the Development of a Methodology and Research of Quantitative Data on the Economics of Security and Resilience in Critical Communications and Information Infrastructures (CIIS) – SMART-SEC, Final Report of the Project Supported by the DG Information Society and Media of the European Commission, FORMIT Foundation, Rome, Italy, 2010.

[5] European Commission, Council Directive 2008/114/EC of 8 December 2008 on the Identification and Designation of European Critical Infrastructures and the Assessment of the Need to Improve their Protection, Brussels, Belgium, 2008.

[6] European Commission, Non-Binding Guidelines for the Application of the Directive on the Identification and Designation of European Critical Infrastructures and the Assessment of the Need to Improve their Protection, Brussels, Belgium, 2008.

[7] G. Hirsch, Modeling the consequences of major incidents for health care systems, presented at the *Twenty-Second International Conference of the System Dynamics Society*, 2004.

[8] Italian National Institute of Statistics, About the Italian National Institute of Statistics, Rome, Italy (www.istat.it/en/about-istat).

[9] Italian National Institute of Statistics, Cause di morte, Rome, Italy (www.istat.it/it/archivio/58063), 2009.

[10] D. Perucchini, M. Porcelli, F. Roberti, D. Stasi, S. Trigila, A. Usai, S. Cavallini, F. Bisogni, R. Bellotti, M. Vichi, M. Bardoscia, R. Zollo and A. Battaglia, Domino Effects Modeling Infrastructure Collapse – DOMINO, Final Report of the Project Supported by the DG Home Affairs of the European Commission, FORMIT Foundation, Rome, Italy, 2012.

[11] Protezione Civile, Guido Bertolaso in audizione alla Commissione Ambiente del Senato, Rome, Italy, 2009.

[12] M. van Eeten, A. Nieuwenhuijs, E. Luiijf, M. Klaver and E. Cruz, The state and the threat of cascading failure across critical infrastructures: The implications of empirical evidence from media incident reports, *Public Administration*, vol. 89(2), pp. 381–400, 2011.

V

ADVANCED TECHNIQUES

Chapter 16

EVALUATION OF FORMAT-PRESERVING ENCRYPTION ALGORITHMS FOR CRITICAL INFRASTRUCTURE PROTECTION*

Richard Agbeyibor, Jonathan Butts, Michael Grimaila, and Robert Mills

Abstract   Legacy critical infrastructure systems lack secure communications capabilities that can protect against modern threats. In particular, operational requirements such as message format and interoperability prevent the adoption of standard encryption algorithms. Three new algorithms recommended by the National Institute of Standards and Technology (NIST) for format-preserving encryption could potentially support the encryption of legacy protocols in critical infrastructure assets. The three algorithms, FF1, FF2 and FF3, provide the ability to encrypt arbitrarily-formatted data without padding or truncation, which is a critical requirement for interoperability in legacy systems. This paper presents an evaluation of the three algorithms with respect to entropy and operational latency when implemented on a Xilinx Virtex-6 (XC6VLX240T) FPGA. While the three algorithms inherit the security characteristics of the underlying Advanced Encryption Standard (AES) cipher, they exhibit some important differences in their performance characteristics.

Keywords: Format-preserving encryption, legacy infrastructure assets

1.   Introduction

Legacy industrial control systems were developed and implemented well before the threats associated with modern networking were recognized. The trend to interconnect industrial control systems, however, has introduced many security concerns [26]. The systems were designed for performance, reliability

---

*The rights of this work are transferred to the extent transferable according to title 17 U.S.C. § 105.

J. Butts and S. Shenoi (Eds.): Critical Infrastructure Protection VIII, IFIP AICT 441, pp. 245–261, 2014.
© IFIP International Federation for Information Processing 2014 (outside the US)

and safety using proprietary hardware, software and communications protocols. The communications protocols incorporate basic error detection and correction functionality, but lack the secure communications capabilities required by modern interconnected systems. Many legacy protocols associated with industrial control systems are incompatible with modern IP-based security such as message encryption. Arbitrarily-formatted data associated with control operations cannot be padded or truncated; this prevents the use of standard encryption that relies on fixed message data lengths (e.g., the 128 or 256 block size associated with the Advanced Encryption Standard (AES)).

The Computer Security Act of 1987 assigned the National Institute of Standards and Technology (NIST) the task of developing security standards and guidelines to secure sensitive federal information and communications systems [15]. Among the most sensitive of these federal systems are those categorized as critical infrastructure assets. According to Executive Order 13636 of February 2013, "the cyber threat to critical infrastructure continues to grow and represents one of the most serious national security challenges" [17]. Executive Order 13636 also defines critical infrastructure as "the assets, whether physical or virtual, so vital to the United States that the incapacity or destruction of such systems and assets would have debilitating impact on security, national economic security, national public health or safety, or any combination of those matters" [17].

In response, NIST started the development of a cybersecurity framework in collaboration with researchers and stakeholders from the telecommunications, energy, financial services, manufacturing, water, transportation, healthcare, and emergency services sectors [16]. The interconnected nature of systems used in these sectors requires comprehensive risk management and infrastructure assurance plans. A major concern in critical infrastructure protection is the ubiquity of systems that employ aging (legacy) technologies with limited security functionality. Many of the legacy communications protocols used in sectors such as energy and transportation are incompatible with modern IP-based security, but are too costly to replace.

An important focus of NIST is the development of cryptographic standards. Cryptography includes the algorithms used to encrypt and decrypt information, and to perform other security functions such as digital signatures, authentication and key exchange [15]. One notable success is the adoption of the Advanced Encryption Standard (AES), the gold standard for symmetric-key encryption.

In July 2013, NIST released Draft Special Publication 800-38G, which recommends methods for format-preserving encryption (FPE) [6]. FPE allows the encryption of data with non-standard formats that are not suitable for modification (e.g., information transmitted in non-IP networks or stored in legacy databases). FPE can potentially provide security to legacy critical infrastructure systems that were not designed with security in mind and that are incompatible with standard encryption technology. This paper investigates the security and performance of the three NIST-recommended FPE algorithms for use in critical infrastructure protection.

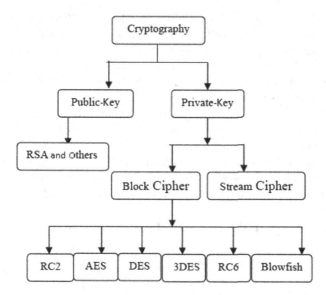

Figure 1. Modern cryptography hierarchy [1].

2. Background

Encryption is the mathematical manipulation of data in a manner that makes it unintelligible to unauthorized parties, yet recoverable by intended recipients [27]. Figure 1 shows the modern cryptography hierarchy. Cryptographic algorithms can be categorized as symmetric or asymmetric algorithms, also known as private-key or public-key algorithms, respectively. Symmetric algorithms use the same key for encryption and decryption; the key must be distributed offline or via a secure key distribution protocol. Asymmetric algorithms use two keys: one for encryption and the other for decryption. One of the keys (private key) is kept secret by one party; the other key (public key) can be distributed openly. This resolves the problem of key distribution, but asymmetric algorithms are typically more complex and computationally intensive than symmetric algorithms.

Cryptographic algorithms operate as block ciphers or stream ciphers. Stream ciphers encipher the plaintext one character at a time and concatenate the independent encryptions to produce the ciphertext. Stream ciphers are fast, but are prone to weaknesses with regard to integrity protection and authentication [27]. On the other hand, block ciphers are slower, but their mechanisms ensure the security properties of confusion and diffusion. Confusion means that the key does not relate in a simple manner to the ciphertext; it refers to making the relationship as complex as possible using the key non-uniformly throughout the encryption process. Diffusion means that changing a single character in the plaintext causes several characters in the ciphertext to change, and vice versa [27]. Block ciphers are widely used in modern cryptography, and three in particular – AES, 3DES and Skipjack – are recommended for use by NIST [6].

AES, 3DES and Skipjack are applied to 64-bit or 128-bit blocks of data. When AES was designed, 128-bit message blocks were commonly used for cryptographic applications [22]. Messages that do not fit the prescribed block size are padded or truncated. However, many supervisory control and data acquisition (SCADA) systems used in the critical infrastructure do not permit padding. SCADA systems traditionally use low-bandwidth links and compact communications protocols such as Modbus and DNP3 [28]. Solutions have been developed to retrofit security in these systems, but they often incur significant processing and buffering overhead that cannot be tolerated in systems with strict timing constraints [28]. A preferred solution is an algorithm that can transform formatted data into a sequence of symbols such that the encrypted data has the same format and length as the original data [22].

2.1   Format-Preserving Encryption

The origins of the format-preserving encryption (FPE) problem go back 32 years. In 1981, the U.S. National Bureau of Standards (later renamed NIST) published FIPS 74 that described an approach for enciphering arbitrary strings over an arbitrary alphabet [2]. The scheme was subsequently proven to be insecure. It was not until 1997 that Brightwell and Smith [5] specifically mentioned the FPE problem and its utility, which they referred to as "datatype-preserving encryption" [5]. In 2002, Black and Rogaway [3] published a seminal paper that proposed three methods for ciphers with arbitrary finite domains: a prefix method, a cycle-walking cipher and a Feistel construction. The first two methods have strong security bounds, but are targeted for tiny-space and small-space messages. In the case of tiny-space FPE, the size of the message space $N = |X|$ is so small that it is feasible to spend $O(N)$ time or $O(N)$ space for encryption or decryption. For small-space FPE, the size of the message space $N = |X|$ is at most 2^w where w is the block size of the cipher underlying the FPE scheme. AES is most often used as the block cipher, so $w = 128$ bits and $N = 2^{128} \approx 10^{38.5}$ becomes the cutoff for "small" [12]. The third method encrypts a much wider variety of data using the Feistel construction that was first examined by Luby and Rackoff in 1988 [10]. The Feistel construction has the desirable property that ciphers built from it can be proven to reduce to the cipher that is used as a round function [19].

In 2003, Spies [24] proposed the FFSEM algorithm that employs the Feistel construction for FPE. The development of FFSEM was motivated by the desire to add security to legacy protocols and systems in the financial services sector [25]. In these systems, one of the barriers to adopting effective encryption methods was the cost of modifying databases and applications to accommodate encrypted information. Applications often expect input in specific formats. Moreover, data such as social security numbers and personal account numbers are often used as keys or indices in databases, so any randomization of these fields by a randomized or stateful algorithm can require significant schema changes [22]. In 2010, Bellare, *et al.* [2] submitted specifications for FFX, a format-preserving, Feistel-based encryption. Note that the

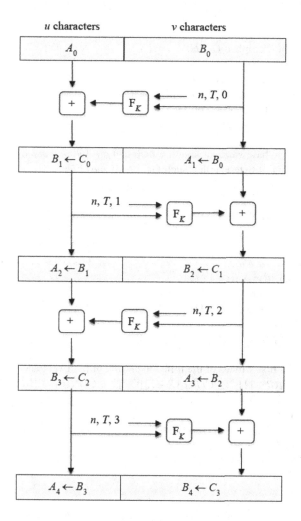

Figure 2. Feistel structure of the FF1, FF2 and FF3 algorithms [6].

"X" in FFX is a placeholder for implementations of the algorithm that are tailored to particular applications.

NIST Recommendations. The release of the FFX specification raised awareness about the FPE problem and encouraged security researchers to develop alternative algorithms. After nearly two years of deliberation, NIST released a draft of Special Publication 800-38 [6] for public comment. The publication specifies three FPE methods: FF1, FF2 and FF3. Each of these methods is a mode of operation of the AES algorithm, which is used to construct a round function within the Feistel structure for encryption as shown in Figure 2.

Algorithm 1 FF1.Encrypt(K,T,X) [4]

Prerequisites:
Approved, 128-bit block cipher, $CIPH$;
Key, K, for the block cipher;
Base, $radix$, for the character alphabet;
Range of supported message lengths, $[minlen..maxlen]$;
Maximum byte length for tweaks, $maxTlen$.

Inputs:
Character string, X, in base $radix$ of length n such that $n \in [minlen..maxlen]$;
Tweak T, a byte string of byte length t, such that $t \in [0..maxTlen]$.

Output:
Character string, Y, such that $LEN(Y) = n$.

Steps:

1: Let $u = \lfloor n/2 \rfloor$; $v = n - u$.
2: Let $A = X \lfloor 1..u \rfloor$; $B = X \lfloor u + 1..n \rfloor$.
3: Let $b = \lceil \lceil vLOG_2(radix) \rceil /8 \rceil$; $d = 4 \lceil b/4 \rceil + 4$.
4: Let $P = [1]^1 \| [2]^1 \| [radix]^3 \| [10]^1 \| [u \bmod 256]^1 \| [n]^4 \| [t]^4$.
5: **for** $i \leftarrow 0$ to 9 **do**
6:     Let $Q = T \| [0]^{(-t-b-1)\bmod 16} \| [i]^1 \| [NUM_{radix}(B)]^b$.
7:     Let $R = PRF(P \| Q)$.
8:     Let S be the first d bytes of the following string of $\lceil d/16 \rceil$ blocks:
       $R \| CIPH_k(R \oplus [1]^{16}) \| CIPH_k(R \oplus [2]^{16}) \| .. \| CIPH_k(R \oplus [\lceil d/16 \rceil - 1]^{16})$.
9:     Let $y = NUM_2(S)$.
10:    **If** i is even, let $m = u$; **Else**, let $m = v$.
11:    Let $c = (NUM_{radix}(A) + y) \bmod radix^m$.
12:    Let $C = STR_{radix}^m(c)$.
13:    Let $A = B$.
14:    Let $B = C$.
15: **end for**
16: Return $A \| B$.

Figure 3. FF1 encryption algorithm adapted from [6].

- **FF1 Algorithm:** The FF1 algorithm is derived from FFX as proposed by Bellare, *et al.* [2]. Figure 3 describes the FF1 algorithm. The NIST recommendation designates a maximally balanced Feistel structure that for an odd length message of size n divides the message into A and B halves of size $u = \lfloor n/2 \rfloor$ and $v = n - u$. The original FFX algorithm uses an alternating-Feistel structure, leaving the user to choose the size of the halves along with eight other parameters. Of the three recommendations, FF1 supports the greatest range of lengths for formatted data and the tweak.

Algorithm 2 FF2.Encrypt(K,T,X) [4]

Prerequisites:
Approved, 128-bit block cipher, $CIPH$;
Key, K, for the block cipher;
Base, $radix$, for the character alphabet;
Base, $tweakradix$, for the tweak character alphabet;
Range of supported message lengths, $[minlen..maxlen]$;
Maximum supported tweak length, $maxTlen$.

Inputs:
Numeral string, X, in base $radix$ of length n such that $n \in [minlen..maxlen]$;
Tweak numerical string, T, in base $tweakradix$ of length t such that $t \in [0..maxTlen]$.

Output:
Character string, Y, such that $LEN(Y) = n$.

Steps:
1: Let $u = \lfloor n/2 \rfloor$; $v = n - u$.
2: Let $A = X\lfloor 1..u \rfloor$; $B = X \lfloor u + 1..n \rfloor$.
3: **If** $t > 0$, $P = [radix]^1 \parallel [t]^1 \parallel [n]^1 \parallel [NUM_{tweakradix}(T)]^{13}$;
   Else $P = [radix]^1 \parallel [0]^1 \parallel [n]^1 \parallel [0]^{13}$.
4: Let $J = CIPH_K(P)$.
5: **for** $i \leftarrow 0$ to 9 **do**
6:     Let $Q \leftarrow [i]^1 \parallel [NUM_{radix}(B)]^{15}$.
7:     Let $Y \leftarrow CIPH_J(Q)$.
8:     Let $y \leftarrow NUM_2(Y)$.
9:     **If** i is even, let $m = u$; **Else**, let $m = v$.
10:    Let $c = (NUM_{radix}(A) + y) \bmod radix^m$.
11:    Let $C = STR^m_{radix}(c)$.
12:    Let $A = B$.
13:    Let $B = C$.
14: **end for**
15: Return $A \parallel B$.

Figure 4. FF2 encryption algorithm adapted from [6].

- **FF2 Algorithm:** The FF2 algorithm is derived from the VAES3 algorithm proposed by Vance [29]. Figure 4 describes the FF2 algorithm, which generates a subkey for the block cipher in the Feistel round function; this can help protect the original key from side-channel analysis [6]. FF2 differs from FF1 in that it employs a larger tweak with an independent tweak radix to allow for additional variation in the cipher.

- **FF3 Algorithm:** The FF3 algorithm is essentially equivalent to the BPS-BC component of BPS [4] instantiated with a 128-bit block and limited to tiny- and small-space messages [6]. Figure 5 describes the FF3 algorithm, which has only eight rounds, but is the least flexible in terms

---

Algorithm 3 FF3.Encrypt(K,T,X) [4]

Prerequisites:

Approved, 128-bit block cipher, *CIPH*;

Key, K, for the block cipher;

Base, *radix*, for the character alphabet;

Range of supported message lengths, [*minlen..maxlen*], such that $minlen \geq 2$ and $maxlen \leq 2 \lfloor log_{radix}(2^{96}) \rfloor$.

Inputs:

Numeral string, X, in base *radix* of length n such that $n \in$ [*minlen..maxlen*];

Tweak bit string, T, such that $LEN(T) = 64$.

Output:

Character string, Y, such that $LEN(Y) = n$.

Steps:

1: Let $u = \lceil n/2 \rceil$; $v = n - u$.
2: Let $A = X[1..u]$; $B = X[u + 1..n]$.
3: Let $T_L = T[0..31]$ and $T_R = T[32..63]$;
4: **for** $i \leftarrow 0$ to 7 **do**
5:     If is even, let $m = u$ and $W = T_R$, **Else** let $m = v$ and $W = T_L$.
6:     Let $P = REV([NUM_{radix}(REV(B))]^{12}) \parallel W \oplus REV([i]^4)$.
7:     Let $Y = CIPH_K(P)$.
8:     Let $y = NUM_2(REV(Y))$.
9:     Let $c = (NUM_{radix}(REV(A)) + y)$ mod $radix^m$.
10:     Let $C = REV(STR_{radix}^m(c))$.
11:     Let $A = B$.
12:     Let $B = C$.
13: **end for**
14: Return $A \parallel B$.

*Where $REV(X)$ reverses the order of characters in the character string X

Figure 5. FF3 encryption algorithm adapted from [6].

of the tweaks that are supported. In particular, the FF3 employs a 64-bit tweak, which is split into right and left halves that are used to add diffusion to odd and even encryption rounds, respectively.

2.2   Evaluation of the Algorithms

One of the criteria used during the evaluation of the AES candidate algorithms in 1999 was demonstrated suitability as a random number generator. Specifically, the evaluation of the output utilizing statistical tests should not provide any means to distinguish it from a truly random source. NIST used several statistical tests to evaluate the AES candidates: frequency test, block frequency test, cumulative sums test, runs test, long runs of ones test, rank test, spectral test, non-periodic templates test, overlapping template test, universal statistical test, random excursion test, random excursion variant test, Lempel-Ziv complexity test, linear complexity test and an approximate entropy test [23]. The Rijndael algorithm performed satisfactorily in all the tests and was selected as the AES algorithm.

Since FPE algorithms are modes of operation of the underlying block cipher, FF1, FF2 and FF3 should benefit from the statistical characteristics of AES. This hypothesis is supported by theoretical results [13, 19, 20]. Our evaluation uses Shannon entropy measurements to assess the security characteristics of the three FFX algorithms. Note that entropy is a measure of unpredictability or information content; Shannon entropy quantifies the expected value of the information contained in a message and is typically measured in bits per byte [27].

In addition to security performance, the computational performance of the algorithms is an important criterion. Several metrics may be used to measure the computational performance: encryption time, processing time and total clock cycles per encryption [9]. The total clock cycle metric was used in this research to evaluate the computational speed of the FF1, FF2 and FF3 algorithms.

3. Experimental Design

In order to determine the security and performance of the FF1, FF2 and FF3 algorithms for critical infrastructure assets, a set of experiments was designed to test the hypothesis suggested by the algorithm designers and NIST [6] that the algorithms inherit the strong security characteristics of the underlying block cipher. NIST has not released details of its internal deliberations and performance assessments.

As such, statistical tests were conducted to determine the ability of the FPE algorithms to provide confusion and diffusion, and to output ciphertext that is computationally indistinguishable from a random process. A dataset containing input plaintext with varying levels of entropy was created. The FF1, FF2 and FF3 algorithms were applied to this dataset. The algorithms were implemented in C using the offspark AES library [18] and the entropy of the resulting ciphertext was measured.

The second objective of our research was to evaluate the computational speed of the three algorithms by measuring the operational latency of a hardware implementation. This was accomplished by implementing the algorithms in VHDL using the Xilinx ISE suite for the Virtex-6 FPGA (XC6VLX240T) [31]. A hardware-agnostic design was used to mitigate effects due to the Virtex-6 CMOS technology and Xilinx FPGA architecture. The operational latency was estimated using the number of clock cycles between the input of plaintext and the output of its ciphertext.

54 2e 7d 45 1e 32 c4 8a e4 e9 75 5f 6e   56 23 75 45 1e 32 c4 8a 2e e9 54 5f 7d
54 2e 7d 83 6a 9a a9 bc 43 de d8 ed 1b   1a 96 41 2e 6a 7d 54 bc 43 de d8 ed 1b
54 2e 7d 3d 62 ec 84 c4 68 3d 40 33 52   2e 7d 4a 3d 62 ec 84 c4 68 54 40 33 52

Figure 6. Plaintext strings in the 3 Front and 3 Random scenarios.

3.1 Plaintext Dataset Design

In 1999, NIST tested the ability of the AES candidate algorithms to encrypt a plaintext avalanche comprising various sequences of random and fixed plaintext bits [23]. Similarly, our research focused on the ability of the FPE algorithms to encrypt a plaintext avalanche comprising various sequences of random plaintext and fixed plaintext bytes. We studied the effect of repetitive and, thus, predictable input data on the entropy of the ciphertext. Input strings of thirteen bytes were used; this non-standard block size is used by a legacy protocol employed in the transportation sector for aircraft transponder messages [8].

Our research employed randomized experiments to enhance the reliability and validity of the statistical results. The True Random Number Generator (TRNG) service provided by Random.org [21] formed the backbone of the experimental design. Unlike pseudo-random number generators that use mathematical formulas to generate sequences of numbers that appear random, TRNG extracts randomness from physical phenomena (i.e., by measuring atmospheric noise), producing 1 MiB (2^{20} bytes) of raw random data. These true random numbers were used to create a dataset of input plaintext strings with varying levels of random and deterministic data. The experimental factor used in the study was the number of deterministic bytes in the plaintext.

The experiments involved eight scenarios in which three, six, nine and twelve bytes of the thirteen-byte plaintext string were held constant at the front or dispersed randomly throughout the string. Each of the eight scenarios was replicated 20 times in unique plaintext files, each containing 4,000 different thirteen-byte strings. In the 3 Front scenario, the first three bytes were the same in all input strings within the file. In the 3 Random scenario, the three deterministic bytes were randomly dispersed throughout the string as shown in Figure 6.

The other six scenarios followed the same design. The 4,000 thirteen-byte strings in each input file repeated the same deterministic sequence; however, each trial used a different deterministic byte sequence. The non-deterministic part of the message was composed of random data extracted from the Random.org sequence of 2013-09-17 [21].

3.2 Implementation and Entropy Measurement

All three FPE algorithms require a NIST-approved block cipher operation CIPH. The 128-bit AES algorithm was used in the implementation. The cryptography community discourages the use of unverified implementations of AES because of its complexity. Therefore, we used offspark, a vetted open source implementation of AES used to encrypt official Dutch Government communications [18]. The offspark implementation is written in the C programming language, which partly motivated the use of C in the research. The research validated the offspark AES implementation by comparing its output with known vectors published in NIST's Known Answer Test [14].

No known answers tests exist for FF1, FF2 and FF3, nor are there any vetted implementations. Therefore, we verified our implementation via decryption. The decryption algorithms provided by NIST were applied to the ciphertext to reverse the encryption process. Satisfactorily-decrypted ciphertext provided confidence that the implementations were accurate.

Entropy is a measure of the amount of information that can be gleaned from ciphertext. The entropy $H(X)$ of a variable or distribution is defined as:

$$H(x) = -\sum p(x) log_2 p(x).$$

Comparisons of the entropy of ciphertext and the entropy of a random distribution were used to assess the security of the algorithms. The ENT tool [30] was used to measure entropy. ENT applied various statistical tests to the sequences of bytes stored in the files and reported the aggregate entropy of the 4,000 output ciphertext strings in each file.

3.3 Hardware Implementation

Hardware performance was another criterion used by NIST in 1999 to evaluate the AES candidate algorithms. The Rijndael algorithm was selected partly because it proved to be one of the fastest and most efficient algorithms, and implementable on a wide range of platforms [7].

A number of different architectures can be considered when implementing an encryption algorithm in hardware or using a field programmable gate array (FPGA). Iterative looping is where only one round is designed; hence, for an n-round algorithm, n iterations of the round are used to perform an encryption. Loop unrolling involves the unrolling of multiple rounds. Pipelining is achieved by replicating the round and placing registers between each round to control the flow of data. A pipelined architecture generally provides the highest throughput [11]. Our research employed a pipelined implementation of 128-bit AES and an iterative looping architecture for the Feistel structure of FPE. Iterative looping saves hardware resources by implementing only one round of the algorithm and using control logic to manage data flow.

The NIST pseudocode description is primarily intended for software implementations. As a consequence, certain operations that depend on previous operations require carefully synchronized logic when implemented in hardware. The pseudocode of algorithm was, therefore, expanded to identify parallelizable modules and blocks that can be implemented with combinational logic. Function calls to AES within the F-block of each round require the use of loop

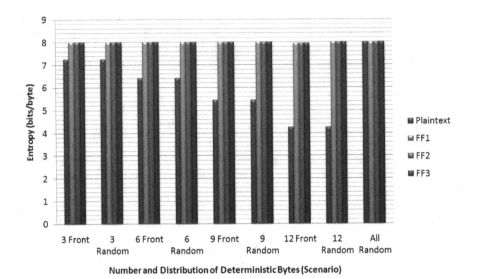

Figure 7. Mean entropy.

counters. The algorithms were coded in VHDL, simulated, placed and routed, and synthesized on a Virtex-6 (XC6VLX240T) device using the Xilinx ISE design suite. Post-PAR static timing analysis and device utilization analysis were performed on each implementation.

The throughput, latency and hardware resource requirements are usually the most critical parameters when evaluating a hardware implementation. Our research evaluated the speed of each algorithm by measuring the operational latency of an encryption cycle. To eliminate bias due to the use of a particular FPGA technology, we estimated operational latency as the number of clock cycles required for an algorithm to encrypt plaintext.

4.   Results and Analysis

This section presents and analyzes the experimental results.

4.1   Security

A thirteen-byte sequence of random data obtained from Random.org served as the control in the entropy experiment. An all-random input plaintext file created with the sequence was determined to have an entropy of 7.996 bits/byte. In the following analysis, the mean entropy was calculated for 20 trials of each scenario. Note that there was no statistical significant variance between the various trials. Figure 7 and Table 1 present the security performance of each algorithm estimated in terms of the ciphertext entropy for each level of the experimental factor. As expected, the entropy decreases in the plaintext as the number of deterministic bytes increases. The input entropy ranges from

Table 1. Mean entropy.

Scenario	Plaintext	FF1	FF2	FF3
3 Front	7.240370	7.996331	7.996487	7.996388
3 Random	7.240221	7.99654	7.996503	7.996498
6 Front	6.402844	7.996482	7.996472	7.996564
6 Random	6.402425	7.996358	7.996373	7.996502
9 Front	5.448800	7.996368	7.996341	7.996511
9 Random	5.448699	7.996375	7.996554	7.996432
12 Front	4.256321	7.942249	7.939892	7.942226
12 Random	4.256166	7.996518	7.996558	7.996404
All Random	7.996332	7.996460	7.996348	7.996424

7.24 bits/byte for three deterministic bytes out of the thirteen total bytes to 4.25 bits/byte for twelve out of thirteen fixed bytes. The distribution of the deterministic bytes, whether located in the front of the string or randomly dispersed throughout the string, does not have a significant effect on the entropy of the plaintext.

All three algorithms provide high levels of ciphertext security with no discernible differences in performance. In all but one scenario (12 Front), the ciphertext is indistinguishable from a random sequence with entropy above 7.996 bits/byte. The plaintext in the 12 Front scenario with entropy of 4.256 bits/byte causes a lower entropy in the ciphertext of 7.94 bits/byte versus the 7.996 bits/byte for the random sequence. The lowered entropy presents an upper bound on the obfuscation capabilities of FPE. Further study is necessary to clarify this performance limitation and categorize suitable plaintext.

The three FPE algorithms provide higher levels of entropy when the same number of deterministic bytes are randomly distributed throughout the string in the 12 Random scenario, These results indicate that the distribution of repeated patterns in the plaintext affects the ability of the algorithms to obfuscate the data more than the amount of repeated information.

4.2 Performance

The performance results shown in Table 2 indicate that the underlying AES core is the principal factor in the area and speed of the implementation. The AES implementation employed in the designs requires 31 clock cycles per encryption and 1,864 slices (slices are the basic building blocks in an FPGA implementation). Each slice contains a number of look up tables (LUTs) that are used to implement AND gates, OR gates and other Boolean functions. In addition to LUTs, slices also contain a number of registers that hold state and are used to implement sequential logic. In the device utilization report, any slice that is used even partially is counted towards the number of occupied slices. A design may be fitted into fewer slices if necessary, but mapping unrelated logic into the same slice may impact the ability to meet timing constraints [31].

Table 2.   FPGA performance.

	AES	FF1	FF2	FF3
Number of Slice Registers	5,801	11,285	11,323	5,592
Number of Slice LUTs	3,452	7,426	6,825	3,587
Number of Occupied Slices	1,864	3,850	3,728	1,820
Number of 18K Block RAMs	172	343	342	170
Maximum Frequency (MHz)	336.315	279.587	284.592	283.427
Clock Cycles per Round	3	68	33	32
Clock Cycles per Encryption	31	707	374	269

The Virtex-6 provides 18 Kb and 36 Kb blocks of RAM for storing data. Our implementations did not require any 36 Kb RAM blocks.

The iterative looping architecture employed in the design minimizes the hardware resources needed for each algorithm. The FF1 implementation uses two cascaded AES blocks per round, which causes the area and number of slices required to be approximately twice those of one AES block. FF2 makes only one call to AES per round, but uses an additional AES block to generate the subkey. FF3 has the smallest footprint of the three algorithms because it relies sparingly on calls to AES.

The maximum frequency is based on the worst path delay found in the design, and it indicates the fastest frequency at which a signal may be toggled given this constraint. A simulation test bench was used to measure to operational latency of each implementation. The numbers of clock cycles required for completing one round and for completing an entire encryption cycle are reported for each algorithm (Table 2). The FF1 algorithm makes two calls to AES per round, which makes it the slowest of the three algorithms. FF2 is faster than FF1 because of its single call to AES in its F-block. FF3 is the fastest of the three algorithms because it uses only eight rounds. The overall results indicate that the FF3 algorithm requires the least hardware resources and has the lowest operational latency.

5.   Conclusions

The FF1, FF2 and FF3 format-preserving encryption algorithms have important applications in critical infrastructure protection. In particular, the algorithms could be incorporated in security modules for legacy protocols and databases that are currently incompatible with standard cryptographic practices.

The experimental results demonstrate that algorithms are secure based on their ability to obfuscate repetitive input data. The algorithms successfully encipher plaintext with twelve of thirteen bytes containing a deterministic sequence. The three algorithms (as recommended by NIST) demonstrate the inherited security characteristics of the underlying AES cipher.

Because the algorithms can be implemented with AES as the underlying block cipher, they are suitable for implementation on any number of hardware platforms. The characteristics of the underlying AES implementation contribute strongly to the security and speed of the three algorithms. The FF3 algorithm requires the least hardware resources, has the lowest operational latency and has similar security performance as the other two algorithms.

The results also demonstrate that the three algorithms can obfuscate data streams with large amounts of repeated data without overhead or significant hardware costs. As such, the FF1, FF2 and FF3 algorithms provide good options for retrofitting encryption in legacy critical infrastructure systems without sacrificing interoperability or performance.

The views expressed in this paper are those of the authors and do not reflect the official policy or position of the United States Air Force, Department of Defense or U.S. Government.

References

[1] D. Abdul Elminaam, D. Abdul Kader and M. Hadhoud, Perfomance evaluation of symmetric encryption algorithms, *International Journal of Computer Science and Network Security*, vol. 8(12), pp. 280–285, 2008.

[2] M. Bellare, P. Rogaway and T. Spies, The FFX Mode of Operation for Format-Preserving Encryption, Report to NIST Describing the FFX Algorithm, National Institute of Standards and Technology, Gaithersburg, Maryland, 2010.

[3] J. Black and P. Rogaway, Ciphers with arbitrary finite domains, *Proceedings of the Cryptographer's Track at the RSA Conference*, pp. 114–130, 2002.

[4] E. Brier, T. Peyrin and J. Stern, BPS: A Format-Preserving Encryption Proposal, National Institute of Standards and Technology, Gaithersburg, Maryland, 2010.

[5] M. Brightwell and H. Smith, Using datatype-preserving encryption to enhance data warehouse security, *Proceedings of the Twentieth National Information Systems Security Conference*, 1997.

[6] M. Dworkin, Recommendation for Block Cipher Modes of Operation: Methods for Format-Preserving Encryption, Draft NIST Special Publication 800-38G, National Institute of Standards and Technology, Gaithersburg, Maryland, 2013.

[7] A. Elbirt, W. Yip, B. Chetwynd and C. Paar, An FPGA-based performance evaluation of the AES block cipher candidate algorithm finalists, *IEEE Transactions on Very Large Scale Integration Systems*, vol. 9(4), pp. 545–557, 2001.

[8] C. Finke, J. Butts and R. Mills, ADS-B encryption: Confidentiality in the friendly skies, *Proceedings of the Eighth Annual Cyber Security and Information Intelligence Research Workshop*, pp. 9–13, 2013.

[9] T. Good and M. Benaissa, AES on FPGA from the fastest to the smallest, *Proceedings of the Seventh International Workshop on Cryptographic Hardware and Embedded Systems*, pp. 427–440, 2005.

[10] M. Luby and C. Rackoff, How to construct pseudorandom permutations from pseudorandom functions, *SIAM Journal on Computing*, vol. 17(2), pp. 373–386, 1988.

[11] M. McLoone and J. McCanny, High performance single-chip FPGA Rijndael algorithm implementations, *Proceedings of the Third International Workshop on Cryptographic Hardware and Embedded Systems*, pp. 65–76, 2001.

[12] B. Morris, P. Rogaway and T. Stegers, How to encipher messages on a small domain, *Proceedings of the Twenty-Ninth Annual International Conference on Advances in Cryptology*, pp. 286–302, 2009.

[13] M. Naor and O. Reingold, On the construction of pseudorandom permutations: Luby-Rackoff revisited, *Journal of Cryptology*, vol. 12(1), pp. 29–66, 1999.

[14] National Institute of Standards and Technology, Advanced Encryption Standard (AES), Federal Information Processing Standards Publication 197, Gaithersburg, Maryland, 2001.

[15] National Institute of Standards and Technology, Critical Infrastructure Protection, Gaithersburg, Maryland, 2002.

[16] National Institute of Standards and Technology, Cybersecurity Framework, Gaithersburg, Maryland, 2013.

[17] B. Obama, Improving critical infrastructure cybersecurity: Executive Order 13636, *Federal Register*, vol. 78(33), pp. 11739–11744, 2013.

[18] Offspark, `offspark`: Straightforward Security Communication, Rijswijk, The Netherlands, 2014.

[19] J. Patarin, Luby-Rackoff: Seven rounds are enough for $2^{n(1-\varepsilon)}$ security, *Proceedings of the Twenty-Third Annual International Conference on Advances in Cryptology*, pp. 513–529, 2003.

[20] J. Patarin, Security of random Feistel schemes with five or more rounds, *Proceedings of the Twenty-Fourth Annual International Conference on Advances in Cryptology*, pp. 106–122, 2004.

[21] Random.org, Random Binary File 2013-09-17, Dublin, Ireland (`www.random.org/files`), 2013.

[22] P. Rogaway, A Synopsis of Format-Preserving Encryption, Voltage Security, Cupertino, California, 2013.

[23] J. Soto, Randomness Testing of the AES Candidate Algorithms, National Institute of Standards and Technology, Gaithersburg, Maryland, 1999.

[24] T. Spies, Feistel Finite Set Encryption Mode, National Institute of Standards and Technology, Gaithersburg, Maryland, 2008.

[25] T. Spies, Format Preserving Encryption, Voltage Security, Cupertino, California, 2008.

[26] K. Stouffer, J. Falco and K. Scarfone, Guide to Industrial Control Systems (ICS) Security, NIST Special Publication 800-82, National Institute of Standards and Technology, Gaithersburg, Maryland, 2011.

[27] W. Trappe and L. Washington, *Introduction to Cryptography with Coding Theory*, Pearson Prentice Hall, Upper Saddle River, New Jersey, 2005.

[28] P. Tsang and S. Smith, Yasir: A low-latency, high-integrity security retrofit for legacy SCADA systems, *Proceedings of the IFIP TC-11 Twenty-Third International Information Security Conference*, pp. 445–459, 2008.

[29] J. Vance, VAES3 Scheme for FFX: An Addendum to the FFX Mode of Operation for Format Preserving Encryption, National Institute of Standards and Technology, Gaithersburg, Maryland, 2011.

[30] J. Walker, Ent: A Pseudorandom Number Sequence Test Program, Fourmilab, Lignieres, Switzerland (www.fourmilab.ch/random), 2008.

[31] Xilinx, Virtex-6 Family Overview, Xilinx Data Sheet, San Jose, California, 2011.

Chapter 17

ASYNCHRONOUS BINARY BYZANTINE CONSENSUS OVER GRAPHS WITH POWER-LAW DEGREE SEQUENCE

Goitom Weldehawaryat and Stephen Wolthusen

Abstract   Consensus problems are of great interest in distributed systems research, especially in the presence of Byzantine faults. While asynchronous message passing is an interesting network model, Fischer, *et al.* [17] have shown that deterministic algorithms do not exist even for single faults, requiring the use of randomization as proposed by Ben-Or [6].

While most approaches implicitly assume full connectivity, the case of non-complete graphs is particularly interesting when studying the feasibility and efficiency of consensus problems. This topic has received limited scrutiny despite the fact that non-complete graph structures are ubiquitous in many networks that require low overall latency and reliable signaling (e.g., electrical power networks). One of the core benefits of such an approach is the ability to rely on redundant sensors in large networks for detecting faults and adversarial actions without impacting real-time behavior. It is, therefore, critical to minimize the message complexity in consensus algorithms.

This paper studies the existence and efficiency of randomized asynchronous binary Byzantine consensus for graphs in the $G(n, \vec{d})$ configuration model with a power-law degree sequence. The main contribution is an algorithm that explicitly utilizes the network structure to gain efficiency over a simple randomized algorithm while allowing the identification of possible additional edges in the graph to satisfy redundancy requirements.

Keywords: Critical infrastructures, Byzantine consensus, power-law networks

1. Introduction

The consensus problem is a fundamental problem in the domain of fault-tolerant distributed systems. It requires the system processes to agree on a common value despite the presence of some faulty processes. Fischer, *et al.* [17]

J. Butts and S. Shenoi (Eds.): Critical Infrastructure Protection VIII, IFIP AICT 441, pp. 263–276, 2014.

have shown that it is impossible to achieve consensus in an asynchronous distributed system that is subject to even a single crash fault. However, Ben-Or [6] has shown that a randomization approach can achieve binary consensus in an asynchronous distributed system that is subject to crash faults.

In applications involving the monitoring and control of electrical power networks, it is critical to detect faults and potential attacks such as sensor manipulations, as well as to ensure that network operations satisfy the mandatory real-time constraints. Existing results have explicitly or, more often, implicitly assumed full or random connectivity, but many large real networks (e.g., electrical power and telecommunications networks) display a scale-free nature, and are sparse and follow a power-law degree sequence. While it is possible to add edges to the graphs (e.g., adding communications links to control networks that partially coincide with electrical power networks), the cost of the additional links must be minimized.

Most critical infrastructure systems require correct interactions among large numbers of geographically-dispersed nodes (e.g., sensors and actuators) as well as at higher levels (e.g., SCADA systems). These systems cannot normally employ fail-stop semantics and must be fault-tolerant; however, robustness to targeted attacks requires a stronger model, namely Byzantine fault tolerance. Byzantine fault detection and tolerance is a known hard problem, as is the consensus problem in the presence of Byzantine faults. The ability to rapidly reach consensus is critical; in most cases, the dominant problem is message complexity.

Castro and Liskov [8], Chun, et al. [9] and Veronese, et al. [27] have proposed replication algorithms to implement highly-resilient services; some of these algorithms can be used to control services such as water, power and gas [18, 26]. Critical infrastructures require highly-resilient services that function correctly even under Byzantine faults that may corrupt some of the computers involved. Asynchronous Byzantine consensus algorithms address this problem by allowing critical services to continue to operate correctly even when system components exhibit arbitrary behavior (e.g., crashes or intrusions by attackers). Recently, the problem of solving asynchronous Byzantine consensus with $2f + 1$ processes has attracted attention [9, 13]. This is possible with a hybrid system model, which extends the traditional model by incorporating a trusted/trustworthy component that constrains the power of faulty processes to exhibit certain behaviors.

One of the core benefits of such an approach is the ability to rely on redundant sensors in large networks for detecting faults and adversarial actions without degrading real-time operations. It is, therefore, critical to minimize the message complexity of a consensus algorithm that reduces latency (e.g., for management of telecommunications networks and state estimation and control in electrical power networks). This has led to the consensus problem being studied in scale-free networks by Wang, et al. [28] using the Barabasi-Albert model [5], which relies on a generative model. However, the preferential attachment model only produces networks with a power-law exponent of three, and some important properties observed in large real-world networks are still missing in graphs that exhibit different exponents while still showing a power-law degree sequence. Therefore, we argue that non-complete graphs are particularly interesting when studying the feasibility and efficiency of consensus problems.

Building on our earlier work on Erdos-Renyi random graphs [29], this paper focuses on randomized asynchronous binary Byzantine consensus for graphs in the $G(n, \vec{d})$ configuration model with power-law degree sequence and presents an algorithm that achieves the desired primary result with reduced message complexity for non-complete graphs. To reach this objective, a refinement of Ben-Or's algorithm recently proposed by Correia, *et al.* [13] is considered. Their approach differs from this work in that it considers fully-connected communications networks. This paper shows that, when choosing a non-complete graph as a communications system, no additional asynchronous messaging assumptions are needed. Moreover, it is possible to increase message complexity efficiency by considering higher degree nodes that forward received messages with high probability P_{high} and lower degree nodes that forward messages with low probability P_{low}.

2. Related Work

The consensus problem is a fundamental problem in the domain of distributed systems. Fischer, *et al.* [17] proved that a deterministic algorithm cannot solve the consensus problem in an asynchronous model even in the presence of one faulty process. In the asynchronous model, each communication can take an arbitrary and unknown amount of time, and there is no assumption of a joint clock as in the synchronous model. However, Ben-Or [6] showed that a randomized algorithm can solve the consensus problem even when a constant fraction of processes are faulty. Interested readers are referred to [1, 4] for a complete proof of correctness of Ben-Or's algorithm and a detailed survey of randomized consensus protocols. Consensus in the asynchronous Byzantine message-passing model has been shown to require $n \geq 3f + 1$ processes in several variations of the basic model. Recently, Correia, *et al.* [13] showed that it is possible to solve Ben-Or's asynchronous Byzantine binary random consensus problem with $2f + 1$ processes. Consensus protocols play an important role in replication algorithms that can be utilized to protect critical infrastructures [14]. Castro and Liskov [8], Chun, *et al.* [9] and Veronese, *et al.* [27] proposed replication algorithms to implement highly-resilient services; some of these algorithms can be used to control services such as water, power and gas [18, 26].

Traditionally, the consensus problem was formulated in the context of random and fully-connected networks, although this assumption is typically not stated. Unfortunately, many large complex networks are poorly approximated by complete graphs or even simple random graphs. Many of these networks also exhibit scale-free properties. This has led to the consensus problem being studied in scale-free networks by Wang, *et al.* [28] using the Barabasi-Albert model [5], which relies on a generative model. However, the preferential attachment model only produces networks with a power-law exponent of three and some important properties observed in large real-world networks are still missing in these graphs, which exhibit different exponents while showing a power-law degree sequence. This paper focuses on the randomized asynchronous binary Byzantine consensus problem for graphs in the $G(n, \vec{d})$ configuration model with power-law degree sequence.

3.   Asynchronous Byzantine Consensus Problem

This section describes the Byzantine consensus problem and its assumptions.

3.1   Asynchronous Byzantine Consensus

Asynchronous Byzantine consensus algorithms are important when constructing Byzantine fault-tolerant systems. The consensus problem seeks to get a set of processes to agree on a common value. Many variants of the consensus problem have been proposed. However, this paper considers binary consensus in an asynchronous environment, where faulty processes can behave in an arbitrary manner and no assumptions are made about the relative speed of processes and the timely delivery of messages. A consensus protocol enables a system of n asynchronous processes, some of which are faulty, to agree on a value.

The consensus problem is solved when the following requirements are satisfied [14]:

- **Agreement:** All the processes choose the same value.

- **Validity:** The common output value is an input value of some process.

- **P-Termination:** Every correct process eventually decides with probability one.

Fischer, *et al.* [17] have shown that a deterministic protocol cannot guarantee agreement even against benign failures in asynchronous systems. Over the years, several techniques have been proposed to circumvent this impossibility result. One of the first approaches to solving the consensus problem was to use randomization. Existing results allow processes to reach an agreement in fully-connected networks. However, the case of non-complete graphs is particularly interesting when studying the feasibility and efficiency of consensus problems in real-world networks such as the Internet, World-Wide Web, metabolic networks and power networks with approximate structures [22], all of which have the power-law form $P(k) \sim k^{-\gamma}$.

Several models have been introduced to generate graphs with power-law distributions. This paper considers a simple generalization of the traditional random graph model called the configuration model [2, 20]. Chung and Lu [10] introduced a modified version of the configuration model, where, given a sequence $(d_1, \ldots, d_n)$, nodes v_i, v_j are connected with probability proportional to $d_i d_j$. Bollobas, *et al.* [7] also showed analytically that graphs constructed according to the preferential attachment rule obey a power-law degree distribution with an exponent of three. The consensus problem has been studied in scale-free networks proposed by Barabasi and Albert [5]. However, the preferential attachment model only produces networks with a power-law exponent of three and some important properties observed in large real-world networks are still missing in these graphs.

The structure of electrical power transmission networks has been studied extensively in a number of countries [22]; despite differences in structure, the efforts have retained an overall power-law degree sequence. This clearly motivates our work on arbitrary power-law degree sequences because it allows the fine-tuning of message complexity and the identification of minimum additional edge requirements.

3.2   System and Network Models

This section describes the system and network models.

System Model.   We consider a distributed system consisting of n processes where $n \geq 2$. The processes may be correct or faulty. Correct processes always behave according to their specifications while faulty processes exhibit arbitrary (Byzantine) behavior.

We consider a Byzantine failure model that does not impose any constraints on how processes fail for a certain fraction of network nodes in a distributed system. This (non)assumption about how processes fail is essential for systems that are exposed to malicious attacks and intrusions. However, only f out of n processes can be faulty with $n \geq 2f + 1$, where n is the number of processes in the system and f is the maximum number of faulty processes [13]. The communications network consists of communications channels used by processes to communicate via messages sending and message receiving primitives. The communication channels are reliable in that messages that sent to and received by the correct processes and are not modified by the communications medium. However, messages may be delayed and may be delivered in a different order than they were sent.

We also consider an asynchronous system in which there are no bounds on the message delays and relative speeds of processes. In such a system, it is impossible to detect missing messages; there is also no way to distinguish between a delayed message and a message that is not sent. This (non)assumption is important because attackers often violate some timing properties by launching denial-of-service attacks against processes and communications. However, we assume the existence of failure detector modules that provide hints about faulty processes. In particular, we employ muteness failure detectors, which suspect that a process is mute either because it crashed or is Byzantine and stopped sending messages according to the algorithm [16].

Network Model.   Power-law (scale-free) networks are characterized by a specific structural feature of power-law degree distributions. Examples of scale-free real-world networks include power networks, the World-Wide Web, email networks, social networks and networks of Internet routers [15]. Scale-free networks usually have nonhomogeneous topologies where the majority of the nodes have few links, but a small number of nodes have a large number of links and $P(k)$ decays according to the power-law $P(k) \sim k^{-\gamma}$ where γ is the power-law exponent [21]. Most real-world networks have the scale-free property with γ satisfying the constraint $2 < \gamma < 3$ [3]. For $2 \leq \gamma < 3$, a network with N nodes has constant or at most $O(logN)$ average degree, but the variance of the degree distribution is unbounded. It is in the regime of γ that power-law networks display many of the advantageous properties, such as small diameter, tolerance to random node deletions and a natural hierarchy where there are sufficiently many nodes of high degree.

Many models have been proposed for representing real networks. One of them is the configuration model, which creates random graphs that can have any generic degree distribution, and can, therefore, capture the degree characteristics of real-world networks. This paper uses the configuration model with a predefined degree distribution to generate static power-law networks.

We consider an undirected simple graph $G(n, d)$ consisting of N vertices with a degree sequence $\vec{d} = (d(1), d(2), \ldots d(n))$. The neighborhood of n_i is denoted by Λ_i and the degree distribution for the graph denoted by $P(k)$ is defined to be the fraction of nodes in the graph with degree k. The degree distribution can be calculated as follows [25]:

$$P(k) = \frac{|\{v|d(v) = k\}|}{N}$$

where $d(v)$ is the degree of node v and N is the number of nodes in the graph. The average degree in the graph is denoted by $\langle k \rangle \equiv \sum_k kP(k)$. The number of edges in the graph is given by $m = \langle k \rangle N/2$.

4.   Reliable Broadcast in Power-Law Networks

This section investigates the performance of an efficient reliable broadcasting algorithm in the configuration model with power-law degree sequence. The performance of reliable broadcasting in power-law networks can be improved by separating nodes into two sets, each set using a different probability when selecting the neighbors to which received messages are forwarded [19]. This allows high-connectivity nodes to forward messages to their neighbors with a high probability and low-connectivity nodes to forward messages with low probability. The idea behind the algorithm is to reduce the number of redundant messages sent to high-degree nodes and, thus, reduce the overall message complexity. The algorithm has two phases. The first phase searches for high-degree node(s) while the second phase disseminates messages. During the first phase, the network is searched using short biased random walks and bond percolation, where a query message is forwarded on each edge with probability higher than the bond percolation threshold of the network.

4.1   Percolation Search for High-Degree Nodes

The percolation search technique is an efficient way of searching for high-degree node(s) in power-law networks. Power-law networks have few nodes with very high degrees. A node is considered to be highly connected if its degree is greater than or equal to half the maximum degree in the network. The percolation search algorithm leverages the power-law property by making queries reach high-degree nodes.

Cohen, *et al.* [11] have shown that, if the power-law degree distribution γ is greater than three, then the critical probability threshold for the integrity of a power-law network system being compromised is one. In other words, they showed that, for a network with γ less than three, the critical value q_c of q where the transition takes place at which a giant component forms is zero or negative (this indicates that the network always has a giant component or the network always percolates). The results ensure the connectivity of an undirected power-law network when γ is less than three.

The percolation search algorithm has three phases [23]:

- **Content Implantation:** During this phase, a node caches or implants its content in some other nodes in the network. The node does this by taking a short random walk through its nodes, starting from itself and duplicating its content at each step. The random walk has size $O(logN)$ where N is the number of nodes in the network.

- **Query Implantation:** When a node issues a query, it first executes a short random walk of size $O(logN)$ and implants its query request in the nodes visited. For a power-law graph, the random walk quickly converges towards high-degree nodes. However, choosing high-degree nodes to traverse first, improves the search. This way, the requester and all the nodes that have the query implanted in them take part in the search. If a query reaches a node that has already received the same query from another neighbor, the query is not implanted; this avoids loops in the query path.

- **Bond Percolation:** All the implanted query requests are propagated independently and in parallel using a probabilistic broadcast scheme. In this scheme, a node receiving a query message for the first time, relays the message on each of its edges with a probability q, which is vanishingly greater than the percolation threshold q_c ($q = q_c\gamma$) of the underlying power-law network [24]. The percolation probability q corresponds to the probability with which network nodes communicate a message to any of their neighbors.

4.2   Message Complexity

In a straightforward parallel search technique, each node, upon receiving a query message, forwards it to all its neighbors, unless a node has already received the query message. This leads to $O(ln(ln N))$ total messages for every

---

Algorithm 1 : Reliable Broadcast Algorithm (Node n_i).

P_{high}: forwarding probability for high-degree nodes
P_{low}: forwarding probability for low-degree nodes
d: degree threshold

Function RELIABLE BROADCAST(id,msg)
Task T1:
$\sigma \leftarrow sign_j(id, msg)$
$\forall_j \neq i :$ SEND INITIAL(i,id,msg)$_\sigma$ to n_j
DELIVER(i,id,msg)
Task T2: {execute only once per message broadcast}
while (message INITIAL(j,id,msg_σ is received) and (verify(id,msg,σ,K_{uj}))) **do**
    if $V_i > d$ **then**
        if $random() \leq P_{high}$ **then**
            for $n_j \in \Lambda_i$ **do**
                SEND (j,id,msg,σ) to n_j
                DELIVER(j,id,msg)
            end for
        end if
    else
        if $random() \leq P_{low}$ **then**
            for $n_j \in \Lambda_i$ **do**
                SEND (j,id,msg,σ) to n_j
                DELIVER(j,id,msg)
            end for
        end if
    end if
end while

---

query. It has been proven that, when $2 < \gamma < 3$, the diameter of the network $d \sim ln(ln N)$ is smaller than small real-world networks ($O(ln N)$) and remains almost constant while the network is growing [12]. The bond percolation step guarantees that a query message is received by nodes in a high-connected component of diameter $O(log N)$ and consisting of high-degree nodes. The content and query implantation steps ensure that the content/message of a node are cached in at least one of the nodes in this high-degree connected component with probability approaching one, and that one of the nodes in the connected component receives a query implantation with probability approaching one.

When a node issues a query message, each edge passes it with probability q. Thus, with $qE = q_c\langle k\rangle N/\gamma$ total number of messages, any content/high-degree node can be located with probability approaching one in time $O(log N)$. After the first phase, the second phase of Algorithm 1 starts message dissemination using the hub node(s). Upon receiving this message and comparing the degree of a node with the degree threshold (d), a high-degree node forwards the received message msg with a high probability P_{high} or a low-degree node forwards it with a low probability P_{low} where $P_{high} > P_{low}$. At each step, the

---

Algorithm 2 : Byzantine Consensus Algorithm (Process p_i).

$est_i \rightarrow v_i$ {current estimate of the value to be decided}

Step 0: $r_i \rightarrow 1$ {round number}

Step 1: RELIABLE_BROADCAST PHASE1(r_i, est_i)

Step 2: wait until (valid messages PHASE1(r_i, -) are received at least $n - f$ processes) and ($\forall_j$: valid message PHASE1(r_i, -) is received from p_j or p_j is suspected by p_i's FD module)

if (more than $n/2$ messages have the same value) **then**

    RELIABLE_BROADCAST PHASE2(r_i, v,*decision*)

else

    RELIABLE_BROADCAST PHASE2(r_i, $\perp$)

end if

Step 3: wait until (valid messages PHASE1(r_i, -) are received at least $n - f$ processes) and ($\forall_j$: valid message PHASE2(r_i, -) is received from p_j or p_j is suspected by p_i's FD module)

if (there are $n - f$ decision messages PHASE2(r_i, v, *decision*)) **then**

    DECIDE(v)

else if (there is one decision message PHASE2(r_i, v,*decision*)) **then**

    $est_i \rightarrow v$

else

    $est_i \rightarrow 1$ *or* 0 with probability $1/2$

end if

    Step 4: $r_i \rightarrow r_i + 1$ **go to Step 1**

---

message is forwarded from n_j to $P_{high}/P_{low}|\Lambda_i|$ other nodes. In a scale-free network, a given node on the average propagates a message to $P_{high}/P_{low}\langle k \rangle$ nodes. The decision about the degree of a node (high or low) depends on a threshold degree d. By changing the probability values, it is possible to control the effective connectivity of the network while information is forwarded. The message complexity of the algorithm can be considerably reduced because only high-degree nodes (e.g., hubs that are few in number in a power-law network) are responsible for message forwarding with high probability. This differs from normal broadcasting algorithms in which all the periphery nodes also forward messages.

5. Consensus Algorithm

This section describes the consensus algorithm and discusses its key features.

5.1 Consensus Protocol

In the consensus problem, each process begins with an initial value $v_i \in \{0, 1\}$ and all the correct processes must decide on one of the proposed values v. This section presents a binary consensus protocol (Algorithm 2) adapted from the Correia, *et al.* variant of Ben-Or's algorithm. The protocol uses the underlying reliable broadcast over power-law networks as the basic communication primitive (Section 4).

The protocol operates in rounds, where each round has two stages. In the first stage of a round, each process p_i reliably broadcasts its current estimate v_i using the high-degree nodes and waits to receive $n - f$ valid messages. If a process receives a strict majority of reports for the same value v, then it proposes v to all the processes; otherwise, it proposes $\perp$.

In the second stage of a round, p_i broadcasts v using high-degree nodes to each destination process, waits for $n - f$ valid messages PHASE2, and then decides on v if there are $n - f$ decision messages PHASE2. If there is one decision message PHASE2 with value v different from $\perp$, then p_i adopts v as its new estimate and a new round is initiated. Otherwise, p_i adopts a random bit (0 or 1) with probability 1/2 for the estimate and a new round is initiated.

5.2   Proof of Correctness

The following is a brief proof of correctness of the consensus algorithm:

- **Agreement:** If a correct process decides v in round r, then no correct process decides $v' \neq v$ in round $r' \geq r$. A correct process p decides the value v in round r if and only if it receives $(n-f)p$ valid decision messages PHASE2 $(r_i, v, decision)$.

- **Validity:** If some process p decides v, then v is the initial value of some process.

- **Termination:** Every correct process eventually decides. It is necessary to prove that the algorithm does not block indefinitely at some point. The only points where a process blocks are where it waits for messages, so it is only necessary to prove that the process does progress and eventually terminates.

Interested readers are referred to [29] for a detailed proof of correctness of an algorithm that has the same basic structure.

5.3   Message Complexity Analysis

This section compares the message complexity of the Correia, *et al.* variant of Ben-Or's algorithm over non-complete graphs using the $G(n, \vec{d})$ configuration model with the original Correia, *et al.* variant of Ben-Or's algorithm, which assumes a flooding algorithm in which every node of a power-law network forwards its first-time received message once to its one-hop neighborhood.

First, we assume that correct processes do not suspect correct processes, i.e., all correct processes receive all the messages from each other. In both algorithms, messages are broadcast in both phases of each round. However, in the original Correia, *et al.* variant of Ben-Or's algorithm, messages are sent to every other process in the system, resulting in $\langle k \rangle N/2$ messages during each phase. On the other hand, in the modified Correia, *et al.* variant of Ben-Or's algorithm, a high-degree node forwards a received message msg with a high probability P_{high} and a low-degree node forwards it with a low probability P_{low}, resulting in a total of $P_{high}\langle k\rangle + P_{low}\langle k\rangle$ messages during each phase.

In both algorithms, there is eventually a round r in which all the correct processes set est_i to the same value v either in Line 13 or in Lines 11 and 13 of the algorithms. When this occurs, in round $r + 1$, all the correct processes broadcast v in Line 3, all the processes receive at least $n - f$ PHASE1 messages with the value (since there are at least that many correct processes), and all the correct processes broadcast PHASE2($r+1, v, decision$) messages, and all receive each other's PHASE2 messages in Line 10. Since in round $r + 1$ all the correct processes broadcast v in Line 3 and PHASE2($r + 1, v, decision$), the original Correia, *et al.* variant of Ben-Or's algorithm sends $\langle k\rangle N^2/2$ messages over the entire graph. In contrast, the modified Correia, *et al.* variant of Ben-Or's algorithm sends only $P_{high}N\langle k\rangle + P_{low}N\langle k\rangle$ messages over the non-complete graph.

It is important to also consider the message complexity of the percolation search for high-degree nodes during network setup in the modified Correia, *et al.* variant of Ben-Or's algorithm. Thus, with $qE = q_c\langle k\rangle N/\gamma$ total messages, any content/high-degree node can be located with probability approaching one in time $O(logN)$. Putting everything together, if no process is suspected by the eventually-perfect muteness failure detector, then the original Correia, *et al.* variant of Ben-Or's algorithm requires $\langle k\rangle N/2$ messages and the modified Correia, *et al.* variant of Ben-Or's algorithm requires $P_{high}\langle k\rangle + P_{low}\langle k\rangle + q_c\langle k\rangle N/\gamma$ messages. In the latter case, the original Correia, *et al.* variant of Ben-Or's algorithm requires $\langle k\rangle N^2/2$ messages and the modified Correia, *et al.* variant of Ben-Or's algorithm requires $P_{high}N\langle k\rangle + P_{low}N\langle k\rangle$ messages. Since $O(P_{high}\langle k\rangle + P_{low}\langle k\rangle + q_c\langle k\rangle N/\gamma) \ll \langle k\rangle N/2$ or $O(P_{high}N\langle k\rangle + P_{low}N\langle k\rangle + q_c\langle k\rangle N/\gamma) \ll O(\langle k\rangle N^2/2)$, there is a significant reduction in message complexity in the modified Correia, *et al.* variant of Ben-Or's algorithm.

6.   Conclusions

This paper has studied the existence and efficiency of randomized asynchronous binary Byzantine consensus for graphs in the $G(n, \vec{d})$ configuration model with power-law degree sequence. A key result is that it is possible to reduce the message complexity in non-complete random graphs using high-degree nodes to forward messages with high probability and low-degree nodes to forward messages with low probability. Additionally, the modified Correia, *et al.* variant of Ben-Or's algorithm over non-complete graphs using the $G(n, \vec{d})$ configuration model with power-law degree sequence yields the desired primary result. Specifically, it is possible to solve the asynchronous Byzantine binary consensus problem with $2f + 1$ processes over non-complete graphs using the $G(n, \vec{d})$ configuration model with power-law degree sequence by employing a reliable broadcast algorithm (that requires a wormhole component, although this has a considerably lower cost than increasing the density of the graph) and an eventually-perfect muteness failure detector without any additional asynchrony assumptions.

The message complexity analysis shows a significant reduction in message complexity in the modified Correia, *et al.* variant of Ben-Or's algorithm over non-complete graphs using the $G(n, \vec{d})$ configuration model with power-law degree sequence. This occurs when high-degree nodes forward messages with a high probability and low-degree nodes forward messages with a low probability. Because the number of the low-degree nodes is much higher than the number of high-degree nodes in a scale-free network, the message complexity is considerably less than that for a flooding algorithm. The significantly lower message complexity for the consensus algorithm reduces latency during network management in telecommunications networks and state estimation and control in electrical power networks.

Our future research will investigate the properties of multiple power-law graphs and efficient consensus algorithms over these graphs. These graphs are commonly encountered in telecommunications networks and electrical power networks, which are nominally distinct, but frequently interconnected.

References

[1] M. Aguilera and S. Toueg, The correctness proof of Ben-Or's randomized consensus algorithm, *Distributed Computing*, vol. 25(5), pp. 371–381, 2012.

[2] W. Aiello, F. Chung and L. Lu, A random graph model for power-law graphs, *Experimental Mathematics*, vol. 10(1), pp. 53–66, 2001.

[3] R. Albert and A. Barabasi, Statistical mechanics of complex networks, *Reviews of Modern Physics*, vol. 74(1), pp. 47–97, 2002.

[4] J. Aspnes, Randomized protocols for asynchronous consensus, *Distributed Computing*, vol. 16(2/3), pp. 165–175, 2003.

[5] A. Barabasi and R. Albert, Emergence of scaling in random networks, *Science*, vol. 286(5439), pp. 509–512, 1999.

[6] M. Ben-Or, Another advantage of free choice: Completely asynchronous agreement protocols, *Proceedings of the Second Annual ACM Symposium on Principles of Distributed Computing*, pp. 27–30, 1983.

[7] B. Bollobas, O. Riordan, J. Spencer and G. Tusnady, The degree sequence of a scale-free random graph process, *Random Structures and Algorithms*, vol. 18(3), pp. 279–290, 2001.

[8] M. Castro and B. Liskov, Practical Byzantine fault tolerance and proactive recovery, *ACM Transactions on Computer Systems*, vol. 20(4), pp. 398–461, 2002.

[9] B. Chun, P. Maniatis, S. Shenker and J. Kubiatowicz, Attested append-only memory: Making adversaries stick to their word, *ACM SIGOPS Operating Systems Review*, vol. 41(6), pp. 189–207, 2007.

[10] F. Chung and L. Lu, *Complex Graphs and Networks*, American Mathematical Society, Providence, Rhode Island, 2006.

[11] R. Cohen, K. Erez, D. ben-Avraham and S. Havlin, Resilience of the Internet to random breakdowns, *Physical Review Letters*, vol. 85(21), pp. 4626–4628, 2000.

[12] R. Cohen and S. Havlin, Scale-free networks are ultrasmall, *Physical Review Letters*, vol. 90(5), pp. 058701-1–4, 2003.

[13] M. Correia, G. Veronese and C. Lung, Asynchronous Byzantine consensus with $2f + 1$ processes, *Proceedings of the ACM Symposium on Applied Computing*, pp. 475–480, 2010.

[14] M. Correia, G. Veronese, N. Neves and P. Verissimo, Byzantine consensus in asynchronous message passing systems: A survey, *International Journal of Critical Computer-Based Systems*, vol. 2(2), pp. 141–161, 2011.

[15] P. Crucitti, V. Latora, M. Marchiori and A. Rapisarda, Efficiency of scale-free networks: Error and attack tolerance, *Physica A: Statistical Mechanics and its Applications*, vol. 320, pp. 622–642, 2003.

[16] A. Doudou, B. Garbinato and R. Guerraoui, Tolerating arbitrary failures with state machine replication, in *Dependable Computing Systems: Paradigms, Performance Issues and Applications*, H. Diab and A. Zomaya (Eds.), Wiley-Interscience, Hoboken, New Jersey, pp. 27–56. 2005.

[17] M. Fischer, N. Lynch and M. Paterson, Impossibility of distributed consensus with one faulty process, *Journal of the ACM*, vol. 32(2), pp. 374–382, 1985.

[18] C. Hauser, D. Bakken, I. Dionysiou, K. Gjermundrod, V. Irava, J. Helkey and A. Bose, Security, trust and QoS in next-generation control and communication for large power systems, *International Journal of Critical Infrastructures*, vol. 4(1/2), pp. 3–16, 2008.

[19] R. Hu, J. Sopena, L. Arantes, P. Sens and I. Demeure, Efficient dissemination algorithm for scale-free topologies, *Proceedings of the Forty-Second International Conference on Parallel Processing*, pp. 310–319, 2013.

[20] M. Molloy and B. Reed, A critical point for random graphs with a given degree sequence, *Random Structures and Algorithms*, vol. 6(2/3), pp. 161–179, 1995.

[21] M. Newman, Power laws, Pareto distributions and Zipf's law, *Contemporary Physics*, vol. 46, pp. 323–351, 2005.

[22] G. Pagani and M. Aiello, The power grid as a complex network: A survey, *Physica A: Statistical Mechanics and its Applications*, vol. 392(11), pp. 2688–2700, 2013.

[23] N. Sarshar, P. Boykin and V. Roychowdhury, Percolation search in power-law networks: Making unstructured peer-to-peer networks scalable, *Proceedings of the Fourth International Conference on Peer-to-Peer Computing*, pp. 2–9, 2004.

[24] N. Sarshar, P. Boykin and V. Roychowdhury, Finite Percolation at a Multiple of the Threshold (`arxiv.org/pdf/cond-mat/0601211v2.pdf`), 2006.

[25] R. Sharan, Analysis of Biological Networks: Random Models, School of Computer Science, Tel-Aviv University, Tel-Aviv, Israel, 2009.

[26] P. Verissimo, N. Neves, M. Correia, Y. Deswarte, A. Abou Kalam, A. Bondavalli and A. Daidone, The CRUTIAL architecture for critical information infrastructures, in *Architecting Dependable Systems V*, R. Lemos, F. Giandomenico, C. Gacek, H. Muccini and M. Viera (Eds.), Springer-Verlag, Berlin Heidelberg, Germany, pp. 1–27, 2008.

[27] G. Veronese, M. Correia, A. Bessani and L. Lung, Highly-resilient services for critical infrastructures, *Proceedings of the Workshop on Embedded Systems and Communications Security*, 2009.

[28] S. Wang, K. Yan and M. Chiang, Optimal agreement in a scale-free network environment, *Informatica*, vol. 17(1), pp. 137–150, 2006.

[29] G. Weldehawaryat and S. Wolthusen, Asynchronous message-passing binary consensus over non-complete graphs, *Proceedings of the Second IEEE Workshop on Network Science*, pp. 9–15, 2013.

Printed in the United States
By Bookmasters